Contents

Detailed Contents

Drugs and Crime

Theories and Practices

Richard Hammersley

polity

First published in 2008 by Polity Press

Polity Press
65 Bridge Street
Cambridge CB2 1UR, UK

Polity Press
350 Main Street
Malden, MA 02148, USA

ISBN-13: 978-07456-3617-7
ISBN-13: 978-07456-3618-4 (pb)

A catalogue record for this book is available from the British Library.

Typeset in 10.5 on 12 pt Plantin
by Servis Filmsetting Ltd, Manchester
Printed and bound in Great Britain by MPG Printers, Bodmin, Cornwall

The publisher has used its best endeavours to ensure that the URLs for external websites referred to in this book are correct and active at the time of going to press. However, the publisher has no responsibility for the websites and can make no guarantee that a site will remain live or that the content is or will remain appropriate.

Every effort has been made to trace all copyright holders, but if any have been inadvertently overlooked the publisher will be pleased to include any necessary credits in any subsequent reprint or edition.

For further information on Polity, visit our website: www.polity.co.uk

Preface

People are often surprised, sometimes shocked, when I do not share fully their grave concerns about drugs and crime. There is often an eagerness to hear from 'an expert' how bad the problems are, maybe even worse than they imagined. Through my research and reading I believe that drugs and crime problems are no larger than many other problems in the world, that they may be unavoidable consequences of the types of society many of us live in today, and that more caring about some of the larger problems, rather than drugs, might be more beneficial to humankind, as well as perhaps having the pleasant spin-off effect of reducing drugs and crime problems. Among those larger problems are poverty, famine, injustice, ignorance and avarice.

My research-based knowledge of drugs and crime has included interviewing over a hundred drug users myself over the years, also analysing interviews with many more conducted by other people. While experienced specialist practitioners and other researchers have had similar levels of exposure to drug users' lives, this amount of experience is not common among generalist practitioners, whether health-care professionals, law enforcement officers or social workers, policy makers, journalists or indeed drug users themselves, or their families. Too often, people play the ace of their lived experience in debate about drugs as if their relatively narrow experiences were the last word, or they simply rely upon a vague consensus that drugs are evils without parallel.

I also believe that many policy actions against drugs and crime have been motivated primarily by the need for policy makers and policy making to be seen to be doing something that looks to the public, particularly the media, to be likely to work. Often, policy simply panders to the crudest, cruellest and most ignorant opinions on drugs and crime, which sells newspapers and satisfies society's most punitive urges, at least in public. One review notes that current UK policy uses prohibitionist rhetoric but implements harm reduction policies (RSA, 2007). This is better than implementing prohibitionist policies, which for example hindered HIV prevention in the USA (Drucker and Clear, 1999), and better too than the archaic and gleeful application of punishment under the guise of deterrence, despite its ineffectiveness.

The author's relationship with the textbook

This book will look at the evidence for my beliefs, drawing on my previous writing, not from vanity, but usually because referencing myself directs the reader to the original paper, where the literature is reviewed in detail. I am deliberately challenging and controversial, although I strive to get my information straight too. The book will also consider alternative accounts of drugs and crime problems, as well as discussing why inaccurate stereotypes about drugs and crime are so persistent in society. It would be crass and inaccurate simply to blame politicians, or the media, for misrepresenting things. When this happens and other people disagree, the media and politicians are usually found out eventually. With drugs and crime, politics and the media perhaps more represent the way that our societies see these problems. There is a long history of demonizing drugs (RSA, 2007) – but why?

The focus of the book is the intersection between drugs and crime, not the entirety of both areas of knowledge, which would be overwhelming for the author and even more so for the reader. In writing the book, I have been very conscious of knowing much less about crime beyond drugs than about drugs in general. It will be interesting and perhaps useful to explain why this is.

I began my academic life as an applied cognitive psychologist. Through opportunism in a scant job market, I got a job with John B. Davies at the University of Strathclyde researching heroin use and crime instead. This appealed to me quickly because of the interest of a topic of obvious practical relevance that so clearly required a multidisciplinary approach to understanding it. I was sympathetic towards such an approach because I, somewhat unusually, studied philosophy and politics with my psychology. I also realized that it was likely to be easier to get funding for drugs research than it was for memory psychology. I quickly felt that drug users were being demonized for activities that only a few months being in the field and reading the literature suggested were no worse than drinking alcohol or smoking, which admittedly makes them pretty bad. To this day it still seems unfair and inhumane to attack those who are in biggest trouble and most distressed. In that early fieldwork I also learned a secret known to many practitioners but rarely made explicit: criminals (and criminal drug users) are not uniformly bad, or even untrustworthy, people. And I was struck early by the number of practitioners who commented that the people I was going to interview were complete liars, so I was wasting my time, then behaved in rather trusting and kindly ways towards them. Practitioners have to manage to be both cynical to protect themselves and caring to do their jobs. Only people who have little first-hand experience of drug users can afford to be completely cynical about them. Actually, almost everyone has first-hand experience of substance users with problems. The majority of extended families in the UK include someone with an alcohol, or these days drug, problem. Of course, that is different! However bad drug problems can be, alcohol problems can match them.

An aside on research funding

I was partly right about funding opportunities in addiction research, but applied research funded by policy makers often comes with many strings attached, and more creative 'blue skies' research on drug problems is too often seen as asking questions to which we already know the answers. The major research councils in the UK fund a little addiction research, but it has to compete with theories and issues more central to individual academic disciplines. Not that I look at the USA with envy. There is major funding of addiction research there via the National Institute on Drug Abuse (NIDA) and other similar bodies, but there are even more strings attached. I have heard several American researchers say that to get funding from such bodies it is almost necessary to have done the research to be funded first, so you can promise the results. Of course scientific inquiry where specific results have to be promised is heavily compromised.

Drugs research is under-funded given even the most modest estimates of the scale and cost of the problems. For example, the UK government estimates that drug abuse costs at least £10 billion annually in England and Wales (Cave and Godfrey, 2005). It estimates that it spends £1.5 billion tackling the problem (RSA, 2007, 39). It is difficult to find out how much is spent on drug problems research because there are a lot of different funders. Guessing from the projects that I knew were being funded as of 2005 (discounting neurological and biological research on drug mechanisms and general surveys and other research with some questions about drugs added in), I estimate that less than £7 million a year was being spent on drugs research, which represents less than a millionth of the estimated costs and about one two-thousandth of the money spent tackling the problem. This is not a level of expenditure commensurate with society's biggest change and challenge. Another possible comparison is that treatment services for drugs and alcohol have an annual cost of about £28 million in Greater Glasgow, which suggests that the costs for the whole of Scotland (population 5.5 million) is conservatively about £49 million. It is recommended that services should be supported by an evaluation/ applied research spend of about 10 to 15 per cent, which would suggest that Scotland should be spending at least £5 million on this type of research about drug and alcohol services. As far as I can tell it spends less than a million. Yet another comparator is that in 2001 in the UK the alcohol industry spent £180 million on advertising (Alcohol Concern, 2004), allegedly to promote different brands but not to:

1 have the alcoholic strength, relatively high alcohol content, or the intoxicating effect as a dominant theme
2 suggest any association with bravado, or with violent, aggressive, dangerous or antisocial behaviour
3 suggest any association with, acceptance of, or allusion to, illicit drugs
4 suggest any association with sexual success
5 suggest that consumption of the drink can lead to social success or popularity
6 encourage illegal, irresponsible or immoderate consumption, such as binge drinking, drunkenness or drink-driving
7 have a particular appeal to under-eighteens
8 incorporate images of people who are, or look as if they are, under twenty-five years of age, unless there is no suggestion that they have just consumed, are consuming or are about to consume alcohol
9 suggest that the product can enhance mental or physical capabilities.
                                                        (Portman Group, 2003)

This expenditure simply to promote different types of alcoholic drink is in stark contrast to that given over to research solutions to the problems caused by alcohol and drugs. These problems would include an understanding of most of the things the Portman Group code of practice excludes from advertising, and proper research should cost, say, ten times as much? As will be discussed in chapter 6, we have no idea how much the illicit drugs industry spends on advertising and promotion of its interests, but it would be false stereotyping of criminals to assume they spend nothing, and the industry certainly has the money to spend. Indeed they sometimes have so much money they cannot do anything with it except bury it in the ground (Strong, 1995).

There is more expenditure on interventions against drug and alcohol problems, but most of it is directed at customs and police work of uncertain effectiveness (RSA, 2007). Neither service is confident that it can control drugs or alcohol problems without more work addressing the underlying causes of these problems, in society and in people.

Research and interventions against crime are similar, also longer on rhetoric than on expenditure, and often tightly controlled for political and publicity purposes. Some have wondered whether political initiatives can impact crime at all – the so-called nothing works period in criminology (e.g., Cohen, 1988; Taylor, Walton and Young, 1973). Nowadays, it is clear that crime can be reduced in a variety of ways (and for reasons nothing to do with deliberate intervention), but it is still unclear that grand political initiatives work. It is also clear that assessing the effectiveness of anti-drug and anti-crime interventions is heavily politicized. By this I mean that those responsible for the interventions do their best to deny or avoid responsibility for failure, seize on any evidence of success, and will readily take the credit for any 'improvement' found, whatever its cause and even if the change was merely an accident or the result of a long-term trend. The politicization of interventions can politicize research also. It can be extremely difficult to fund research that challenges common-sense definitions of drug use or offending.

The need for pluralism

To understand drugs and crime we need to engage a huge range of academic disciplines, from politics to biology, not forgetting philosophy, social policy, law, sociology, geography, anthropology, sociology, criminology, psychology, psychiatry, public health, forensics and neurosciences in between. Every advance and discovery about drugs and crime in one discipline has to be framed by the others. Personally, I am a health psychologist with an interest in criminology and a sophisticated training in cognitive psychology. I bridge science and social science on purpose, and am truly comfortable with both quantitative methods and qualitative ones. Within the bounds of one discipline, there are many examples of theories that seem wrong or confused from the understandings of another discipline. For instance, the sociology of 'risk society' (Beck, 1992; Giddens, 1991) fits poorly with the psychological decision-making approach to risk (e.g., Slovic, 2000), which fits poorly again with the influential but flawed 'risk factors' approach to predicting offending and substance use (see Armstrong, 2004) and poorly again with understandings of risk as socially constructed (e.g., Adams, 1995).

There are also important issues about the extent to which drugs and crime problems are set up and thought about within common but sometimes incorrect sets of social assumptions about them. A theme of this book will be that, to an extent, drugs and crime problems are manufactured by these social assumptions. This morass of complexity appeals to me, and I remain suspicious of offers of simple solutions to a complicated problem that should include very central and serious debate about the definitions that we are using to study it. I hope this book will prepare readers to think about and discuss drugs and crime in a more critical manner.

Acknowledgements

Thanks to Emma Longstaff at Polity Press for persuading me this was the book to write. I would also like to thank my colleagues at Glasgow Caledonian University for giving me space to write it, as well as my many collaborators and co-authors on relevant topics over the years, including: Simon Anderson, Niall Coggans, Phil Dalgarno, Norman Davidson, John B. Davies, Jim Dignan, Lawrie Elliott, Frances Finnigan, Alasdair Forsyth, Mary Gilhooly, Jean Hine, Simon Holdaway, Richard Jenkins, Furzana Kahn, Tara Lavelle, Louise Marsland, Pete Marsh, Keith Millar, John Minkes, Michael Morgan, Val Morrison, Ken Mullen, John Oliver, Stephanie Pearl, Peter Raynor, Marie Reid (also my spouse and support), Anna Stallard, Iain Smith, David Teeman, Paul Wiles and Paul Wilner. Particular thanks to Jason Ditton and David Shewan for reading and commenting on chapters of the book, as well as being stout-hearted collaborators, and to three anonymous referees. Finally thanks to my parents, Mary and George Hammersley, for the gifts of compassion and reason.

Glasgow and Cockburnspath, September 2007

1
Constructing the Problem of Drugs and Crime

This is the problem: drugs and crime are consistently related to one another in different studies. Even when different places and different forms of drugs and crime are studied, the conclusion is consistent. Some general surveys, for example, show that the same people who admit to doing drugs also commit crime, particularly in youth (e.g., Elliott, Huizinga and Ageton, 1985; Jessor and Jessor, 1977; Willis, 1971; Kandel, Simchafagan and Davies, 1986). Similarly, drug users admit more crime than non-users (Bean, 1971; Gordon, 1973), while criminals admit more drug use than non-criminals (Noble, 1970; Bass, Brown and Dupont, 1972; Lightfoot and Hodgins, 1988; Spunt et al., 1995; Lamb and Weinberger, 1998). There are studies that reveal that some people who are drug dependent commit high levels of crime (Inciardi, 1979; Jarvis and Parker, 1989) and use much of the proceeds to buy drugs (Rajkumar and French, 1997). This applies to those on heroin most commonly, but also to some cocaine users, particularly crack cocaine users, and to people dependent on other drugs or alcohol. Here I'm giving only a handful of illustrative examples, mostly from the USA and the UK, but studies around the world in places as different as Chile, Hong Kong, Australia, Russia and Thailand all find that drug use and crime are correlated.

However, despite what people may believe, the connections are in fact far too complicated to summarize as a straightforward 'drugs–crime' relationship (Bennett and Holloway, 2005a). This book looks in depth at the complex issues surrounding these phenomena. For example, drug-dependent people who are also known to commit crimes tend to be clustered in areas that are socio-economically deprived (Burr, 1987; Curtis, 1998; Ihlanfeldt, 2007) in the same way as people known to commit crimes without drug use. When people who are known to be drug dependent and commit crimes are treated for their drug problems, then both offending and drug use tend to improve (Inciardi, Martin and Butzin, 2004; Dijkgraaf et al., 2005; Ribeaud, 2004; Gossop et al., 2000), although this more often involves reductions in both than complete non-offending and complete abstinence. Indeed, there are problems of defining 'non-offending' and 'abstinence' which cloud the findings. Moreover, when heroin is in short supply then offending can reduce, rather than increasing in order for the users to be able to pay the resulting higher price (Donnelly, Weatherburn and Chilvers, 2004), and when habits shifted away from crack cocaine in New York, then violent crime fell (Bowling, 1999). However, reduced availability does not have uniform beneficial effects everywhere. For instance, it can lead to people switching to more problematic substances, as when expensive Scottish heroin in the 1980s led to the injecting of insoluble temazepam (Hammersley, Lavelle and Forsyth, 1990). Or, it can lead to further criminal professionalization of the black market. Moreover, some people argue that drugs–crime connections are largely a product of the illegality of drugs, which criminalizes supply, inflates prices and abdicates the sorts of controls over drugs that are exercised over alcohol, tobacco and medicines.

It is clear that crime would exist without drugs because other social forces create and stimulate demand for stolen goods and because the same psychological and social pressures form criminals and people with serious drug problems: drugs and crime exist in a 'common causal nexus' (Elliott, Huizinga and Ageton, 1985) where it is impossible to blame one for the other in any simple way.

Many people looking at drugs–crime connections conclude that it is obvious that the same risk factors predispose people to both drug use and offending, and that drug dependence causes crime because users need money to buy drugs. Indeed, the consistency of links challenges strongly socially constructed explanations of drugs–crime relationships, as one would surely anticipate more variation across different cultures and social conditions. However, perhaps consistency is in the eye of the beholder. While the behaviour of drug-dependent offenders is reasonably similar everywhere it has been studied, links between drug use and offending at the population level are unpredictable (Martin et al., 2004). The sheer scale of drugs and crime problems is often held to be justification for action, yet their magnitude is partly a matter of assumption and definition. Furthermore, whatever the scale of the problems, even if drugs cause a lot of crime, it does not necessarily mean that eliminating drugs will reduce crime, or have only

Previous generations seemed to believe that people could drink hot coffee without advice. Nowadays, people allegedly want their coffee hot enough for enjoyment, but not so hot as to scald – a tricky if not impossible balance for caterers afraid of litigation. The management of potential risks has sometimes led to bags of peanuts labelled 'Warning – may [sic] contain nuts', swing parks without swings, all rectal examinations taking place in front of two health-care professionals (one of each gender so all patients are equally embarrassed) to avoid sexual harassment or allegations thereof, teachers doing drugs education required to refer any pupil mentioning their own drug use to the head teacher, all metal sharpish objects being banned from air travel, and parents being worried about taking pictures of their children nude. Risk management is usually well intentioned, but can have strange consequences.

There are a number of serious points (see Adams, 1995, and chapter 6). First, definitions of risks that are worth managing vary from place to place, so people do not agree. Second, the information needed to calculate what the risks of harm really are is always incomplete and is always difficult and often impossible to obtain, so people have to guess. Third, making things seem less risky can cause people to behave more dangerously. If coffee is routinely labelled 'hot' then the server doesn't have to bother warning the customer if the cup seems unusually hot, and liability is passed to the customer; if the swing park has a padded floor, then children jump from higher up because landing might hurt less. Fourth, developed societies are increasingly centralizing risk, security and safety, moving away from a 'modernist' view that innovation, novelty and technology are generally good. Since Beck (1992) identified these trends, they have intensified. For example, around 80 per cent of UK citizens now favour spying on terrorist suspects and detaining them without trial (National Centre for Social Research, 2007).

In this cultural context, drugs and crime are useful for policy makers because disliking drugs and crime might unify us and divert attention from more problematic and complex changes that have occurred over the past thirty years. These include a widening of the poverty gap between richest and poorest, with resultant health and other inequalities both globally (globalissues.org, 2007) and within affluent countries (Luxembourg Income Study, 2000). However, it is relevant and perhaps not coincidental that New Labour policies have reduced child poverty in the UK across the same period as crime has broadly fallen (Hills and Stewart, 2005). Another problematic change has been the debasement of the educational system, partly through under-funding. For example, in England and Wales A-levels are easier than they were (*The Economist*, 11 August 2005). In 1993, 49 per cent of degrees in England were upper seconds or firsts. By 2004 this figure had risen to 58 per cent (Department for Education and Skills, 2005), suggesting lowered standards, as the numbers attending university also rose over that time – so presumably the mean ability fell. Yet another change is the erosion of secure career-type employment for most people, which has been replaced by jobs that are temporary and often part-time, requiring both adults in a family to work to make ends meet securely and thus making it difficult for people to be full-time parents (Ermisch and Francesconi, 2001).

An additional headache for national policy makers is that the power of nation states is diminishing in the world against the rise of global capitalist organizations, among which it is sensible to include organized crime and drug trafficking (Castells, 1998). Actually, it may be old fashioned to talk of 'drug trafficking', because increasingly trafficking in illegal cargo has become a global industry that will transport anything from a stolen kidney to shiploads of hazardous waste, to fake designer goods for street markets (Naim, 2005). The many skills required for trafficking may have been honed supplying drugs, but they can be used to conceal and ship anything. Crime is a more perennial problem, but it too is influenced by major social inequalities (Chamlin and Cochrane, 2005; Baron, 2006). It is unclear whether politicians can do anything about the changes over the past thirty years and whether the public want them to. Drugs and crime concerns are diversionary activities that unify us against these 'incontrovertible' dangers, rather than leaving us to worry too much about where our society is taking us in terms of inequality, exploitation, fearfulness and ignorant consumerism. This perhaps applies even more so to policy makers, who may be loath to concede impotency and difficulty foreseeing the global future.

Pragmatic realism

The idea that drug abuse and crime are socially constructed phenomena is threatening or incomprehensible to many people. Both clearly exist and are clearly related. I do not accept that the universe is constructed entirely from discourse, but I do accept the much weaker but more reasonable suggestion that all our thinking about and understanding of the universe is constructed from discourse of one sort or another. That is, the real world surely exists independently of our attempts to understand it, and there is a convincing philosophical argument to this effect (Husserl, 1977), but there are no guaranteed methods for finding out 'the facts' or 'the truth' of the real world. This approach to research can be called 'weak social constructionism' or 'realism' (Harré, 1970; Bhaskar, 1997), but to confuse things other philosophical positions are also called 'realism'. The Bhaskar and Harré form I will call 'pragmatic realism': I do not want to abandon the idea of a real world independent of our discourse, because then there would be no point researching it, but I do want to abandon the idea that scientific or other research methods of any kind guarantee truthful knowledge of the real world.

The topics of drugs and crime are weakly socially constructed throughout and aspects of our understanding are strongly socially constructed; some drugs and crime 'problems' may not exist at all – the anticipated crack cocaine epidemic in the UK in the 1990s being one example.

There is considerable resistance by policy makers and the media to acknowledging any form of social constructionism, because 'spin' – managing discourse about events – is a main tool of their trades. Therefore it is often very difficult to show which concerns and problems are entirely illusory without being attacked for it. More widely, the management of information is a potent form of social power (Douglas and Wildavsky, 1983) – perhaps the only fundamental form of power in addition to raw violence (Galbraith, 1985). Scientists, health-care professionals and criminal justice professionals also wield information as power, so are also resistant to social constructionism. Of course, appreciating that social constructionism is accurate is itself power, but of a rather lame variety, as it leads to uncertainty about what to do, which in turn often causes social constructionists to be passed over in favour of those willing to present themselves as more certain. People readily confuse a person's confidence with their knowledge, hence their power. Some people who understand social constructionism very well choose a positivistic presentation of knowledge. The most extreme form of social constructionism, which is often called postmodernism, poses a threat to science because it proposes that all accounts/discourses/texts compete equally. This may be an account of how contemporary societies tend to work, but it should not diminish the power of expertise, including science. For example, the discourse of some newspaper leader writers is unlikely to rehabilitate anyone from offending or substance dependence, whereas psychological and psychoanalytic discourse can. Architects are not generally encouraged to abandon engineering principles for postmodern playfulness.

Many practising scientists find social constructionism offensive to their belief that truth can be found in a consensus among experts that can be replicated in research and 'works' in operating the world. Weak social constructionism does not undermine this idea of truth, but it makes it extraordinarily difficult to achieve, potentially fallible and very vulnerable to human conceits among scientists, such as that their particular methods are superior. Scientists' grandest conceit is that they are somehow above vanity, power and avarice, or that somehow their superb research methods cancel out such petty human vices and prevent bias from creeping into their thinking and writing. Common sense (and the literature on scientific fraud) suggests that bias is most likely when intricate and expensive research technology is involved, raising the stakes considerably. Social scientists are quick to spot vanity in policy makers, but often slower to recognize this weakness in themselves.

In the long haul, objectivity may be achievable to an extent in the natural sciences – with much scope for vanity, power, avarice and debate along the way – which do not study things that themselves have ideas and opinions. But in the social sciences, scientists' theories can be understood by people – the very people being researched – and they can consequently alter the ways in which they behave or how they talk and think about what they do. Drug-dependent criminals come to talk of themselves in the language of health- and social-care professionals (Davies, 1997). Social constructionism cannot be ignored for very long without doing extremely poor social science or science relevant to people. Few theorists with social constructionist or post-modern positions apply this criticism soundly to their own ideas. The fallibility of research evidence does not mean it can be replaced with somewhat informed opinion.

Social constructionism has caused something of a split among social scientists. In psychology this has been characterized by the distinction between 'social social psychology' and 'experimental social psychology' (Sapsford et al., 1998). Social social psychologists embrace social constructionism and are wary of naïvely 'scientific' research on social behaviour. Experimental social psychologists reject social constructionism and believe that objective scientific methods will prevail. There is an equivalent, if less overt, split in criminology. Policy and government-funded research tend to favour the scientific, experimental, quantitative researchers over the critical social constructionists, to the point that, in the USA, qualitative sociological research often occurs in places with names such as the National Development and Research Institute and the Institute for Scientific

Analysis to veil their nature. As a pragmatic realist, I accept that both approaches can be useful, but that neither are guaranteed to be true, correct, or even sensible. Progress in drugs and crime research would benefit from improvements of many types, including better use of existing methodologies, better understandings of socially constructed biases in our thinking and research, and the development of new methods.

Another aspect of pragmatic realism is the tolerance of a world that contains a multitude of diverse real things and caution about trying to reduce one level of reality to another. In criminology and mental health research there is often an excess of enthusiasm to reduce human activity to biological explanations such as genetics or neurological differences. Drugs and crime are classes of phenomena where the social and cognitive levels of explanation are important in their own right (see Morton, 2004).

It is also important to appreciate that science is a fallible human and social activity. All too often science, and social science, is presented as resulting in some form of accurate truth. Instead, pragmatic realism suggests that it is important to be wary of the following:

1 grand, single-theory explanations of complex human activities, such as drug use or offending. One should be cautious of assuming that any substance has inevitable effects on human behaviour (Davies, 1992; Shewan et al., 1998) or that any one factor 'causes' offending (Armstrong, 2004).
2 reductionist theories that seek to explain complex social activities in terms of individual neuropsychology, without considering the setting and social meaning of the activity. Substance use is a social activity as well as a pharmacological one and can sometimes occur purely for social reasons, without sufficient consumption of an active drug for specific pharmacological effects to be relevant. Examples include injecting heroin too dilute to be active (Johnson et al., 1985) and placebo effects (Stewart-Williams and Podd, 2004). That anything that affects behaviour must have neuropsychological effects is a tautology, not a causal explanation.
3 empiricism, which assumes that with sufficient methodological sophistication the data or the facts can be gathered accurately, without bias, including the conceptual bias inherent in the ways that the problems are labelled. For drugs, this is exemplified by documentation of the 'risks' of drug use, as if drug use, the associated risk factors and the consequences could all be measured without problem. All three are often dependent upon self-report data and,

even when other harder sources of data are available, these too may be prone to sampling and measurement bias. For example, some people tend to deny or downplay all deviant activities and in surveys will tend to seem neither to use drugs nor to offend.

The biological metaphor

The triple mistakes of grand theory, reductionism and empiricism are common in drugs and crime research. Most research into substance use and dependence is biomedical science. Hammersley and Reid (2002) estimated that 85 per cent of journal articles on key illicit drugs are biomedical in orientation (including animal studies), rather than being concerned at all with the clinical, psychological or social correlates of use. Biological science offers an impressive combination of theory, including the ability to explain how one thing causes another, classification and detailed empirical observation. Sadly, biomedical research has as yet delivered little of use in tackling drug problems. Psychopharmacology has made mistakes historically, such as believing that methadone was a non-addictive substitute for heroin, and has not yet delivered well-targeted theoretically based chemical interventions against drug misuse, although these are repeatedly promised. Over the same five decades there have been considerable advances in the understanding and treatment of substance problems, based upon clinical and non-clinical research on drug users, reviewed in chapter 8. Among these are the widening acceptance of controlled substance use as a possibility, the use of brief interventions, of motivational interviewing and other cognitive behavioural interventions, and harm reduction as a viable approach. Techniques work at rates comparable to the treatment of other mental health problems and have been achieved with relatively modest funding and little or no reference to neuropsychopharmacology.

The brain is increasingly attractive to researchers and policy makers alike. Perhaps the photogenic nature of brain scans appeals to a society whose culture is increasingly visual rather than being concerned with complex verbal constructs. Crime cannot be entirely about the brain, but criminology is often attracted to a type of thinking about social problems that mimics biological thinking without appreciating that social problems and biochemistry are different – as are human and animal behaviour.

Criminology's roots were in sociology and psychology, but it quite rapidly separated from these themselves immature disciplines.

Relevant psychology theory has continued to develop and relevant sub-disciplines include forensic psychology and applied cognitive psychology, which studies issues such as eyewitness testimony and face recognition. As criminology developed into a discipline taught widely at universities, relevant sociology theory began to decline. Up to the 1960s there was considerable interest in deviance, which grounded early criminology, but by the 1970s Foucault described criminology as 'entirely utilitarian' (Foucault, 1980, 47) and observed that its mode of operation was to suggest that the practical problems were so pressing that there was no time, perhaps no need, to develop relevant social theory. Rather, criminology is driven by repetitive policy and practice problems. One foreword puts it like this:

> Another development in criminology . . . has been the gradual secession of criminology from the field of sociology. The reasons for this rift are complex, but they include . . . the eagerness of many universities to exploit the explosive demand among students for courses and degrees that have the word 'crime' in them. Many universities have created entirely new programs, departments and degrees around the topic for reasons that make little intellectual sense and that inspire little confidence in the integrity of administrators . . . if criminologists fail to expose their students to the core disciplines of the social sciences, the long-term consequences could be catastrophic. (Warr, 2002, xii)

'Catastrophic' is perhaps overestimating the powers of social researchers and policy makers and underestimating the difficulties of a discipline even recognizing its foundation assumptions. However, thinking about complex social phenomena as if they were well-defined biological ones is a serious mistake.

At this point it is necessary to mention the 'disease model' of addiction, given that it remains influential on policy and treatment, particularly in the USA. According to the model, addiction is a disease caused by changes in the brain, perhaps more likely in some brains than others. More detail will be given in chapter 8; suffice it to say for now that the 'model' is really more of a metaphor, and 'disease' as used in the model is really just the claim that biology is paramount in addiction. Thinking about substance use may be refreshed by describing, then challenging, this more general and endemic 'biological metaphor' for substance use, which can be summarized as follows:

> Because substances have demonstrable effects on biological systems, it is tempting to believe that use of a substance and its consequences are robust phenomena that meet scientific data quality criteria, operate

consistently across people and can be explained by causal reductionist models.

This metaphor is too limited to encompass substance-use behaviour and fails to consider the impact of individual differences or the contexts where use occurs (the 'set' and 'setting', Zinberg, 1984; see chapter 2). Biological effects of substances are often necessary for substance use (although use of non-active substances, or debatably active substances such as herbal remedies, is widespread) but they are not sufficient.

The model is a 'metaphor' because, in both academic and non-academic discourse about substance use and substance problems, biology is applied only loosely. The most obvious example of this is the very use of the term 'drugs', as if this applied to some natural biological category that resulted in harm.

Although the biological metaphor fits drugs badly, it is widely used as if literal. Furthermore, there are signs that the biological metaphor is being reapplied to criminology as well, to suggest that a person's drugs and crime problems are diagnosable conditions of that individual with a predictable development and prognosis. Allegedly, drugs and crime problems are *not* complex and unpredictable problems with substantial social, systemic and cultural contributions, as well as major influence from the immediate social and physical environment, but rather personal problems that can be prevented by appropriate child rearing, diagnosed unambiguously and treated with medical and psychological interventions.

Summary

Drugs and crime are linked, but the size, seriousness and causes of this link cannot be taken for granted. Interpretations of the linkage are socially constructed, as are society's concerns about drugs and crime rather than about other problems. These interpretations influence the very nature of the problems. The biological metaphor that locates 'problems' in the constitution and experiences of the person is too simple. A pragmatic realist approach will be used in this book, which considers all relevant types of facts and attempts to understand both drugs and crime themselves and society's often fearful and negative amplifications of those problems.

Discussion points

- Find a piece of discourse about drugs and crime, preferably of local relevance to you, and analyse it for naïve assumptions, simplifications and exaggerations.
- Would it be preferable for society (a) to accept that drugs are not as big a problem as feared or (b) to fund research and treatment at a level appropriate for the alleged scale of the problem?
- How useful is biology, including genetics and neuropsychology, in understanding crime?

Further reading

Davies, J. B. (1992). *The myth of addiction.* Reading, MA: Harwood Academic.

Zinberg, N. E. (1984). *Drug, set and setting: the basis for controlled intoxicant use.* New Haven, CT: Yale University Press.

RSA (2007). *Drugs – facing facts: the report of the RSA commission on illegal drugs, communities and public policy.* London: Royal Society for the Encouragement of Arts, Manufactures and Commerce.

Runciman, R. (ed.) (1999). *Drugs and the law: report of the independent inquiry into the Misuse of Drugs Act 1971.* London: Police Foundation; www.druglibrary.org/schaffer/Library/studies/runciman/default.htm [accessed 31 May 2007].

2

What Are Drugs?

Even more than crime, drugs form a topic where all sources of information are biased. Official sources tend to take a pessimistic view, emphasizing problems and addiction, and hypothesizing that biological factors are primary. For example, the National Institute on Drug Abuse (2006) defined addiction as follows:

> Drug addiction is a complex brain disease. It is characterized by drug craving, seeking, and use that can persist even in the face of extremely negative consequences. Drug-seeking may become compulsive in large part as a result of the effects of prolonged drug use on brain functioning and, thus, on behavior. For many people, relapses are possible even after long periods of abstinence.

Many writers in the academic literature are dubious about the usefulness of the disease model of addiction (see further reading), and at minimum not only the drug but also the mindset of the user and the setting of use are important (Zinberg, 1984).

Definitions

The collective noun 'drugs' is often used as if it referred to something clear and concrete. It doesn't. Imprecise thinking about 'drugs' is hardly extraordinary in everyday life, but it is surprising in supposedly educated and informed writing about drug problems. In everyday life 'drugs' has two meanings. The most relevant one roughly means 'substances that have some sort of psychological effect that make people want to take them and are illegal to take in this way'. But many experts would include alcohol and tobacco at least with other drugs, although they are legal to take in many countries, at least by adults under defined conditions. Others see the legal status of substances as irrelevant to scientific definitions and prefer to classify all substances that have some sort of psychological effect that make people want to take them as 'drugs', whether they are illegal or not. This should incorporate many 'drugs' not in widespread use (see Dalgarno and Shewan, 2005) and probably many natural and synthetic pharmaceuticals that have not yet been used as 'drugs'. For such reasons some people prefer to refer to 'chemicals', as in 'chemical dependence', or 'substances' instead of drugs. Both these terms seem to me unable to capture the special issues of 'drugs'. 'Chemicals' is problematic for the consumption of plants and other materials where we are unsure about the biochemistry. It is also problematic because it is feasible that some 'chemical dependencies' involve only placebo effects, sugar being one example (Reid and Hammersley, 1999), so many chemicals are not 'drugs' and some 'drugs' are not chemicals (even if they are made of chemicals like everything else). 'Substances' is really too wide and potentially includes any food, drink, cosmetic or other substance ingested which might directly or indirectly have psychological effects. If face cream makes users feel happy, is this a 'mood-altering substance'? Does it matter if it really penetrates the skin or not? A final reason for sticking with 'drugs' is that the legal status of substances can have major effects on use. If heroin were legal, inexpensive and freely available without prescription, then different people would use it, in different ways, and different problems would result. It might not be considered a 'drug'. Alcohol use in Saudi Arabia is not the same behaviour as alcohol use in the UK. At the time of writing, in most of Europe, North America, Australia and New Zealand, tobacco is moving towards being a 'drug', having not been classified as such for some eighty years, while cannabis is gravitating in the other direction, towards not being a drug, like alcohol. It is becoming good practice to ask about cannabis separately in surveys and interviews, as young people in the UK (and reportedly in the USA) who use cannabis sometimes believe that they do not take drugs, only 'blow'.

Unless otherwise specified, when this book mentions 'drugs', then it means drugs, alcohol and tobacco, as well as other chemicals or substances that are used sometimes for their psychological effects, but generally not things too far removed from 'drugs', such as face cream.

The second, more neutral meaning of 'drug' is merely some kind of medicine or possible medicine. This meaning is useful here to remind us that 'drugs' have generally been of benefit to humankind. If we could not drug pain, then not only would millions of people suffer from chronic pain but surgery would also be impossible and terminal illnesses such as cancer unendurable. If 'mood-altering drugs' did not exist, then more millions would have no relief from the miseries of depression and other psychological problems. It is difficult to get the right statistics, but there seem to be something like 12 million operations in the UK National Health Service every year, of which a large, but unknown, proportion will receive an opiate such as morphine or codeine for pain relief. This compares to an estimated 200,000 to 300,000 people who are problem heroin users. In other words, at minimum there are something like fifty times more medical opiate users than there are problem users, not even counting the many millions of chronic pain sufferers prescribed opiates, or buying weaker forms over the counter. 'Drugs' in its more sinister meaning can be a side effect of medicine. Cocaine, cannabis and amphetamines have all been popular medicines in their time.

People who make sweeping generalizations about 'medicines' are not generally taken seriously. The advantages and disadvantages of medicines are clearly dependent upon the specific substance being offered as medicine, the dose, what it is supposed to treat, its side effects, and so on. The same applies to drugs. Two oral paracetamol and codeine tablets for pain relief are not the same as injecting dihydrocodeine (DF-118s) as a heroin substitute. Or, take two very contrasting scenarios of use: that by a fifteen-year-old homeless person who has run away from care and that by someone who is terminally ill and in chronic pain. Ignoring issues of legality, people are likely to be concerned about drug use by the homeless child, whether it is of heroin, cannabis or alcohol, and less concerned about use by the terminally ill person.

Some people find it laudable to avoid drugs entirely, including caffeine drinks such as tea, coffee and colas. If one widens 'drugs' slightly more, then this becomes problematic. Should one avoid also medicines that help manage mood, like antidepressants? If you should, how badly depressed or unwell should a person be before it is acceptable to take mood-altering drugs? Should one avoid painkillers (analgesics) such as paracetamol, ibuprofen or aspirin? Again, how much pain makes their use acceptable and when does pain permit the use of opiates? The side effects of chronic aspirin use can be very serious – gastric bleeding can be life-threatening. Fear of getting patients addicted can lead to under-dosing patients with opiates, even when they are in serious pain or terminally ill, despite the finding that very few people prescribed morphine for acute serious physical pain become opiate addicts once the pain is over (Nicholson, 2003; Bressler, Geraci and Schatz, 1991).

What about using a drug that can alter mood or relieve pain, but employing it for other purposes, such as taking aspirin to thin blood and reduce the risk of heart attack? Is morality dose-dependent, or contingent on *not enjoying* the effects of a drug? What about the people who take over-the-counter analgesics daily, perhaps despite not being in pain or having other medical needs for them (Dowling, Storr and Chilcoat, 2006)? Purportedly they do so because they feel better. How much 'better' does one have to feel before a medicine is potentially addictive? What about medical marijuana use? As of 2006, eleven US states had passed laws permitting this (see medicalmarijuanapro-con.org). Californian law includes 'any other illness for which mari-juana provides relief' (California Proposition 215, 1996, Section 1), and most of the eleven states license its use for chronic pain. Does using cannabis to relieve pain (or other conditions) involve not enjoy-ing it? Can medicine be fun? A complete avoidance of medicines seems irrational in the modern world. Avoiding intoxicants is more feasible, but there is a wide grey area.

People who have recovered from a chemical addiction with Narcotics Anonymous, Alcoholics Anonymous, Cocaine Anonymous or Marijuana Users Anonymous differ in their choice of 'abstinence'. Some avoid intoxicants entirely, some avoid the substances they had problems with, but continue using others. 'Avoiding' intoxicants includes avoiding tea, coffee and tobacco for some, but not for others. Some recovered heroin users avoid alcohol and marijuana. Others do not consider moderate use of these drugs to be a problem for them. Some people stop drinking by turning to marijuana. Some AA members continue to use prescribed mood-managing medication, such as Prozac, while others regard this as perpetuating chemical dependency. There are also now substances that can block all or part of the neuropsycho-logical effects of specific drugs, such as naltrexone for heroin. Should taking these be regarded as a form of chemical dependency or not?

If people with personal expertise and experience in drug abuse dis-agree about what constitutes unacceptable use, then perhaps drugs and patterns of their use need to be judged on an individual basis. This is highly inconvenient for law making because it is much easier to regulate a chemical by banning or controlling it than by permitting its use under some conditions but not others.

It is also unrealistic to try and draw a watertight distinction between drugs and medicines. Take the following case history, of the Holly-wood film producer Don Simpson:

As autopsy reports and pharmaceutical records would later reveal, Simpson . . . the summer before his death, was on a regimen that included multiple daily injections of Toradol, for pain; Librium, to control his mood swings; Ativan, every six hours, for agitation; Valium, every six hours, for anxiety; Depakote, every six hours, to counter 'acute mania'; Thorazine, every four hours, for anxiety; Cogentin, for agitation; Vistaril, every six hours, for anxiety; and Lorazepam, every six hours, also for anxiety. He was also taking, in pill and tablet form, additional doses of Valium, plus the pain relievers Vicodin, Diphenoxylate, Diphenhydramine and Colanadine; plus the medications Lithium Carbonate, Nystatin, Narcan, Haloperidol, Promethazine, Benztropine, Unisom, Atarax, Compazine, Xanax, Desyrel, Tigan and Phenobarbital. (Simpson's pharmaceutical records for July 1995 show billings of $12,902 – from one pharmacy, through one psychiatrist, at a time when Simpson was using at least eight pharmacies and several doctors, receiving medications using the aliases Dan Gordon, Dan Wilson, Don Wilson and Dawn Wilson, in addition to his own name. A law enforcement source who investigated Simpson's pharmaceutical records estimated his monthly prescription medication expenses at more than $60,000. One ten-day period in August 1995 shows Simpson's pharmacy expenses at $38,600.) Police and coroners' documents also show that Simpson was experimenting with prescription doses of Morphine, Seconal and Gamma Hydroxybutyrate, or GHB. These medications were being ingested, autopsy reports would show, in addition to large quantities of alcohol and cocaine . . . More ominously, Simpson was using heroin. (Fleming, 1998, 8–9)

This is the heaviest drug use I have ever heard of. One would be hard-pressed to decide which parts of this massive cocktail were medically required and which constituted drug abuse, although presumably some of Simpson's prescribing doctors had some illusions that they were helping him. It also illustrates stereotypes about the grave dangers of certain drugs that Fleming (1998) regards heroin as 'ominous' when on top of everything else it would perhaps hardly be noticed. Simpson's prescriptions included several different benzodi-azepines – which are commonly abused – several natural and synthetic opiates, several medicines generally used to manage severe mental illness with psychotic symptoms (delusions, hallucinations and other oddities of thought) and even a barbiturate, which is noteworthy because barbiturates were not generally prescribed by 1995. Most of the prescriptions, broadly speaking, appear to be attempts to calm him down or sedate him. While he may have been naturally over-aroused or perhaps suffering from mania, it is feasible that his very heavy cocaine use had led to extreme over-arousal along with an irrational lack of recognition that the cocaine had caused this. There are certainly cases of cocaine users being able to consume vast quantities of alcohol that would render a non-user unconscious. Or Simpson may simply have enjoyed the drugs and lied to doctors to get them. Like other nearly as extreme users, Simpson seems to me to be beyond enjoyment and into some type of obsessive consumption that was occurring largely for its own sake. Being drug-free for the day would have seemed to him like an altered state of consciousness.

Simpson also illustrates a common tendency for some more extreme drug users to tend to take such a variety of drugs that it becomes increasingly unrealistic to pinpoint a particular drug or drugs as 'the' problem. For example, heroin users often take large quantities of cannabis, alcohol and other drugs as well, particularly when heroin is in short supply. Other drug-dependent people strongly favour a single drug, most commonly heroin, cocaine or alcohol, and use it to the exclusion of almost everything else. The case also illustrates some of the complications in the drugs–crime relationship. Simpson was not a criminal in the ordinary sense of the word, but a respected film producer with an extreme private life. Being rich, he did not need to commit crime to fund his drug use, although could he have sustained a $30,000 a month drug habit indefinitely? This compares to a mean monthly drugs spend of about £1,400 (including alcohol and tobacco) by heavy (and often criminal) opiate users in Glasgow in the mid-1980s (Hammersley et al., 1989). However, Simpson did break the law in various ways to get the drugs.

Another complication for defining 'drugs' is that, as a new drug appears in a society and use spreads, its potency, methods of use and contexts of use tend to change. New drugs are often adopted first by relatively intellectual and artistic but marginalized groups, who may be opposed to mainstream cultural values. Among historical examples are coffee, initially linked via coffee houses to seventeenth-century broadsheet writers, cartoonists and other dissidents (Barr, 1995); cocaine, initially adopted by Sigmund Freud among many other intellectuals at the turn of the twentieth century; LSD, initially promoted in the USA by writers and academics such as Timothy Leary and Ken Kesey (Wolfe, 1989); and ecstasy (MDMA), associated with a new dance-music scene in the UK (see ecstasy.org). At first the drugs tend to be taken at high doses and are described as having very marked psychological effects.

Use then tends to spread out into wider society. As this happens, in the mass market potent drugs tend to be diluted or taken in ways that reduce their effects, and become cheaper per dose; many users take the drug for a mild 'buzz' rather than for very marked effects. Stronger forms of use continue to exist but involve some expertise and usually more expense. For example, these days some people in Scotland still take ecstasy, wanting its strong positive effects, as were associated with dance culture, but others take a small dose as a pick-me-up while drinking in the pub, which was unheard of in the early 1990s. Sometimes the mass-market, industrialized forms of drugs are more problematic than their initial forms, because they are easier to take, cheaper or more habit-forming. Examples are cigarettes compared to pipe tobacco and cigars and crack cocaine compared to powder cocaine or coca leaf. There are similar concerns about the mass consumption of weaker, highly palatable, usually sweet, forms of alcohol such as alcopops.

Which drugs?

There are about twenty different drugs in common use in most developed countries, although the exact list varies from place to place. These can be reduced to the categories shown in table 2.1. The list is likely to change over time. For example, Quat, a leaf that when chewed provides mild stimulation, is common in Somalia and has migrated with Somalis. So far, it has not become a mainstream drug of abuse, but it could, or a purified version of its active ingredients might. Table 2.1 summarizes 'the facts' about sixteen types of drug, inevitably simplifying to squeeze them all in, and illustrates two important points for the argument of this book: drugs are diverse and should not be lumped together in thought or word, so drug–crime links differ for different drugs.

Moving on, motives for use differ for different drugs, and the dangers are often worsened by specific methods and particular styles of use. Regular use of any drug throughout every day is inadvisable. Finally, people use drugs because they make them feel good, or have effects that users like. Broadly, effects can include arousal, sedation, happiness and other alterations of mental state that involve hallucinatory and psychedelic experiences of various kinds. People do not take drugs that make them feel miserable, but many drugs that usually cause happiness can also cause sadness, which most readers will have seen with alcohol. This merely illustrates that moods are not directly caused by drugs alone, but are mediated by the user's cognitions and the setting of use. Being high on cocaine may be elating at the party but terrifying on the road.

Table 2.1 Drugs of abuse

Drug	Benefits of use	Risks include	Harm-reduction measures	Dependence propensity	Links with crime (other than supply offences)	Quality of evidence base	Quantity of evidence base
1 Alcohol	Relaxant, reduces anxiety, lightens mood, painkiller, promotes sociability, demonstrates social status, very widespread	Overdose, coronary heart disease, liver damage, brain damage, mental health, accidents and violence, rash sexual and other behaviour, malnutrition, poverty	Drinking within sensible limits; drink-free days; controlled drinking; avoid use under stress or other mental health problems	Medium – but because it is so widespread it causes the most problems	Chronic effects facilitate violence and give courage for offending; petty crime to buy alcohol; impaired judgement leads to dangerous behaviour; drink-driving	Medium	Very high
2 Caffeine – coffee, tea, colas, other drinks	Increases arousal and improves concentration and cognitive performance (perhaps only relieving effects of caffeine	Minimal, except as side effects of some specific methods of use; physical agitation and tremor on overdose	Keep intake to reasonable levels	Dependence can be demonstrated in many users, but it is benign; none of the symptoms are normally severe or	No, but historically coffee houses were linked to criminal and dissident activity	High	Low

Table 2.1 (continued)

Drug	Benefits of use	Risks include	Harm-reduction measures	Dependence propensity	Links with crime (other than supply offences)	Quality of evidence base	Quantity of evidence base
	withdrawal), helps set biological clock taken in the morning			problematic and stopping is tolerable			
3 Tobacco	Improves concentration and cognitive performance (perhaps only relieving effects of nicotine withdrawal)	Cancer, cardiovascular diseases (CD)	Nicotine-substitute products; quit smoking; reduce amount smoked – smoking bans help here	Very high – problems are primarily very serious damage to long-term health that is often fatal	No? But most drug-dependent people and many offenders smoke	High	High
4 Cannabis/marijuana (blow, draw, spliffs, hash, grass)	Relaxant, lightens mood, painkiller, promotes sociability, facilitates sensual enjoyments (e.g., food, music, sex), is	CD from mixing with tobacco, mental health (particularly psychosis among vulnerable people), accidents,	Smoking without tobacco; alternatives to smoking – vaporizers, eating; sensible limits; cannabis-free days; avoid use	Low – but because it is so widespread even low risks will result in a large number of cannabis-dependent people, like	Its acute effects do not facilitate offending; cannabis users consistently report more offending than non-users, despite not	Medium	Medium

	rebellious and fashionable	violence related to drug dealing, rash sexual and other behaviour	if previous bad experiences, or mental health problems	alcohol does	being dependent – a theoretical challenge (see chapter 4)		
5 Psilocybin mushrooms (magic mushrooms)	Hallucinogenic, but generally in a fairly mild way, highly positive mood, feeling connected to other people and the environment	Toxicity from overdose or ingestion of other fungi, mental health, accidents	Quality assurance of product; avoid use if previous bad experiences, or mental health problems; use in non-threatening settings	Very low	No	Low	Low
6 Ecstasy (MDMA, MDA)	Arousal, positive mood, empathy with other people, openness to new experiences, appreciation of surroundings	Hyperthermia, mental health, long-term depression or cognitive deterioration due to damage to serotonin systems	Use lightly; do not mix with other substances; stay cool if dancing	Very low	No. Acute effects probably reduce the likelihood of crimes against other people	Medium	Low
7 LSD (acid, trips)	Positive mood and effects,	Mental health, can	Avoid use if previous bad	Very low	No chronic effects;	Medium	Low

Table 2.1 (continued)

Drug	Benefits of use	Risks include	Harm-reduction measures	Dependence propensity	Links with crime (other than supply offences)	Quality of evidence base	Quantity of evidence base
	otherwise like ecstasy and Psilocybin; however, high doses can have dramatic hallucinogenic effects	trigger psychosis in vulnerable people, accidents	experiences or mental health problems; use small doses at first; use in non-threatening settings		occasional acute offending due to delusions or hallucinations		
8 Amphetamines (crank, speed, wizz)	Alertness, arousal and wakefulness, often talkativeness and high activity levels	Mental health, including effects of chronic insomnia, rash sexual and other behaviour, malnutrition, aggression, accidents and violence, acute heart problems	Avoid use for days or weeks on end; moderate doses	High	More perhaps than for any other drug, set and setting are important; some users are dependent and offend, most are not; occasional violence or other acute offending, generally not	Low	Low

Drugs are highly diverse substances that can be used in diverse ways. When people talk of 'drugs', that talk often makes generalizations that oversimplify or assume unsafely that what applies to one drug or form of use applies also to another. The next section will look at drug discourse.

Understanding discourse about drugs

While 'information' and 'facts' are presented as if they were value-free accounts of how the world really is, social constructionism assumes that all communication is discourse and that most activities, including the presentation of self, have a communicative component (Potter and Wetherell, 1987; Jenkins, 1996). This encompasses writing about drugs, talk about drugs and the ways that drugs are presented (and indeed not presented) visually and in other media.

For example, given that in the UK cannabis use has become common among young people, it is unrealistic that in the main evening TV soap operas one rarely sees people smoking cannabis, although people are drinking alcohol in almost every episode (the same applies to US shows). It is as if cannabis has been deliberately edited out of the stories. This is interesting because soaps cover most other potential human stories, including people with drug problems, or drug supplying. The message by omission is that drug use is not mundane or normalized and when it, occasionally, appears it usually leads to problems of one sort or another. The accuracy of this position can be debated (Dalgarno and Shewan, 2005; Parker, 2005). Table 2.2 shows systematically the main ways in which discourse about drugs can vary.

Table 2.2 is not offered as an exhaustive list of how discourse can vary, and the simplest action points are to recognize that it does vary and to be prepared to interpret discourse about drugs critically, whether it is in an academic paper, a journalistic account, a policy document or what a user says. Drugs discourse is complex, the form and content of the discourse is motivated, whether the producer intends it to be or not (Davies, 1997), and discourse that offers itself as the truth or the facts should be considered cautiously.

Drug

It is a commonplace of drugs discourse that individual drugs are different in their effects and dangers, although often a unifying theme is that all drugs are dangerous in one way or another. For example,

Table 2.2   How discourse about drugs varies; a systemic mapping

Dimension of variation	Examples	Comments
Drug	Alcohol, tobacco, cannabis, heroin, cocaine, ecstasy	And many others
Set: who is using	Addict, parent, role model, peer, child, anti-model, stranger, criminal	Can be fixed or fluid roles, also mere labels, or socially functional attributions – (Davies, 1997)
Setting: where is use occurring?	Home, al fresco, club, pub, car	And many others; see Zinberg (1984)
Perspective: who is observing or describing?	Self, parents, health, criminal justice, education, peer group	An important issue is the credentials and credibility of different perspectives
Timing	Past, current, future	Distance from present may matter too
Level: what social level of explanation is being offered?	Social, psychological, biological	And what social functions do explanations serve?
Narrative tone	Tragedy, comedy, irony, romance	See McAdams (1993)

there are many sets of objective or scientific leaflets giving basic information about drugs, and these often follow a common, repetitive
format, with more space given to health and other problems than to
the pleasurable and other effects that lead people to use them in the
first place. It both matters and doesn't really matter which substances
'drug' discourse is about.

Believing that all drugs are equivalent is ill-informed and potentially
dangerous. Most obviously, it results in cannabis users being the predominant recipients of laws and policies written with heroin and
cocaine in mind (see Runciman, 1999). Other dangerous mistakes
have included believing that smoking drugs is safe, whether that be
cannabis or brown heroin (Pearson, 1987), and that, as 'addicts',
people dependent on heroin will conform to stereotypes of 'alcoholics'
and generally be incapable of moderating their behaviour – hence
harm-reduction programmes would be a waste of time that only
encourage heroin use, when they often succeed in reducing morbidity and mortality (Neale, 2000).

life and its difficulties, as ultimately unpredictable but enjoyable. *Romance* involves a struggle that works out all right in the end because people are in control of their lives. Much self-help literature is romantic in tone. *Irony* involves a view of life as mysterious, bleak and entertaining, but without a goal or purpose.

The predominant tone of public discourse about drugs is tragic. Informal and private discourse can take other tones. The public expression of tragedy may bias thinking about drugs towards the tragic and make other tones and modes of thought seem unacceptable. Yet, more public discourse about alcohol is expressed in comedic terms, and it is likely that other drugs are viewed similarly by their users. Comedy shows nowadays occasionally portray drugs as a comedic issue, and there was even a US sitcom, 'Weeds', about a respectable widow who turns cannabis dealer (Glaister, 2005). The gulf between 'having a laugh' and the possible tragic future consequences of drug use is very wide. The romantic tone is most widely employed in accounts of recovery from substance problems, where the person struggles against overwhelming odds in order to overcome their addiction. This is a widespread theme in celebrity biography, examples being Ray Charles (Hackford, 2004), Johnny Cash (Mangold, 2006) and Boy George (Bright and Boy George, 1995). The ironic tone in my experience is widely utilized by practitioners in private: people are as they are, and among the more spectacular human weaknesses and stupidities is drug use. The advantage of irony is tolerance; it is non-judgemental about the 'tragic' inevitability of problems and the consequent need to intervene. The ironic tone is rarer in writing, one exception being Howard Marks's account of his activities as a cannabis trafficker (Marks, 1997). There are also ironic as well as romantic elements in Burroughs's autobiographical novel *Junky* (Burroughs, 1977). These four narrative tones are not the only tones possible, but they are useful and widespread examples.

Conclusions

Drugs are chemicals or mixtures of chemicals that have a variety of effects on users' mental functioning. However, there is no clear mapping from their neurophysiological effects to the behaviours to which they are linked, including crime. Nor is there any scientific classification scheme that separates drugs from other substances, medicines among them. As we will see in chapter 4, nor is there evidence that any specific drug has effects that necessarily link it to crime. It is therefore unlikely that drugs cause crime, if we are using 'cause' in the way it is used in hard science.

There are, however, a myriad of theories, ideas and assumptions that drugs are problematic for their users and 'cause' crime, but 'cause' and its synonyms are usually proffered as a rhetorical device to assert the truth of the ideas being put forward. Discourse about drugs is very diverse and usually highly motivated; this applies to scientific discourse as much as to everyday concern. To advance thinking about drugs and crime, it will be important to avoid confusing widespread consensus with truth and also to consider all ideas carefully and in detail. Different drugs have quite different chemistry and effects.

Summary

Drugs cover a very diverse range of substances. In discussions of drugs and crime, these tend to be lumped together in inappropriate ways. While many users use many substances, it is important to be clear about which substances link to crime, and how. Also, drugs–crime links depend not only on the psychopharmacology of the drug involved, but also on the mindset of the user and the setting of use. Additionally, the form and nature of discourse about drugs need to be considered carefully, as much drug discourse makes implicit assumptions about the nature of drugs, users and use that promote taking drugs–crime links for granted, rather than trying to understand when they do and do not occur.

Discussion points

- If heroin were legal, inexpensive and could be bought over the counter, then what might happen? Would more or fewer people use it? Would it be linked to crime? Would more or fewer people die as a result of use? Would there be more or fewer heroin-dependent people? Would more people inject heroin, or fewer? Would heroin dependence be the big social problem it is today?
- Is it better to get high on cannabis than suffer chronic pain?
- What would a drug one could take all the time without being addicted be like?

there is a serious risk that the drugs–crime relationship is mainly a matter of definition. Perhaps a circle of reasoning connects them in ways that almost guarantees that they are related. Perhaps, to use one explanation of many, 'crime' and 'drug use' are labels applied to the socially undesirable activities of marginalized groups – often working-class or ethnic minority young men (e.g., Pearson, 1983). Other people, perhaps, do similar things but their behaviour is labelled differently.

Crimes are socially constructed actions (yes, even murder) which are motivated, usually involving people in power defining their powerful positions by diminishing or controlling those not in power (Douglas and Wildavsky, 1983). Practically speaking, in post-industrial societies 'power' is no longer based in brute force, threatened or applied, but in control of resources, including money, and control of knowledge or information. 'Knowledge' and 'information' are often used interchangeably, but it is important to distinguish them. Information is the glut of undigested data we receive in the 'information age', while 'knowledge' is material that has been digested or understood in some sense, which is generally more useful and contributes more to power. Often, we have a lot of information about crime (and drugs) but little digested knowledge.

To suggest that crime is defined according to power structures is not to suggest some paranoid conspiracy between individuals meeting in secret, but to sketch how societies tend to work, whether the powerful and the weak realize it or not. Right-wing and left-wing political theory do not disagree about this, though right-wing theories tend to propose that the wielding of power is inevitable, supernaturally justified, natural, unavoidable or necessary, while left-wing theories tend to propose that it is undesirable and needs to be checked or radically altered, by controlling or preventing the power of an elite minority from dominating. For the maintenance of power to be important in society, it is only necessary that people generally do not act against their own self-interests on purpose and that this applies to everyone, including politicians, policy makers, criminology researchers and practitioners, even if they usually try their best to help others. For example, few politicians would implement a policy that they believed would lead to radical improvement in society if this were also electoral suicide. It is fairly easy for non-politicians and politicians with minimal chance of power to criticize this and suggest radical policies, such as legalizing all drugs, which they believe would be beneficial. Whether it would or not, the media and the general public would probably hold politicians accountable for the drug-related deaths that would occur after drugs became legal. Shrugging those deaths off as similar to the alcohol-related deaths that already occur would not be an adequate political response.

Crimes are against the law, but laws vary

Crime is very simple in one way – crimes are acts that are against the law. As this is not a book about crime per se, we will skip over most issues about who can define and impose law, upon whom, and we will also ignore conditions where who is entitled to make laws and enforce them is in dispute – in places such as Iraq occupied by American and British forces, for example. Laws are most commonly assumed to apply across some sort of geographical area, such as a city, a region, a state, a nation or a federation of states. There are also various attempts to develop and apply international legal standards, about human rights for instance. International agreements about drugs, drug trafficking and organized crime are among these (see United Nations Office on Drugs and Crime, 2006; Bean, 2004). In most places there is potential for there to be confusion and even conflict between laws made by different bodies. There is also the potential for quite different local interpretations of laws. For example, Netherlands law considers tolerance of drug use and users, without tolerance of supply and trafficking, to be compatible with international treaties on drugs, while the USA tends to take a stricter view. Yet, individual states in the USA have different laws about possession of marijuana. When laws are broken, they are normally sanctioned as if each single law (and offence) could be defined by itself. However, problematic cases abound that show that adhering to or enforcing one law often occurs with costs to others. For example, how much violence is a person entitled to use in self-defence? If that force leads to the death of another, is that murder, manslaughter or not an offence at all? What about conditions where the killer goads the victim into an attack? Another example is that a country could in theory enforce international drug laws and largely prevent drug use by searching everyone and everything that entered the country extremely carefully, rather as the UK proceeded for some weeks in summer 2006 to prevent a terrorist attack on transatlantic flights. However, this would violate human rights treaties, damage trade and tourism, be extremely expensive and probably generate massive corruption.

changing networks of contacts and activities. In this context, laws and law enforcement are usually playing catch-up. For example, media and law enforcement agencies tend still to present a view of organized crime and international terrorism that emphasizes a hierarchical structure headed by evil masterminds. This, a staple of popular fiction and a distorted mirror of the hierarchical structures of many law enforcement agencies, is easy to understand. Both international crime and terrorism tend to conform more to a network model (Castells, 1998; Naim, 2005).

Second, the possibilities for global trade and travel apply to drug use and crime too (Castells, 1998). The citizens of a country may collude in criminal activities elsewhere, travel abroad to offend or take drugs, or strategically place themselves where the laws are most convenient. Examples include sex tourism (Naim, 2005), the use of tax havens and travelling to Amsterdam or across state lines in the USA to smoke cannabis. Ordering objects and substances that are illegal in one's own country over the internet is a growing activity. In Europe, tax differences on alcohol and tobacco lead to smuggling on a large, but hard to estimate, scale (Anderson and Baumberg, 2006). Similar activities occur in the USA, where tax laws vary across states. Legitimate enterprises also exploit differences in the law around the world and do their utmost to influence local laws in their favour. Legitimate enterprises are often accused of crime or immorality, when for example they move production to a country with weak labour laws and cheap labour costs. Illegitimate enterprises may perhaps mirror this and show signs of being law-abiding, when this is useful to them, and also moral. 'Good' and 'bad' are highly problematic in network society. For example, the CIA flew al-Qaida suspects to Morocco to be interrogated because the interrogators there understood how to frighten, depersonalize and humiliate Muslims and because torture is not strongly regulated in Morocco (Chambraud, 2005). It is difficult to understand, justify or criticize this sort of activity within a framework of absolute laws applying across a delimited country.

Globalization leads often also to an extreme diffusion of responsibility for criminal acts, as none of the people involved feel that they are breaking the law that much. Why should Moroccan interrogators be concerned about breaking the laws of another country? Illegal audio or video recordings may be copied by people who are breaking no local laws, the people who ship them may not feel they are breaking the law either in any serious way, the people who distribute them and sell them may feel they are offering a grey service rather than committing a crime, and the buyers may simply want a bargain. There is only profound criminal intent in this network if one or more evil masterminds plan the whole thing, which may not always be the case. As we will see later, this applies to drugs too.

All this needs to be said to make a simple point strongly: laws and hence crimes are not some form of natural category that require no thought, discussion or criticism. In consequence, crime should not be taken for granted in discussions of drugs and crime, but it often is. Too often debate is about drugs–crime links without questioning the nature of the things that are supposedly linked, or thinking beyond the assumption that crime (and drugs) are the personal activities of people that can be labelled as 'criminals'.

If crimes should be judged by the harms they cause, then some of the worst crimes of the twenty-first century will probably be perpetrated by people who believe they are simply making money at the edges of the law. Arguably this applies also to the worst humanitarian and ecological crimes of the twentieth century. Yet, crime by individuals will continue to fascinate because it diverts attention away from these much more troublesome grey areas.

Developed societies are becoming safer

Global social, informational and economic inequalities are widening (e.g., Castells, 2002; Bauman, 2006). It is in developed and affluent societies, where most of the research discussed in this book has occurred, that drugs–crime connections are at the forefront of social concerns. Setting aside the most impoverished and marginalized groups in those societies for the next few sentences, life expectancy and absolute affluence have increased greatly over the past 100 years. Tolerance of person-to-person violence and abuse has generally fallen. Corporal and capital punishment are rarer, police officers are discouraged from fighting with offenders, bullying is often of national concern. Children should not be hit, should not hit others and should not taunt or tease others. Sadistic initiation rituals are supposed to be a thing of the past, whether into the army, a trade apprenticeship or a school. Crime rates may have fallen too, insofar as it is possible to compute a 'rate' for transactions labelled differently across history. Many people can afford insurance to cover themselves against mishaps. Many of the most personally hazardous activities of earlier centuries, such as mining and manufacture, have been outsourced to other places.

as they are for those that are recognized offences. For instance, the financial loss to a company of paper taken home and wasted might be much larger than the loss due to stolen pens.

Such difficulties lead on to an important tendency, in both academic and applied criminology, to focus on relatively dramatic offences that are easier to agree about and so to neglect mundane law-breaking that not everyone agrees is *really* an offence, and which they dismiss as a conventional rather than a moral offence. It should not be otherwise, but while the laws and commandments that define crime can be quite simple and black and white – 'Thou shalt not kill' – the practice of crime and its detection occur in complex ways and require working with ambiguity. For example, how much involvement in killing constitutes 'killing'? Is there a distinction to be drawn between accidental and deliberate killing, and how long after does the person have to die for the act to be 'killing'? Somebody drives their car at a rival in love, knocks them down, and they die within minutes. That is the favoured type of crime scenario. Somebody accidentally bumps a stranger with their car, to no obvious harm. They then die years later of a condition that may or may not have been caused or worsened by the bump. This kind of scenario is very problematic. One of the last men executed for murder in the UK was hung because he said 'Let him have it', but he might have meant either 'Shoot him' or 'Surrender the gun'.

There may additionally be disagreements about exactly what acts are crimes, and there are certainly variations from country to country. There are also often limits on who can commit crimes and under what conditions. For example, young children may not be held to be criminally responsible for their actions. Soldiers in times of war may be allowed – indeed trained – to do things that are crimes in peacetime. As of 2005, US and British soldiers occupying Iraq as 'peacekeepers' were clearly sometimes confused about whether they were dealing with an active enemy whom it was acceptable to intimidate and dominate abusively, or with civilians or prisoners of war who needed to be treated according to peacetime laws. In peacetime, law enforcers, including the police, customs and excise and various spying agencies, are often granted powers to do things that would be illegal if private people did them. They may be able to kill people in certain circumstances, invade privacy, access confidential information, imprison people on suspicion only, break motoring speed limits, and so on.

Luckily, this is not a book about crime in and of itself, but the key point is that in defining and recognizing crime there is clearly space for various kinds of bias that will affect how 'crime' is linked to drugs.

Suppose, for example, that for some more minor offences the police are more likely to proceed formally if they believe that the offender is a drug user. If the store agrees, trivial shoplifting by a fifteen-year-old might not go as far as the police station, but if the fifteen-year-old has heroin in her pocket then this might be different. Indeed, the dual offence – possession and shoplifting – is usually regarded as more serious, hence requiring proceeding. Such prejudice might come into play even more where 'attempted' offences are concerned. It is extremely difficult to document such informal biases and prejudices, as they will not be reflected in the official records. It is unlikely that front-line classification of crime is entirely the cause of the drugs–crime relationship, but it plays a part and the size of the part is unknown. It would be a mistake to adopt the common assumption that because this bias is unknown and rarely discussed in any serious way it must be small (Adams, 1995).

For example, the Metropolitan Police in London were particularly concerned about racial crime after the case of Stephen Lawrence (a young man who was stabbed from racist motives and bled to death; McPherson, 1999). Officers were instructed to refer suspected racial crimes to a special unit. Officers were reluctant to make this judgement and tended to refer all crimes where any victim was not white to the unit, swamping it. Well intentioned as it was, this was clearly not a successful way of defining 'racially motivated' crime. Similarly, when new assessment forms (ASSET) were introduced to Youth Justice in England and Wales, they included questions about drug use. Youth Offending Team staff who felt unable to judge the importance of this drug use tended to refer everyone who admitted using drugs to a drugs service (Hammersley et al., 2004). These are blatant examples; it is much harder to document subtle or 'informal' ones.

At least since the 1970s (Young, 1972) it has been widely believed that the police do not target people randomly as possible offenders. The police, sensibly from their point of view, target people who somehow seem suspicious. Of these people, some are indeed carrying drugs, driving a stolen car, or whatever. The problem is that the levels of crime by whoever passes locally as seeming innocuous are largely unknown and relatively unlikely to be detected. If pensioners in affluent suburbia take illegal drugs or steal cars, then all we really know about these behaviours is that the perpetrators have the sense to lie about them in surveys and are rarely detected. In contrast, we know a huge amount about offending and drug use among deprived youth, who most often offend and hence are even more often detected. Amplifying the truth can become a kind of lie.

To sum up, there are very substantial problems in defining crime or, even when definitions are broadly agreed, in recognizing that a particular crime has occurred or that a particular event was a crime. The problems of definition and recognition generally tend to exaggerate the links between crime and drug use because the activities of the same people tend to be defined or recorded as 'drug use' and 'crime'.

Violence

There is not a crime called 'violence' but there are violent crimes. Among animals, there are four interrelated forms of aggression (e.g., Archer, 1988), and some of these have look-alikes in crime, although one should be wary of assuming that they are similar underneath. First, there is predatory violence, which is calculated, skilled and intended to serve as means to an end, so it tends to be as minimal as necessary. The predator does not waste energy or risk injury by getting carried away. In crime, there is instrumental violence that is intended to achieve some specific purpose that might, in another situation, be achieved by other means. Among common reasons for instrumental violence are the enforcing of criminal debts, including drug debts, frightening people to facilitate crimes and escaping detection or arrest. Instrumental violence tends to be learned and planned, although it may occur spontaneously when an opportunity presents itself.

Second, there is aggression in defence against a predator attacking the animal or its young. This usually occurs only if escape or avoidance is not feasible. Particularly in defence of young, animals will behave very aggressively towards predators with the aim of driving them away while remaining uninjured themselves. Predators tend to give up kill attempts when the risks of injury seem too high. People who believe that they are about to become the victims of violence, including those who know that there are reasons for them to be the victims of instrumental violence, may behave like this. But their beliefs may be exaggerated or false. For instance, it is not unusual for armed police officers to shoot unarmed or innocent suspects because they have strong expectations that they are confronting someone who is armed and dangerous and they misinterpret an innocent move.

Third, there is aggression within a community of a species. Within a community, aggression is to manage resources, notably mating opportunities, and social status. Mostly this is restricted to displays of aggression, and the weaker party usually concedes defeat before damage is done. Many species have explicit signals for conceding defeat. Sometimes, however, the aggression interaction causes serious physical harm, and this is more common among males of some species than others (e.g., Gros-Louis, Perry and Manson, 2003).

In human communities there are differing learned norms and expectations about displays of aggression and admissions of defeat. These may require some actual violence to seem convincing. A friend of mine caught his wife with another man. He was actually pleased, because they had not been getting on and this gave him the excuse to leave completely. But, as he said, 'I didn't really hurt him, but I had to kick him about a bit or I would have looked bad.' Getting aggression right is difficult.

Using violence for aggression is often regarded as being a problem of men, particularly young, less well-educated, working-class or ethnic minority men. It is true that, disproportionately, it is these men who are caught being violent. This does not mean that they are more bellicose than others in society; rather, they may lack alternative means of successfully expressing aggression by more socially tolerated means. When they speak in a hostile manner they will lack the forms of pronunciation and expression that are considered appropriate for 'proper' verbal aggression. This does not mean that they are not articulate, but that they speak the wrong code (Labov, 2006). Other means of dominating or expressing social status may also be denied to them. For example, they are unlikely to own a 'nice' car – nice cars often looking aggressive and being driven aggressively by more affluent young men. They may lack any defensible private space, such as their own home, which can be aggressively protected.

Fourth, there is aggression against strangers of the same species. This is intended to drive the stranger away from the animal's territory but, at least among chimpanzees, it can involve severe violence (Watts and Mitani, 2001). Humans remain surprisingly territorial, despite the fact that most of the resources they need no longer come from the geographical place where they live. This is problematic. The laws of nations tend to assume idealistically that all citizens are equal, strangers or not, but human aggression may be different towards strangers and kin.

Animal aggression and emotion

Even if the analogies between animal and human aggression are tenuous, animal aggression illustrates that disorder and violence are not simple behaviours that turn on and turn off, but describe a complicated spectrum of interactions. The relevant crimes are defined by outcome, but the interactions very rarely began with the intent of outcomes such as grievous bodily harm or murder, which is why establishing intent is so important in determining the extent of guilt. Even when legally the offender fully intended to hurt or kill the victim, this was often supposed to achieve a result that in another interaction might have been achieved by less tragic means. Aggressive interactions are to achieve something, or to dominate or control someone, or to avoid the expectation of harm to oneself or one's family. Additionally, Nell (2006) has speculated that there is a drive for cruelty, originating in the reinforcing arousal and excitement of predation. However, most predation or hunting attempts are unsuccessful (Nell, 2006), which means that one reason that hunting or predation might be strongly reinforcing is that it is a partial reinforcer, with rare success. This also raises the question of whether it is the hunt or the kill that is reinforcing, as well as issues about vicarious excitement, including fantasy, being reinforcing too.

Our culture has a fascination with evil, cold-hearted people who love to hurt and kill for its own sake. A few people do learn to enjoy hurting and killing, but most do not. This even applies to trained soldiers. While it is perhaps possible to coerce and reinforce most people into cruelty under the right conditions, many soldiers are deeply traumatized by their experiences of cruelty (e.g., Foy et al., 2002).

As the intended outcome of an aggressive interaction is not usually violence, trying to teach people to not want to be violent is somewhat beside the point. Most people do not want to be violent, but they do want certain things that require some level of aggression, ranging from hunting to acquiring money by robbery.

Another stereotype of violence is that it can be caused by an explosive rage during which the person is so aroused that they have only minimal awareness of what they are doing. The person has, purportedly, 'completely lost it'. This form of violence is particularly important for drugs–crime links because it is feasible that the effects of some drugs might facilitate such violence. There are clearly cases of people who fall into rages of this kind, during which they may harm themselves and others in ways that do not look like well-planned activity. Most such tantrums occur among children. However, adults with truly uncontrollable rage are relatively rare. A simple test perhaps is whether during their rage they genuinely harm themselves more than they frighten, harm and intimidate others. Children do this more often than adults.

Drugs and violence

Much drug-related violence is an instrumental part of other criminal activity, such as drug dealing or escaping from a crime scene. General drugs–crime connections will be discussed in chapter 4. Additionally, a number of drugs have psychological effects that may make aggression and violence more likely. First, many drugs impair cognitive functioning. Consequently, the intoxicated person may make poor judgements about the threats of the situation that they are in and become aggressive or violent more easily than usual, or less appropriately. Or, they may fail to recognize the severity of their actions at the time. For example, they punch instead of slapping. It is important to appreciate that no drug simply impairs or improves. For example, alcohol can improve cognitive function by reducing anxiety, but can also impair it by suppressing coherent thought. It can make people braver, without thought of the future, but also more cowardly in the face of immediate risks (Steele and Josephs, 1990). Cocaine and amphetamines can both improve cognition, but can also produce grandiose or paranoid thoughts that lead to faulty judgements (e.g., Kalayasiri et al., 2006), and long-term use and deprivation can impair reasoning (Pace-Schott et al., 2005). Drugs like cannabis, ecstasy and the true hallucinogens can lead to delusions and derangement but also to creativity, insight and problem-solving (see Robson, 1999; Ghodse, 2002). Consequently, no drug in common use has guaranteed effects on violence. However, many drugs numb or anaesthetize at larger doses. Once violence has begun, this may make it easier for it to continue with less awareness of pain.

There are also chronic effects that may cause aggression and violence. Long-term use and withdrawal from long-term use, including alcohol hangovers and withdrawal from cannabis, can make the person more irritable and put them in a negative mood, which can lead to overreaction towards other people. Additionally, many drugs interfere with sleep, which may be relatively harmless for one or two nights, but can cause irritability, low mood, cognitive impairment and delusional thinking if deprivation is sustained (e.g., Scott, McNaughton and Polman, 2006).

It has regularly been claimed that various drugs have more direct and pernicious effects on behaviour, literally *making* users aggressive and inconsiderate of others or eroding their moral sense. It has even been claimed that some drugs give people superhuman strength (e.g., Kinlock, 1991). None of these claims have stood up to careful research scrutiny. The effects of drugs on violence are more subtle and situational.

Defining crime in practice

Moving beyond the false idea of a crime as a natural and easily defined act, it may be useful to take a contemporary approach and think about the different stakeholders who are involved when crime occurs. These are the criminal, the police, the legal system – both prosecution and defence – and the health- and social-care system, also the victims of the crime, their families and social networks, as well as the families and social networks of the criminal. A final stakeholder is that rather nebulous entity 'society', which it is easier to speak about, or claim to speak for, than it is to define. Principles of restorative justice (Dignan, 2004) suggest that the ideal outcome of a crime is that the social equilibrium, disrupted by the crime, is restored to the satisfaction of all stakeholders, or even improved. Restorative justice tends to think of crime as a transaction between people rather than focusing on 'criminals'.

A focus on criminals can be unhelpful because thinking about criminals rather than crimes tends to differentiate 'criminals' from other people, who are allegedly normal law-abiding citizens, and to locate the primary causes of 'crime' within criminals. Hence, rather than restoring equilibrium, justice tends to become concerned with treating criminals to prevent their offending in the future – that is, repair whatever was dysfunctional within them that caused their crime. The drug-dependent offender is a stereotypical case of the 'criminal' in this sense. It is important to be cautious in assuming that criminals, even drug-dependent ones, are fundamentally different from other people.

In nation states, the definition of crime usually involves a considerable power imbalance between the offender and the official stakeholders who define them as criminals. The imbalance comes from the offender's comparative lack of information, knowledge, resources and access to physical sanctions. This is not to bemoan injustice. Criminals have indeed often offended. One question is whether their actions would have been treated and labelled as the same sorts of offence if they were different people. Another question is why particular acts become of concern to society when others do not.

For example, in Scotland the drinking of Buckfast tonic wine has become linked with 'ned' culture and hence violence and disorder (http://en.wikipedia.org/wiki/Buckfast_Tonic_Wine; accessed 1 June 2007). This has extended to calls for banning this particular drink, although it actually accounts for only a small percentage of alcohol sales, could readily be replaced by something else, and is only 1 to 2 per cent stronger than most modern New World red table wines. Furthermore, young people report systematic differences in the policing of groups of al fresco drinkers, depending upon whether they look like 'neds' or not, with drinking Buckfast being one sign (Galloway, Forsyth and Shewan, 2007).

Another UK example is that a response to knife crime has been to ban the sales of knives to the under-sixteens, as if they were most likely to wound or kill others with knives. In Scotland, about half the murders are committed with knives (Knife Crime Consultation Team, 2005), but the data are not available to show that knife carrying among the under-sixteens is a special problem deserving a special response. Rather, knife carrying among that nebulous group the 'young' is supposedly the problem. Yet, many 'young' people, including those over sixteen, carry knives for their own protection (Insight Security, 2007).

Researching crime

All the preceding means that researching crime is difficult, and there are usually compromises to be made between getting bogged down in complexities of definition to the point of hopelessness or cynicism and defining crime and criminals so conventionally or naïvely that these definitions virtually determine the research findings. In my view, there is more of the latter type of research than the former. This is in part because much criminological research is commissioned by governments. Civil servants tend to prefer uncomplicated and standardized definitions that will connect with politicians' ideas, and it is research by those definitions that is usually commissioned. For example, there are lots of studies of young, deprived men, but few of law-breaking and immorality by women over sixty. There is much use of a long standard list of questions about specific crimes, but little investigation of how people judge whether or not they have committed or been victim of a crime or not. Is that scratch on the car vandalism or was someone careless in the supermarket car park? Was the fight a 'square go' using violence in culturally accepted ways to resolve a matter of honour between two men, or was it a serious assault? Is losing hundreds of pounds on a misleadingly marketed pension investment scheme less the result of a crime than having the same sum removed from your purse in a bar? We have absolutely no idea how people make such judgements. Instead, most criminology research unhesitatingly assumes that the perspectives of some stakeholders count more than the perspectives of others.

To finish, it is interesting to draw a relevant analogy with psychiatry. Psychiatry developed as a humane alternative to the imprisonment of and contempt for lunatics, who were viewed in nineteenth-century asylums for entertainment by paying members of the public (Neve, 1997). Psychiatry has wrestled with extremely difficult problems of the classification of mental disorders, often taking an inappropriately high-handed, moralistic and arbitrary view of 'mental illness' along the way, frequently relying upon treatments discovered by accident and entirely lacking a credible theoretical basis, and often imposing inappropriate cultural norms, largely belonging to the psychiatrists, on people suffering from mental disorders. Much of this maltreatment occurred (and still occurs) under the guise of science. Nonetheless, psychiatry has made advances: first, in developing a systematic and revisable understanding of mental disorders, with two grand classificatory schemes, the *Diagnostic and Statistical Manual of Mental Disorders* (DSM-IV) and the *International Classification of Diseases*, mental health sections (ICD-10) (such schemes are important because it is possible for researchers and practitioners to agree on what they are studying, which in turn sometimes allows progress, even if and when the classifications are abandoned or considerably revised); second, in developing psychological and physiological models that may help to explain many forms of mental illness; and third, in developing practices that involve, empower and listen to sufferers and attempt to integrate them into society rather than excluding them as mad.

In contrast, criminology is some decades behind psychiatry. It has no systematic classification of crimes, but is instead wracked by attempts to relate moral standards, often arbitrary laws and natural-sounding labels such as 'theft', all of which vary across cultures and history. It lacks convincing models of offending, and those that are available are borrowed from psychiatry and hence apply to criminals, but not to crime transactions. It is also defective in practices that engage and integrate offenders.

If this reads like harsh judgement, try translating some recent policies against crime into mental illness, when they immediately seem rather unjust. 'Three strikes and you're out': *The first two bouts of major depressive illness will be treated in the community. A third bout will result in compulsory hospitalization for at least two years.* 'Disclosure (police checking) if working with children or other vulnerable people': *Before you can obtain employment you need to consent that your health records are checked. If you have suffered from a major mental illness, then you may not be employed.* 'Drug testing and treatment orders': *If you break the law as a result of your mental illness, then you may be required to take medication to treat your mental illness and be tested regularly to ensure that you are taking the medication.* At which point the distinction between mental disorders and offending becomes blurred. One aim of this book is to avoid using drugs as a way of understanding 'criminals' and placing full blame for a wide class of social transactions on specific, stigmatized people.

Summary

Crimes are best understood as transactions between people, rather than as entirely objective events. It matters who defines crime, and how. The nature of those definitions will partially determine drugs–crime relationships. Often, transactions involving certain types of people, often the more socially excluded, including younger people, are more readily defined as 'crime' than similar transactions involving others. Drug problems – defined similarly – also coincide with social exclusion. Crime is often defined to serve the interests of the more powerful in society and control the less powerful. Left-wing and right-wing theories differ only in whether this is the proper thing or not: it may be unavoidable. In consequence, better ways of thinking about crime may actually help resolve crime problems, sometimes by reconceptualizing them.

Discussion points

- In the UK there is currently a lot of concern about violence and disorder in city centres at night, which are blamed on drunkenness and binge drinking. Is binge drinking related to disorder by coincidence – both occur in crowded city centres at night – by society's reduced tolerance of violence, or because alcohol makes people violent? What do we need to find out to be sure about this?
- Would it be feasible to reduce crime by becoming more tolerant of certain transactions currently labelled as crimes?
- Does being tough on crime mean being hard on criminals?

Further reading

Castells, M. (1998). *End of millennium.* Oxford: Blackwell.

Maguire, M., Morgan, R., and Reiner, R. (2007). *The Oxford handbook of criminology.* 4th edn, Oxford: Oxford University Press.

Burke, R. H. (2005). *An introduction to criminological theory.* Cullompton, Devon: Willan.

Newburn, T. (2007). *Criminology.* Cullompton, Devon: Willan.

4

Drugs–Crime Connections

Until recently, most reviews of drugs and crime simply documented the associations between them, with little concern about cause and effect. Nowadays, they are more likely to focus on the outcomes of attempts to intervene. Whether one can intervene successfully without a causal model of the problem is a moot point (Morton, 2004; Pawson and Tilley, 1997).

Detailed drugs–crime connections

The detailed research findings do not suggest that drug use simply leads to drug dependence or problems, which in turn lead to crime. When one goes into depth, there are many different theories that need to be considered. The chapter will be organized by a number of different phenomena that are known to link drugs and crime, some more commonly mentioned than others. Violence was discussed in chapter 3. General phenomena include:

1 the extent to which people are willing to admit deviance
2 the existence of deviant subcultures where in some ways drugs and crime are regarded differently and more tolerantly
3 labelling of the activities of specific undesirables as offending and drug use
4 personality traits that incline the same people to behave in more extreme, more stimulating and possibly more deviant ways
5 a disturbed or disrupted childhood as common cause of both drug use and crime

6 both offending and substance misuse as responses to stress, including the stress caused by becoming an official case in health, social-care and justice systems
7 being more affluent and better adjusted providing protection of various kinds against both drugs and crime, meaning that the same people tend to do, or to be labelled as doing, *neither*
8 mutual social facilitation of drugs and offending, so that offending makes drug use easier and drug use makes offending easier
9 high disposable income from crime leading to extravagant substance use
10 heavy use of drugs encouraging becoming involved in supply, which in turn facilitates extravagant use
11 dependence on drugs requiring money often obtained from crime
12 the psychopharmacological effects of specific drugs facilitating certain types of offending.

Without yet going into detail, it is clear that interventions to reduce drugs–crime links that address only one or two of these twelve phenomena may fail to reduce crime or weaken drugs–crime links, which are often heavily overdetermined. This overdetermination means that, while it is correct that drugs and crime are strongly associated, it is false that one causes the other. It is also worth appreciating the diversity of the phenomena, rendering grand theoretical explanations of drugs and crime unlikely, unless they can encompass a range of phenomena from discourse to biology, taking in psychology in between. Moreover, it would be remarkably difficult to construct a realistic social scenario where drugs and crime were *not* associated. For example, were poverty to be made history, perhaps crime and drug use would fall, but whatever relative poverty was left would tend to be correlated with whatever new behaviours came to be classified as drug use and crime: in the near future, people convicted of criminal water wastage will also be more likely to smoke tobacco. Each of the phenomena and the underlying theory will be discussed in turn.

Willing to admit deviance?

People who admit to, or are willing to discuss, drug use of any kind are more likely to report drug use of other kinds. For example, people who drink alcohol are more likely to admit smoking tobacco and marijuana and more likely to admit offending, but the same association can be found when comparing users and non-users of almost any substance. This non-specific association has been found repeatedly in surveys and in other types of research. It is also important to remember that what people say they do, whether in a survey or to a practitioner, is not necessarily what they really do. There is some evidence that drug use and offending are disassociating as some forms of drug use, such as cannabis smoking, become more normal behaviour (Hammersley, Marsland and Reid, 2003), and that cannabis use and alcohol use are emerging as activities distinct from use of other drugs (Patton et al., 2007). Correlation between different deviant activities suggests either a general tendency to deviance or, perhaps, that some people are less willing to admit to antisocial behaviours than others.

Responding in socially positive ways to questions about drugs and crime seems likely, particularly when it is socially functional to do so. Indeed, when a lie scale is included in drugs surveys, then people who answer in a socially positive way tend to under-report drug and alcohol use (Dalla-Dea, de Miceli and Formigoni, 2003). Admitting other forms of deviance where there is no supposed causal link also tends to be correlated with substance use. Examples include men who admit having sex with men tending to report more substance use than those who do not (Cochran et al., 2004), teenagers with left-wing political views (in 1960s and 1970s USA) tending to report more use of marijuana (Jessor and Jessor, 1977), and people with physical disabilities having higher rates of substance use and other mental health problems (Turner, Lloyd and Taylor, 2006).

This systematic variation in willingness to admit, or even research, deviance is coupled with social conditions where law-abiding, middle-aged, middle-class people are also collectively in a stronger position to define normality and deviance for everyone, particularly in terms of formal laws, rules and regulations. They are relatively unlikely to define their social transactions as being criminal and, when they do, the resultant offences are often regarded as understandable and requiring no special explanation.

For example, even large-scale tax fraud is not studied from the angle that the fraudsters have deep psychological or social problems that 'explain' their behaviour. The most affluent people often pay very little income tax because they have the financial resources to exploit every loophole in the law with the aid of the best lawyers and accountants. This is regarded as conventional offending at worst, if not downright admirable. In contrast, people who work while claiming benefits, with rather more modest losses to the public purse, commit 'crime'. Yet, the extremely wealthy are arguably more deviant, unusual anyway, than benefits fraudsters, and many of them are driven to extreme affluence by complex psychological problems.

Beyond a certain limit there are no sane reasons for pursuing further wealth. More floridly peculiar successes have included Howard Hughes, Robert Maxwell and Michael Jackson. The Duke of Westminster allegedly has his egocentricities (Levy, 2007), while the organizations headed by the two richest men in the world, Bill Gates of Microsoft and Robson Walton of Wal-Mart, have both been accused of unethical and harmful business practices (see www. wikipedia.com), which do not suggest unlimited and inclusive honesty and respect for the rights of others.

The propensity for people to evade the reality of their own deviance tends to be neglected in most research, causing problems in interpretation. Suppose, for example, that schoolchildren who are more conventional, intelligent and prudent use drugs too but are more likely to lie about this in surveys because they are more aware of and concerned about the risks of being honest. This might suffice to cause the well-known inverse relationship between conventional social functioning and drug use. It can be difficult to research such issues of bias and psychological association. When it is possible, it is much harder to fund and enable such research than research about more striking problems such as drug use itself. Many non-researcher stakeholders care more about the findings than about the methods used to obtain them. Good academics tend to care more about the quality of the methods than the meaning of the findings, as they strive to be impartial and honest according to the moral order of science (Harré, 1970). In addiction research and criminology there are always tensions between academic impartiality and the, often extreme, partiality of other stakeholders. Consequently, corruption and debasement of scientific quality is fairly common. Among the corrupting influences are the increasing requirements for the quantification of 'quality' in research (see chapter 9), which leads to pressure always to find something out that can be published, rather than failing to find anything out or concluding that what is already known is sufficient. It is even better if what is published is evidently 'new' or 'important'. The awkwardness for research of deviance evasion should not lead to its being ignored as a serious difficulty for numerating drugs and crime problems.

Deviant social networks

The sociology of deviance has proposed since the 1920s that there are subcultures that tolerate or promote activities which others find deviant. One classic is Howard Becker's (1953) paper on becoming a marijuana user. In some neighbourhoods and social networks, some forms of drug use and drug dealing are normal activities in which people engage to get by (Agar, 1973; Johnson et al., 1985; Bourgois, 1995). There, people may be respected because they have served time in prison, and drug dealers may be regarded as successes. It has been suggested that the life of a criminal heroin user, although hazardous, can be more fulfilling than the realistic alternatives, which amount to welfare or dead-end, low-paid jobs. Within some subcultures it is the more enterprising and successful people who become criminal addicts, not the abject failures (see Golub, Johnson and Dunlap, 2005; Agar, 1973). For example, successful drug dealers may be rewarded by being promoted to the gang board that franchises local dealerships (Levitt and Dubner, 2005).

So, drug users and criminals have social lives and social networks that help sustain their behaviours, and many of their actions may be socially rational and supported. However, policy and the media can be quick to equate 'deviant subculture' with specific deprived neighbourhoods that contain poor, socially excluded people, often from families who have not been in steady employment for more than a generation and often with high proportions of residents of minority ethnicities. This linking of place and subculture is too simple for four reasons.

First, the most visible or dominant culture in a neighbourhood does not necessarily condone or generate most offending or drug use. For example, in a predominantly 'black' neighbourhood there may be a higher proportion of white drug users than black drug users – colour being an index of poverty rather than of drug-sanctioning culture. It is also a problem that the locally dominant subculture may itself be relatively marginalized and may be unable (or unwilling) to obtain support for sincere anti-drugs or crime work that would be readily available in a less marginalized neighbourhood. For example, Rastafarians may not like crack smokers at all, but they may hesitate to call for a local crackdown on drug dealing.

Second, criminal activities penetrate the economics of legitimate life. Money and goods obtained illegally do not go only to criminals. For example, car stereos are typically stolen by children, who do not own cars. Where do the car owners upgrading their stereos think these come from? This illustrates the problems of defining 'crime', which led Ditton (1979) to argue that crime could only be considered to have occurred if it involved arrest and prosecution. Otherwise there is simply behaviour. Additionally, Johnson et al. (1985) offered a case for theft stimulating the economy. A stolen TV is business for insurance and for the police, provides a cheap TV for someone who could not afford to upgrade, and leads to the purchase of a new TV sooner than otherwise for the victim. Despite such points being made repeatedly in criminology, they are usually rejected by policy and the general public as unpalatable.

Moreover, drugs and crime can bring cash into social networks and neighbourhoods that may have very few other economic resources. Forsyth et al. (1992) described how the dealing of harder drugs involved travelling further, to more deprived areas. Pull the drug dealing from some areas and there would be almost no economy at all. Dealers and criminals who have cash are likely to share some of it with family and friends (McKeganey and Barnard, 1992) and also spend in local service industries. Clichés about heroin users spending all their money on drugs are inaccurate: lots of it, yes; all of it, no (Hammersley et al., 1989). Cash from family or friends may be accepted, 'no questions asked', or it may be passed off as gambling winnings, cash in hand from casual work, or the result of other strokes of fortune. Somewhat inconsistently, therefore, some of the outraged mothers against drugs may be profiting from drugs by not wondering sufficiently where the money comes from. This is of course far easier when their children are discreet, are well behaved at home and do not fit the junkie stereotype.

Third, assuming that people acquire values from their neighbourhood has always been simplistic and has broken down further over the last fifty years, with improved communications at a distance, cheaper travel, TV, other mass media and, most recently, the internet. Social stratification often precludes the free mingling of different 'types' of neighbours. People have long and often maintained social contacts at a distance by the telephone and other means (Castells, 2002, 120). While more people in more deprived neighbourhoods may have relatively few links outside their home locality, this is far from uniformly true. Indeed, drugs and crime themselves can generate national or even global links. For example, people may form gang and other criminal contacts in prison that become the basis for criminal networks inside and outside (Fong, 1990). Within a neighbourhood, gang membership can form a powerful social grouping and provide social and personal identity (Cloward and Ohlin, 1961; Branch, 1997), but not all people, or even all young men, are affiliated to a gang.

Fourth, if a person's social and cultural identity ever was a consistent representation of a coherent local culture, then those days have vanished. At least since the industrial revolution and urbanization, there has been a myth of a self-contained and cohesive local community that was somehow different from the modern neighbour-hood, with its transience, uncertainty and anomie. Nowadays, rather ironically, the closest fit perhaps lies in localities that are coherent mainly through lack of choice and opportunity because relatively few inhabitants can acquire the financial and educational means to leave or develop wider social networks. For instance, this fits the deprived US inner-city areas studied by Golub and Johnson (1999). In the UK, there are some drug injectors even in leafy suburbs and charming country towns. If their activities are normalized in a subculture, rather than merely tolerated, it is not one based on place.

In a large, complex society, it is not clear who defines cultural values; it is no longer simply those in power – the priests, kings, military or politicians. Instead, there are a number of competing voices, usually including politicians, religious leaders, the media, educationalists and various kinds of celebrities. Often, these spokespeople are pronouncing upon a nostalgic fantasy of society where their kind truly wielded power, which fails to recognize the contemporary importance of a multiplicity of networks implemented with the aid of the internet, telephones and other technology. In some Islamic states, people also watch 'Baywatch' on satellite TV, featuring scantily clad Californian lifeguards. It is unrealistic to believe that networked people (Castells, 1998) garner their values from their local neighbourhoods, for an increasing number will have more than one home over their lives, just for a start. Instead, networked people assemble values according to the networks with which they are currently affiliated. It may also be unrealistic to assume that individual people's values are durable or consistent across different social situations or networks (Jenkins, 1996). It is likely that people are honest in some situations and dishonest in others, are substance users in some situations and not in others. At the extreme, people are capable of overseeing mass murder while also being kindly family men. The media eternally delight in the stereotype of a political figure or celebrity whose private life does not match their public values, whether it be the socialist who loves luxury or the religious leader promoting family values and visiting prostitutes. (See Hammersley, Jenkins and Reid (2001) for discussion of the situational meanings of cannabis and Reid and Hammersley (2000) for a general discussion of the social construction of personal identity.)

Castells (1998) emphasizes that non-networked people who have limited access to computer and other global networks have become socially excluded and predicts that this gap will widen. For people from impoverished neighbourhoods with poor infrastructures and limited educational or economic opportunities, it may make more sense to talk about a neighbourhood culture or set of values. It is those values that are often most criticized by society's spokespeople, usually themselves networked. To an extent, this is a double standard based still on the class system.

Positive values common in socially excluded neighbourhoods include:

- loyalty to family and close friends, sometimes with the downside of xenophobia and distrust of most outsiders
- sharing of whatever limited assets are available
- cunning and fortitude in getting by in very adverse life circumstances, but including tolerance of activities that are not fully within the law and being willing to act the fool, or play helpless, to the authorities when it is expedient to do so
- a down-to-earth practical approach to life that mistrusts grand pronouncements, religious edicts and the like, at the expense of not living for future health, wealth and respectability.

This can lead to a tolerance of hedonism and widespread hedonistic behaviour, including heavy substance use (see, for example, Bourgois, 1995; McKeganey and Barnard, 1992; Wight, 1993). The more negative label for this approach is 'fatalism', although Buddhism proposes that acceptance of life is a route to peace and contentment. In the UK and the USA at least, this is considered non-problematic when acceptance involves a passive accommodation of one's lot, but can become a social problem when it involves making the best of a bad job by any means necessary, including active, deviant means that are not healthy.

What complicates the mix yet further is that society's values are increasingly ascertained or invented by research or journalism of one kind or another, as when market research organizations hold focus groups to discuss a politician's presentation of self, which is fed back to her advisors and causes changes in presentation that are discussed in the newspapers, or, more pertinently to this book, when journalists visited early UK Acid House clubs, noticed that nobody was drinking alcohol and inferred that they were taking drugs. Which drugs? At this point there did not appear to be significant quantities of MDMA in the UK, but journalists popularized 'the love drug' anyway, and soon the newly christened 'Ecstasy' was being marketed in mass quantities (see Hammersley, Khan and Ditton, 2002).

One must be wary of assuming that 'conventional society' exists or has a list of values on which its members would agree. Values are probably subject to continuous renegotiation in interpersonal transactions (Jenkins, 1996). Part of that renegotiation is to define values by contrast with their opposites. People often find it easier to point to the deviant than they do to describe the normal, because they tend to be more aware of difference and anomaly. In this context, criminals and drug addicts are useful horror examples that help us decide what we are not. Such stereotypes impede a sensible approach to tackling drug and crime problems. These problems belong to society, they are not alien to it.

Social identity is defined by test cases at the boundaries of acceptability. For example, even a quick look at the pictures of women/girls in mainstream women's and men's magazines in the UK suggests considerable conflict over the boundary between finding young women sexually attractive, naturally, and finding under-age girls sexually attractive in a paedophilic way. Many of the models look barely pubescent, which is all the more deviant because children are reaching puberty younger than they used to. When twelve-year-olds can look sixteen it is odd that eighteen-year-old models often look fourteen and are selling clothes to 35-year-olds. It is also interesting that the rise in this glut of images of childlike bodies occurred at the same time as the rise in obesity, along with a detestation of paedophiles. People both love and hate what they cannot have.

The same clearly applies to drug use. Substance users (i.e., almost everyone) are keen to define their activity as within the boundaries of acceptability, and one means of doing this is to define other, purportedly more extreme or dangerous, forms of use as over the edge. So, contrasts are set up between the harmful and dangerous substance use of the young and the sensible practices of the mature, between social drinking and binge drinking, between alcohol and cannabis, between cannabis and 'hard' drugs, between cocaine and heroin and, ultimately, between the latest, so naturally worst, drug craze and whatever came before, as when crack cocaine was judged even worse than heroin. I recall a 1990s TV documentary about the US Drug Enforcement Agency. Heavily armed officers burst into an apartment seeking crack dealers. The man in bed exclaimed anxiously, 'Hey man, I'm just a junkie, there ain't no crack here.'

A similar analysis might be applied to many crimes. Tolerance of violence is falling and perhaps has been falling for as long as there have been historical records. William the Bastard (rebranded in England as William the Conqueror after the Norman invasion of 1066) broke the siege of Alençon by having the hands and feet of his captives chopped off and catapulted into the besieged town, which surrendered (http://members.tripod.com/~GeoffBoxell/willie.htm; accessed   18

Personality traits

Certain personality traits are related to drug use and offending. One widely accepted way of modelling general personality is with the 'big five' personality dimensions: Calm – Nervous; Extraverted – Introverted; Closed-minded – Open to new experiences; Disorganized – Conscientious; Disagreeable – Agreeable (Costa and McCrae, 1997). Several of these dimensions look as if they might be related to drugs and crime, and indeed they are, but matters are complicated by the fact that the five-factor questionnaire is just one of many measures of personality that have been used to research crime and substance use. Different measures are related to each other in complex ways. To abbreviate the story, offenders tend to be nervous, extraverted, disorganized and disagreeable. Substance users tend to be extraverted, nervous, disorganized and open to new experiences. However, a lot of the research has been done in normal populations, usually students, correlating personality with consumption of alcohol and perhaps marijuana and tobacco as well – but not extending to problem substance use. Alternatively, research has been done in clinical or criminal populations. Furthermore, psychology is more interested in personality disorders, such as psychopathy, than in offending itself. So there is more work describing the psychopathic criminal's personality than describing any personality traits that might be related to offending in a more mundane manner. To understand drugs–crime–personality links in general, a study would have to survey self-reported offending and substance use and measure general personality traits in a large sample. This does not appear to have been done. When surveys of offending or substance use include personality measures, then these are typically tailored towards measuring undesirable traits such as aggression, rather than assessing personality comprehensively.

According to some studies, extraverts, who, the theory goes, are naturally less highly aroused and hence require more stimulation to achieve their optimal level of arousal, tend to use substances more (De Winne and Johnson, 1976; Spotts and Shontz, 1984) and to offend more (Rushton and Chrisjohn, 1981). An alternative measure that resembles extraversion combined with openness to new experiences is sensation-seeking, which is a tendency to enjoy and pursue new sensations and experiences, even odd, frightening or dangerous ones. Not surprisingly sensation-seeking too is correlated with alcohol and cannabis use (Hittner and Swickert, 2006; Donohew et al., 1999) and offending (Knust and Stewart, 2002). Sensation-seeking/extraversion

might explain substance use for pleasure or recreation, while introversion might predict heavier or more problematic use, for example to
escape problems or anxieties.

Nervousness, or neuroticism, is also related to drugs and crime in
surveys (Rushton and Chrisjohn, 1981; Spotts and Shontz, 1984;
Ruiz, Pincus and Dickinson, 2003), and neurotic problems such as
depression and anxiety occur at high rates among substance-using
offenders (e.g., Pelissier and O'Neil, 2000). In some cases, depression
or anxiety precedes offending or substance use, but in most cases all
the problems develop at the same time, usually across the teenage
years, making it meaningless to label one cause and the other effect.
A problem with interpreting the evidence is that depression and
anxiety occur at high rates in the general population. Studies of
depression and anxiety do not always assess substance use well, so the
seeming association could be coincidence, or, more plausibly, some
of the depression and anxiety found in surveys might actually involve
substance use problems too. Furthermore, what if people more
readily admit depression than addiction in surveys? Disagreeableness/
hostility is also related to substance use and offending (Samuels et al.,
2004; Ruiz, Pincus and Dickinson, 2003; McCormick et al., 1998).

Impulsiveness   Organization/disorganization connects to a number of
thoroughly studied personality links to drugs and crime. People who
are impulsive tend to be disorganized, to commit offences and to use
substances more (Carroll et al., 2006; Brotchie et al., 2003). Also,
people with attention-deficit hyperactivity disorder (see below) tend
to be impulsive and disorganized and, perhaps in consequence, offend
and use substances more. Strictly, one should say that people who
admit to, or are caught, offending or using substances tend to be more
impulsive and disorganized. Highly organized people may be less
likely to do these things, or merely less likely to get caught, or more
likely to avoid the transactions commonly labelled 'crime' and choose
other morally dubious activities that are less likely to be sanctioned.

Early temperament   A number of features of temperament in infancy
and early childhood are predictive of substance use when older, but
again not in a specific way (Werner and Smith, 1982). Infants who are
'easy' and do not get upset or fearful in novel situations tend to
develop better social skills than infants who get upset. An early indicator of likely problems is that young children prone to temper
tantrums fare less well and are more likely to have substance problems
and offend as adolescents and adults, as well as being more likely to

have other mental health, behavioural and social problems. It is not easy to map 'temper tantrums' in toddlers on to the big five adult personality measures, but neurotic, non-conscientious, disorganized, disagreeable extraverts might be predicted to be more likely to have temper tantrums, to the extent that personality is stable over the life course.

Addictive personalities?   The idea of an addictive personality has slid into popular language to describe someone who has difficulty both in resisting temptations, particularly sensual ones, and in engaging moderately in enjoyable activities. This is more a generic description of 'addiction' than an explanation of it, and is applied loosely to activities such as eating, sex, work and extreme sports as well as the classic addictions. Indeed, someone who is inclined to temperance and moderation is unlikely to work, play, gamble or consume excessively, but why do people differ in this regard? Studies of the 'addictive personality' have generally failed to find a consistent personality profile to describe people with drug or alcohol problems. Rather, the quite general traits reviewed above modestly predict substance use. Additionally, there are a number of different psychological problems that involve extreme traits and predict offending and substance use problems among other difficulties. These include the personality disorders and attention-deficit hyperactivity disorder. Lay use of the term 'addictive personality' to describe someone may describe their behaviour, but does not describe a consistent underlying personality structure. *Trainspotting* (Welsh, 1993) provides an excellent novelistic portrayal of the diverse personalities who can become heroin users. A small group of friends include a psychopath (Begbie, who doesn't use heroin), a narcissist (Sick Boy), someone a bit socially and intellectually inadequate (Spud), someone who is quite capable but struggling to break free of his dysfunctional peers (Renton) and various other personalities.

Personality disorders   When used correctly, the term 'personality disorder' is applied to a person whose philosophy of life and approach to the world is both different from the norm and in some sense dysfunctional, usually because it severely impedes their normal psychological growth and harms their relationships with other people. Thanks to horror movies and action thrillers, many people have a lurid conception of these disorders, picturing lunatics brandishing chainsaws and merciless assassins. In fact most people with personality disorders go about the world unnoticed and largely harmlessly. As many as 11 per cent of the population may have a diagnosable personality disorder (Lenzenweger et al., 1997). An important general link to drugs and crime is that all personality disorders make it harder for sufferers to develop stable, successful careers. Not working makes crime more tempting and drugs easier to get into. There are a number of different labels for these disorders, although some people exhibit mixtures of them, and the labels are to an extent categories of convenience. Three key ones particularly related to offending and substance use will be described in turn.

ANTISOCIAL PERSONALITY DISORDER (ALSO CALLED 'PSYCHOPATHY' AND 'SOCIOPATHY')   Someone suffering from antisocial personality disorder has difficulty empathizing with other people as having equal rights and feelings as themselves. Rather, they consider other people as resources to be exploited and manipulated to further their own ends, whether sexually, financially or otherwise. Lacking empathy, they often think that people who do not behave like them are stupid, or that other people do secretly behave like them, or wish they had the courage to do so. Some people with antisocial personality disorder are intelligent, calculating and ruthless manipulators who rise to the top of their careers, while others are less intelligent, more impulsive, or less effective and repeatedly come to grief by failing to appreciate the consequences that their actions will have. For example, they will hurt someone to get what they want, without recognizing that this will be considered grievous bodily harm and lead to their imprisonment. Antisocial personality disorder is related to offending because sufferers may be motivated not to offend only by the harm to them of getting caught. It is related to heavy substance use and substance . . . use problems because sufferers see no reason why social norms of temperance and moderation should apply to them, and they care little about any psychological, social or financial damage that their substance abuse may cause to others. They are also willing to offend in order to buy their drugs. So a large minority of drug-dependent offenders have antisocial personality disorder – over 30 per cent in one study of imprisoned substance users (Pelissier and O'Neil, 2000). But, the majority have different problems.

There ought also to be concern that the term 'antisocial personality disorder' may sometimes be applied to people behaving normally within a deviant subculture, particularly if diagnosis is not undertaken carefully and in a culturally sensitive manner. A heroin-using thief who persistently violates the rights of others by stealing from them and has only heroin-using friends, whom he will rip off sometimes, may have a personality disorder, or he may be behaving according to the norms of the subculture (where people with true antisocial personality disorder will also thrive). It is not going to be that easy to tell. 'Antisocial behaviour' does not necessarily mean antisocial personality. Furthermore, when offenders are studied there is a risk of taking their antisocial behaviour to be evidence of antisocial personality, which is circular reasoning (Cooke et al., 2004).

NARCISSISTIC PERSONALITY DISORDER People with narcissistic personality disorder can empathize with others, but they have an exaggerated sense of their own importance and entitlement in the world. This includes having unrealistically high expectations of what other people should give, or owe, them, coupled with little expectation that such giving should be reciprocated. Consequently, their very high expectations are often disappointed, leading to frustration, sadness and repeatedly broken relationships when people fail to live up to their expectations. They are often puzzled about why the world is not the way that they think it should be. They may resort to more and more extreme means to force the world to live up to their expectations, which can include making dramatic demands of other people, such as threatening suicide or otherwise forcing a crisis that will push them onto centre stage. Narcissism is related to offending, because people with this disorder may offend to obtain what they feel they are entitled to – why should *they* pay tax? – and they may also offend as part of their self-centred acting-out. Additionally, they can sometimes be aggressive towards others who fail to meet their high expectations. Sometimes this can be disproportionate to the perceived failure. For example, they might assault a service industry worker because they *should not* be kept waiting. Among the things to which they may feel entitled is excessive quantities of drugs or alcohol. They may fail to accept that health risks apply to them, and additionally they may use drugs or alcohol to manage the stress caused by their frustrating condition.

BORDERLINE PERSONALITY DISORDER People with borderline personality disorder have a fragile sense of self that needs frequently to be bolstered by the regard and concern of other people. They also tend to feel that, of themselves, they have little or no worth and that their identity depends on the regard of others. Thus, they are needy of other people and hypersensitive to rejection and abandonment. Consequently, when other people like them and treat them nicely they tend to worry that the other people are either stupid or will stop being nice once they discover their real natures. One result of this is that people with borderline personality disorder often test intimate relationships to destruction by behaving badly to see if the other person will stick with them. As is the case with those suffering from narcissistic personality disorder, they may self-medicate with drugs or alcohol and use drugs as part of their destructive acting-out. If they offend, it also tends to be as a form of acting-out, revenge or destructiveness. However, if they are substance dependent then they may additionally offend to buy drugs or alcohol.

Personality disorders are topical in the UK because there is currently debate concerning what to do about people whose disorders are so severe that they are difficult to treat and pose a threat to themselves or others unless they are incarcerated. Personality disorders used to be considered very hard to treat and to be more or less permanent. For instance Bowlby's ([1963] 1997) attachment theory postulated that antisocial personality was formed by failed early attachment, as can occur among institutionalized orphans or the children of deeply depressed parents. Recently, it has been found that the disorders can change and improve over time (Lenzenweger, Johnson and Willett, 2004), and there are advances in treating them with cognitive behavioural techniques (Linehan, 1993). There is probably more of a continuum from normal to 'personality disorder' than previously thought. The implication of this is that there needs to be extreme caution about detaining people on the assumption that they cannot change and may offend again.

Attention-deficit hyperactivity disorder   This is not a personality disorder, but the symptoms are often confused with personality disorder symptoms. Sufferers from ADHD (also known as ADD) are believed to have abnormalities in their brain frontal cortex that impair the ability to plan and control their behaviour (Barkley, 2006). These abnormalities may be acquired during early brain development and are probably in part inherited. They are not caused by poor parenting or other mainly environmental factors, although the impact of ADHD can be lessened by good parenting and management. However, management can be challenging for parents, so problems are liable to be worse in poorly functioning families, and the presence of someone with the disorder can worsen family function. Symptoms can also be exacerbated by stress and tiredness, so lifestyle management and good routine are also important.

Sufferers tend to have difficulty concentrating for long periods of time and in organizing their activities, are easily distracted and can be restless, fidgety, excessively talkative and impulsive. This often causes them problems at school and at home and can lead to their being continually reprimanded for misbehaviour that they find difficult to control, such as constantly interrupting, which can damage their self-esteem. Doing badly at school and low self-esteem can predispose young people to drugs and crime. Additionally, impulsivity predisposes people to drugs and crime. Finally, stimulant drugs can be used to treat ADHD. This may sound paradoxical, but these drugs stimulate the parts of the frontal cortex that inhibit undesired behaviour, calming the person down. So, sometimes ADHD sufferers, even undiagnosed ones, learn to use amphetamines or cocaine to self-medicate their condition. They may also use other drugs and alcohol to cope, rather than self-medicate. ADHD is probably under-diagnosed and common in the population, with perhaps 5 per cent of children having it (Barkley, 2006), so it is probably a frequent unrecognized contributor to adolescent behavioural problems, although it can also be applied inappropriately as a label for disorderly children.

Summary   There are difficulties in relating different measures of personality to each other, but it is clear that similar personalities share inclinations to substance use and to offending. It is not clear that there is a distinct 'addictive personality' beyond the fact that what inclines to one form of substance use inclines also to another. Additionally, a number of different personality traits, in various combinations, predispose people to substance use and crime. At the extreme, some personality disorders and ADHD also predispose individuals to substance use and crime, but they are not simple causes of either.

Disturbed or disrupted childhood

Child and adolescent development may be related to both drug use and crime in a number of ways, which will be explored in detail in chapter 5. Broadly speaking, adverse life circumstances in childhood challenge childhood adjustment and make both substance use and crime more likely.

Donohue and Levitt (2001) controversially argued that freely available abortion led to a drop in crime rates in the USA because the never-born children included many whose life chances would have been slender and who would very likely have become criminal. The accuracy of their statistical analyses has been debated (Foote and Goetz, 2005). Moreover, the causal chain described to explain the association between abortion rates and crime rates should also apply to substance dependence, if not substance use itself, as dependent people often have multiple problems originating in difficult child-hoods. This does not seem to be the case: indeed, drug use rose in the USA over the period when crime fell.

A less sensational but more plausible explanation is that both offending and substance misuse are responses to stress, including the stress caused by becoming an official case in health, social-care and justice systems (see Hammersley, Marsland and Reid, 2003). The impact of stress on mental and physical health is additive, cumulative and chronic (Holmes and Rahe, 1967): different causes combine to produce stress, protracted stress is worse than brief stress, and the effects of serious stress can persist for months or years after it has ceased. In the case of very serious trauma, such as being imprisoned in a concentration camp, the effects can persist for an entire lifetime (Levi, [1947] 1991). Major positive events are stressful, as well as major negative ones. For example, a parent giving up drinking or drug use can impose strain on the family even although the overall effect is positive (Velleman, 2006). The same applies to a parent being released from prison, as well as being imprisoned in the first place. It is likely that many of the risk factors that predict drug use and offending are actually varied sources and indirect signs of stress. It is stress that causes the problems, rather than a specific structure of risk factors. This would explain why the impact of risk factors tends to be non-specific and overdetermined. Risk factors tend to predict a range of social and psychological problems in adolescents and adults rather than being specific to specific problems, and many people who have drug problems or are persistent offenders have multiple risk factors.

Affluence and good adjustment protects

As already discussed, it is also important that being in a more affluent and better-adjusted family provides protection of various kinds against both drugs and crime, meaning that the same people tend to do *neither*. A primary explanation for this may be that the child's stress levels tend to be lower. Also, when they engage in the activities and transactions that might be defined as drug use or crime, their families are more likely to be able to call upon their social capital to protect the child against these definitions. There are various ways in which this occurs, including the family being able to provide better emo-tional support, being able to dispute the definitions in appropriate ways, and being able to call upon their wider social network to support and testify on behalf of the possibly delinquent child.

However, family functioning is influenced by the functioning of all family members. When a family has a child who is oppositional and defiant or has ADHD, then this can be as stressful for the parents as parenting a child with a more overt disability such as autism (Barkley, 2006). Furthermore, some such disorders appear to have a substantial genetic component, meaning that families not unusually contain more than one person with similar problems. All this can impede adjustment and cause stress for everyone, worsening all problems. In short, dysfunction in the family can make the family dysfunctional and may lower their affluence and increase their social exclusion. Similarly, a drug or alcohol problem in the family can have wide repercussions.

Thus, the discovery of the protective value of good family and affluence does not necessarily mean that these can be engineered for families that are already struggling. Such families may, for example, be unreceptive to parenting programmes and may wreck attempts to increase their prosperity. When interventions are offered that actually address major family concerns and appreciate the severity of their difficulties, then these can have an impact (e.g., Schumacher & Kurz, 2000). Perhaps it is simplistic interventions that are the problem.

Social facilitation

Drugs and crime are socially connected as long as drugs are criminalized, in that obtaining and consuming drugs may require more association with people also willing to commit other offences than the drug user would prefer. Also, criminals may have more exposure to drugs and drug users because other criminals are more likely to use drugs than are the general population. Furthermore, because they are illegal, drugs are supplied by people who are willing to break the law. Some drug suppliers are only willing to break anti-drug laws (Potter and Dann, 2005), but they may nonetheless be more tolerant of law-breaking than the norm and may have to consort with criminals to supply drugs. Drug supply can also involve highly organized criminals motivated by illicit profit rather than provision of a desired but illegal service to their peers. In this mix, it is feasible for criminals to develop drug problems and for drug users to escalate their criminality. For example, skilled cannabis growers motivated by an alternative lifestyle can be lured into cultivation for profit.

Some national drug policies, notably that of the Netherlands, are explicitly aimed at reducing these links, for instance by providing access to drugs, particularly cannabis, without recourse to the black market. As found in the Netherlands, such policy does not usually

reduce drug use, and may even increase it, but the intent is not erad-
ication of intoxication (anyway what about alcohol?) but minimization
of the harm caused (see Reinarman, 2000).

The current climate for drugs is generally like that for alcohol in
some Middle Eastern countries, where drinking is banned. Where
alcohol is more widely and routinely consumed, it tends to be worse
for health but less coupled to crime, violence and other social problems. Squeezing alcohol, by introducing tighter controls and more
temperate traditions, tends to lead to drinking by fewer people, less
often, but consuming more when they drink at all. It tends to increase
links to crime, deviance and other social and health problems for
drinkers, but at the benefit of reduced health problems in the general
population. Were drug laws to be relaxed, it is most likely that links
with crime would weaken – indeed this may already have happened
where drug use has normalized (Parker, Aldridge and Measham,
1998) – but at the cost of health problems increasing in the population, with more people having problems related to drug use, of a less
severe kind.

It is also likely, but under-researched, that deviance generally promotes wider deviance. People who already believe that some of their
behaviours are socially problematic and unacceptable may be more
likely to engage also in other deviant activities because they feel that
they have less to lose.

Were some drugs to be more tolerated, then perhaps their links to
crime would be weakened. However, the costs would include (1) more
health problems related to drug use and (2) the continued or even
worsened linking of crime and whichever substances or forms of use
were *not* tolerated. For it seems unlikely and unwise that a society
should tolerate any and all forms of substance use.

High disposable income from crime leading to extravagant substance use

Crime provides funds that can facilitate a growing and eventually very
large drug habit. Many drug users would be unable to develop a full-
blown dependence without being competent criminals because this
can easily cost upwards of £80 per day. When more funds are available from crime, then heroin injectors tend to take more heroin; when
little cash is to be had they may not be able to get any heroin at all
(Johnson et al., 1985). At least in this sense, drug-dependent criminals are as dependent on crime as they are on drugs. It is a matter
of economic logic. Furthermore, users developing a big habit can

sometimes get into serious debt to dealers. Repayment is policed with threats, ultimately of serious physical harm, although these are not necessarily enacted immediately (Denton and O'Malley, 1999). This can force users to offend or be hurt.

Heavy use of drugs encouraging becoming involved in supply

Johnson (1973) found that cannabis use was not linked to crime, but that cannabis dealing was. The pathways were that cannabis dealing led to heavier use of a wider range of drugs and that dealing led to associating with skilled criminals. Furthermore, it is relatively easy for a dealer to consume their supply rather than selling it, get into debt and be required to repay substantial sums of money through other criminal activity, or face even worse sanctions. Dealers are also more likely to be exposed to the widest range of drugs available.

Dependence

Eventually, we arrive at what used to be considered the primary explanation for drugs–crime relationships. People offend because they are dependent on drugs to a level that makes the drugs feel like a necessity and results in the necessary quantities of drugs being expensive. Consequently they offend to get money to take drugs, feeling that they have little choice in the matter. The popular portrayal of this link is that, as they experience withdrawal, the desperate addicts are driven into action and rush out to rob or steal by any means necessary. This happens sometimes, but according to our respondents in one study (Hammersley et al., 1989) the problem is that crime requires skill and cunning, both of which are impaired during withdrawal, so the withdrawing person is likely, out of desperation, to make mistakes and get caught or commit crimes at which they are not skilled. Sensible drug injectors keep a small quantity for the morning to sort them out so that they can go to work before enjoying their drugs afterwards – more like the hair of the dog than the frantic drug fiend. Similar findings have been reported elsewhere (e.g., Johnson et al., 1985). Dependence certainly fuels a sizeable want of money, but effective criminality requires holding it together (Agar, 1973). When the habit becomes too much to hold together can be the point when things can start to go wrong with criminal activities. For example, one respondent claimed he was a skilled pickpocket who had never been successfully prosecuted for that particular crime. He was in jail for trying to break into an off-licence through its roof, desperate because he was out of cash and drugs.

Pharmacological effects facilitating crime

The acute and intoxicating or chronic and cumulative effects of drugs might facilitate some types of crime. Some drugs might damage people's moral sense or decision making and render them less capable of distinguishing right from wrong. An obvious example would be someone so drunk that they do not realize that they are urinating in the street. Intoxication may reduce anxiety or fear and thus facilitate behaviours the person would find difficult when sober. It may be easier to hit other people, or find the banter to con one's way into a building to steal things. Some drugs block pain and make it easier to do things that would usually hurt, such as fighting the police or hitting people. However, it is possible to get the dose wrong, usually too high. For example, the sleeping pill temazepam is a popular drug of abuse in Scotland. When it is taken in excess users 'think they are invisible', offend carelessly and get caught (Hammersley and Pearl, 1997). Finally, drug use and crime simply co-occur. Criminals meet in pubs and drink alcohol before offending, because where else would they meet? People with drug problems offend when high on drugs because they do *everything* when high on drugs. The people caught while driving drunk or stoned often did not crash or get arrested simply because the drug impaired their judgement or ability, but because they get stoned or drunk so often that they are not even going to refrain before driving, which is indeed a warning sign of having a problem (Hammersley and Leon, 2006).

There is a long history of exaggerated claims made for the powers of drugs. Earnest claims that a drug directly causes bad behaviour tend initially to be taken at face value, even when scientific evidence is lacking. In methodologically adequate research it is surprisingly difficult to show that any of the commonly misused drugs directly 'cause' any behaviour. For instance, one would expect it to be easy to demonstrate that alcohol facilitates violence rather than merely being correlated with it. It is not easy, and the relationship seems to be subtle and complicated, in part because violence is complicated, as discussed in chapter 3.

Summary

Drugs and crime are linked in many ways. The problems are socially constructed together using the same assumptions, cultural values, power structures and discourse, tend to occur in similar social conditions, and tend to be outcomes of similar psychological development (see also chapter 5). Each tends to facilitate the other in a number of ways. Large drug problems are difficult for most people without money from crime, which further ties the two together. A drug problem can focus some people excessively on acquiring drugs. While some forms of drug use in theory could depart from a society entirely, all modern complex societies include intoxicants and there is a massive demand for them. Were the drugs currently linked to crime to disappear, they would probably be replaced by others, notably alcohol. Crime probably cannot be eliminated from any society, because it lies across contemporary social boundaries, whatever those are. The boundaries can shift, and intolerance of crime tends to make the acceptable area within the boundary smaller. People who transgress the boundaries tend also to use drugs and may take use to extremes. It is not clear that this is the first, or the worst, of their problems, despite its often being the most dramatic and most vilified.

Discussion points

- Do you always tell the truth about your substance use? Why not?
- Why do people like the idea of an addictive personality?
- What would a society that had drugs but no crime look like?

Further reading

Bean, P. (2004). *Drugs and crime.* 2nd edn, Cullompton, Devon: Willan.

Bennett, T., and Holloway, K. (2005). *Understanding drugs, alcohol and crime.* London: McGraw-Hill.

Lightfoot, L. O. (2005). *Programming for offenders with substance abuse and dependence problems.* Ottawa: Correctional Service of Canada.

Stevens, A., Berto, D., Kerschi, V., Oeuvray, K., van Ooyen, M., Steffan, E., Heckman, W., and Uchtenhagen, A. (2003). *Summary literature review: the international literature on drugs, crime and treatment.* Canterbury: University of Kent, European Institute of Social Services.

Stevens, A., Trace, M., and Bewley-Taylor, D. (2005). *Reducing drug-related crime: an overview of the global evidence.* London: Beckley Foundation.

RSA (2007). *Drugs – facing facts: the report of the RSA commission on illegal drugs, communities and public policy.* London: Royal Society for the Encouragement of Arts, Manufactures and Commerce.

5
Drugs, Crime, Adolescence and Youth

Understanding deviant and delinquent behaviour in adolescence has been hindered by four conceptual problems. First, there is the concern, discussed in chapter 4, that the activities of youth, particularly young socio-economically deprived men, tend to be labelled as more problematic than equivalent activities by other social groups. What superficially looks like change due to age may sometimes be a change due to how society labels the activities of the maturing person. For drugs and crime, this often amounts to paying less attention to adult misbehaviour and over-focusing on the transgressions of the young.

Second, to understand how behaviours develop we would need a better understanding of what is normal for adults. Work on drugs and crime often muddles three senses of 'normal': the typical, the legitimate and the tolerable. Typical adult behaviour is diverse, and many activities neither completely legitimate nor fully tolerable are common, including dishonesty, heavy drinking and some forms of drug use. Among legitimate behaviours are those that are legal and, more problematically, those that are acceptable in some contexts, but questionably legal – for example, a 'lock-in' drinking session in a bar. Arguably, society offers fewer legitimate venues for the illegal activities of young people, which tends to problematize their offending and substance use. Tolerable activities are those that are widely accepted, whether or not they are legal or typical. Cannabis use is widely tolerated, even by non-users. As discussed in previous chapters, the boundaries of the typical, legitimate and tolerable vary. Cannabis use is not, and should not be, tolerated anywhere, anytime. Furthermore, cannabis use that would be tolerated were the smokers aged twenty-five may be viewed with grave concern should they be thirteen, even if the setting was otherwise tolerant (e.g., a music festival).

While many activities are typical, tolerated and legitimate, the three are not logically connected. Typical activities, such as sexual infidelity, may be neither tolerated nor legitimized. Tolerated activities, such as fiddling taxes, may not be typical or legitimized. Legitimate activities, such as high bank charges, may not be typical or tolerated. Data on the reported prevalence of activities, which are often all that is available, do not clarify these meanings.

Third, there is the problem of 'naturalism', which is thinking that we know what is natural for human beings and therefore can readily identify that which is deviant or unnatural. In understanding adolescence and youth, naturalism can involve confusing biological maturation with an inevitable progression towards being a 'normal' adult. It is widely assumed that only when this maturation is disrupted somehow do drugs, crime or other abnormalities come about, and the basic research question is often 'What is wrong with these young people that offend and/or take drugs?' Then, once what is wrong is identified, interventions are designed to prevent, repair or redress it. This common-sense approach is hindered by the lack of a coherent theory of what a normal adult is, or should be. Often, moralistic judgements about how young people should behave appear in criminological research as if it were self-evident that adults do not generally behave in such ways. This can lead to earnest discussions among policy makers and researchers that part company from common-sense observations of people on the street. For instance, much concern about drugs seems to assume that drugs are generally so unenjoyable and dangerous that only people under intense pressure or who are somehow disturbed of mind would take them, which ignores adults' eager intoxication most weekend nights in most city centres and holiday resorts. Of course, that is mostly about alcohol (is it?), which is somehow different (is it?).

Fourth, building on the previous difficulties, there is often lack of clarity about whether research is supposed to be explaining the development of 'problems' in adolescence and adulthood, or whether it is supposed to be explaining the entire spectrum of substance use and delinquency, including the many activities that are widespread, but disapproved of. Widespread activities may have no special causes that can be addressed with interventions. In contrast, the career of a heavily substance-dependent persistent criminal may be depressingly overdetermined to the point that many interventions are a spit in the ocean of their problems. Too often, research lacks conceptual clarity on these points and consequently struggles to offer a coherent theory of the development of substance use and crime which could inform intervention.

Theories of development of drugs and crime

Maturation theories

Maturation theories assume that human development is largely a matter of the natural unfolding of what is genetically determined, although this may vary according to the limits and opportunities of the environment. A recent example of this type is the finding that the brains of people in their late teens are immature, as the frontal lobes, containing planning and other executive functioning, continue to mature into a person's twenties, and this has been used as an explanation of adolescent impulsivity and misbehaviour. The Coalition for Juvenile Justice (2006) provides a useful summary.

In this biological theoretical frame, some level of misbehaviour or acting-out is to be expected, and drugs and offending are just extreme examples of this. Wait, this theory says, and most young people will settle down. There have been similar attempts to explain the behaviour of young, middle-aged and older adults as maturation. For example, the cessation of heroin dependence has been attributed to maturation, but this is due not to a natural process but rather to the long-term challenges and instabilities of the heroin-dependent lifestyle (Mullen and Hammersley, 2006; Anderson and Levy, 2003). It is length of career, not neuropsychological maturity, which leads to quitting.

Maturation theory is wrong as an approach to behaviour. Most adolescents are not troubled, do not act out, and even get along with their parents (Steinberg, 2007), and there is a risk of stereotyping and bending observations to fit the stereotype. Related to stereotyping, there is a problem of assuming 'naturalism' in maturation theories for people. We do not know, and there is no way of knowing, how fifteen-year-olds or any other age group would or should naturally behave. Nor is it possible to build norms for their behaviour by close observation. This can be done with animals but not with people, because people are reflexive. If you observe fifteen-year-old behaviour and report it, then the report may change the behaviour. For example, reporting that cannabis use by fifteen-year-olds is increasing may lead fifteen-year-olds to assume cannabis use is normal and become more likely to take it.

Looking further backwards in time for evolutionary purposes, presumably the neuropsychological development of an eighteen-year-old was 'mature' in prehistory, when life expectancy may have been about twenty and what is now 'mature' neuropsychology was a rarity. So, it is not safe to assume that 'mature' neuropsychology and behaviour are normal and developmentally proper and that adolescents are deficient in some way. According to evolutionary speculations, it could as easily be that anyone over thirty is past their biological sell-by date and their survival is a cultural phenomenon that is nothing to do with their individual brain or behaviour.

Stage and gateway theories

Not dissimilar to maturation theories are stage theories of psychosocial development. The best known are Piaget's stages of intellectual development (e.g., Piaget, 1952), Erickson's (1968) stages of emotional development and Kohlberg's (1969) stages of moral development. Substance use has also been subject to stage theories of a sort, in theories that propose that there is some sort of progression from one type of drug to another (Kandel, Yamaguchi and Chen, 1992). Similar progressions have been noted in offending patterns (e.g., Elliott, Huizinga and Ageton, 1985), but I am not aware of anyone who has gone as far as to argue that these are distinct developmental stages – despite the fact that most burglars will first have shoplifted.

Stage theories are an advance on maturation theories, because they attempt to specify some sort of logical order to stages, rather than assuming that they just unfold naturally. It is usually unclear whether this logical order really exists. When it does not, then the stages are really just normative descriptions of children's behaviours. There is a temptation to apply the stages prescriptively to individuals so that, for example, somebody who has tried tobacco aged thirteen is considered to be 'at risk' of trying cannabis aged fourteen. This is a description of population norms, not of individual behaviour. A specific fourteen-year-old who has tried tobacco may be at any level of risk from zero to very high, depending upon what she thinks about smoking, whether she has access to cannabis and many other factors.

Modern developmental psychology has focused more on issues of cause and logical order to development and placed less emphasis on stages or the natural unfolding of different behaviours. In this rethinking of development, a key change has been to become wary of the tendency to assume that certain common behaviours are natural things that were the purpose of development and are caused by tailor-made representations in the brain. This is occasionally true, but many widespread behaviours do not constitute neurological natural categories and are extremely recent, artificial results of language, discourse and culture. Literacy itself is one major example. The human brain did not evolve and does not develop *in order* to be able to read; rather, it draws upon a range of brain processes that originally had evolutionary value for other purposes, such as the ability to make fine visual discriminations. Because reading requires a range of processes and is quite challenging, people vary in their precise methods of reading, and when people struggle to read, quite a variety of things may be the problem, from needing glasses, to lack of motivation, to specific neurological deficits. Seeing adequately is necessary for reading, but this does not mean that it is wise or cost-effective to buy spectacles for all children with low reading scores. But nor will 'practice, practice, practice' work for someone who cannot see.

Similarly, people did not evolve and do not develop *in order* to have specific patterns of behaviour that are not criminal and specific patterns of ingestion that are not drug use. Nothing specific has to be broken or mis-developed in order for offending, drug use or drug problems to occur. It is likely that there are many pathways by which people come to offend, use drugs or have drug problems. Some pathways probably involve very serious developmental pathology; other pathways may involve only normal developmental processes, or be entirely a matter of the negative labelling of developmentally and culturally normal activities, or be due to the fact that all cultures must have boundaries and some activities must lie closer to those boundaries than others. Cognitive and social development in a society that contains drugs, alcohol and tobacco is likely to be different, but we lack much understanding of how. An absence of appreciation of these complexities leads to a futile search for simple explanations of drugs and crime.

For substance use and crime the challenges of understanding development are different from reading because, first, the nature of reading is not subject to the major conceptual and definitional problems outlined in earlier chapters. Also, people are supposed *not* to develop those behaviours. The developmental question is often framed in terms of naturalism. Are drugs and crime unnatural behaviours that only happen because something is wrong with the person, or natural behaviours, within specific types of society, that need to be governed and regulated to protect society from people's natural 'instincts'? Illogically, media, moralists and policy makers often prefer both answers together.

Reading research illustrates that this polar opposition is not particularly useful. Reading cannot be natural, but it must use natural cognitive processes. It is important not to confuse what is normal developmentally with what is natural. Given practice with reading, one can make reasonable predictions about how well children of different ages will read, and even normal variations are understood. Given a culture that includes drugs and crime, we can also make reasonable predictions about what people of different ages will do, as will be described shortly. However, what is documented as developmentally typical is often treated as evidence of a serious moral problem, which is presumed to be unnatural.

The most recent modification of stage theory of substance use is 'gateway theory' (Kandel, Yamaguchi and Chen, 1992), which proposes that different substances tend to be tried in some sort of logical order, and that trying one increases the likelihood of trying the next, rather than simply being the results of a common cause (Rebellon and Van Gundy, 2006). To the extent that cannabis statistically increases the chances of other drug use, controlling for preceding common causes, the reasons for this remain unclear (Fergusson, Boden and Horwood, 2006) and the developmental acquisition of different drugs is not invariant. For example, in the UK, tobacco is a gateway to smoking and tends to be tried before cannabis, whereas some smokers in the USA start with marijuana (Golub and Johnson, 1994). It is true that the great majority of heroin or cocaine users have tried alcohol and marijuana before they tried harder drugs. This is sometimes presented as a progression, like having to sit up and crawl before you can walk (although some babies slide along on their bottoms instead of crawling). In reality, the development of substance use involves a widening of substance use behaviours. For example, many heroin users also smoke cannabis and tobacco and may actually consume these more heavily than they do heroin (Hammersley et al., 1989). 'Gateway' drugs are those that are most widely accepted, available and affordable for younger teenagers, as the different tobacco–cannabis sequence in the USA and the UK illustrates. Adolescents will rationally take what they consider to be the least risk first. This is not special to substance use. In sexual behaviour first kissing and petting also tend to come before first intercourse. There is no psychological or biological causal path that makes heroin or LSD more serious drugs than cannabis. Even in the same neighbourhoods, progressions are variable (Tarter et al., 2006).

One implication of gateway theory is that if you delay use of gateway substances you may also delay or prevent use of harder drugs. This probably depends upon how you achieve delay. If you change young people's attitudes to substance use, then perhaps this will work, because they make more informed decisions and delay and minimize risks taken. If you delay by compulsion, for example by making alcohol or tobacco less available to young people, then it is possible that they will switch to other even more undesirable substances instead, as when youth turn to glue or petrol sniffing because alcohol is not available to them (Watson, 1986).

A less popular implication of gateway theory is that society ought to promote safer drugs and forms of drug use as less harmful alternatives to more dangerous ones. Probably also useful would be a graduated and controlled exposure to different forms of substance use, rather than the current free-for-all or a stampede for intoxication at age eighteen or twenty-one. One scheme for changing the law to reflect this is proposed by the RSA report on drugs (2007, 310–24). A major difficulty remains that adults generally do not want their children to use any substances for some years after the children want to use them. Were cannabis to be sold in shops and cafes, minors would not be allowed to buy it and would continue to turn to tobacco first or the black market, unless tobacco were no longer sold widely.

Environmental theories

Another type of theory of drugs and crime is implicitly a-developmental. Such theories propose that drug use and crime occur because the social and physical environment facilitates, promotes, or fails to prevent such activities. Consequently, the best interventions for youth will alter the environment to make offending or substance use less likely. Such interventions include 'target-hardening' approaches to crime prevention – if car stereos cannot be removed they cannot be stolen – and regulation of legal access to alcohol and tobacco. As will be discussed in chapters 7 and 9, regulating the environment is a powerful way of managing behaviour, but regulation by complete prohibition is more problematic. Many contemporary initiatives against drugs and crime unrealistically strive to prevent undesirable activities altogether. There is no fundamental reason why this should not work, but for drugs and crime, desirable to some young people, and with long histories and traditions, suppression has generally failed. It is possible to achieve largely weapon- and drug-free schools with sufficient security, but this is not the same thing as weapon- and drug-free children. To achieve the latter, it may be necessary to influence children's hearts and minds, as well as their environments.

Risk factor theories

Youth justice policy in many countries is heavily influenced by risk factor theories of youth crime, although many other theories exist (see

Shoemaker, 1990). Risk factor theories assume that delinquency and substance use are multiply caused by a variety of factors, including individual biological and psychological factors, social/familial factors, situational factors and neighbourhood factors (e.g., Sprott, Jenkins and Doob, 2000; Hawkins, Catalano and Miller, 1992; Farrington, 1995). Risk factor theories have also been influential in psychiatry (see Rutter, 2006). As applied to policy, they can be problematic (Armstrong, 2004).

Proponents of risk factors consider their theories to be sophisticated descriptions of the data in the form of the correlations that can be established between different factors at different times in the life course; they are assumed to be empirically derived. One of their supposed advantages, and appealing selling points to policy makers, is that large sample sizes, validated measures and sophisticated statistics can be used as objective standards of the strength and power of the research. This evades, but does not resolve, questions of whether the right variables were successfully measured and analysed in their proper order. The types of multivariate statistical analyses that are used, such as regression analysis and path analysis, require a theoretical model of how the variables might relate to each other. The refusal to use an explicit theoretical model simply means that a tacit one is used instead (Cohen et al., 2002), which often amounts to the common prejudices of the researchers and the commissioners of the research. Furthermore, to apply risk factors, it is at minimum necessary to consider relative rather than absolute risk (Frisher et al., 2005). For example, people who are violent in city centres at night may mostly be drunk, but this does not discriminate them from those around them, over 90 per cent of whom will have consumed at least some alcohol, making drunkenness a useless 'risk factor' for predicting violent behaviour. Indeed, not drinking in that context, being socially deviant, may actually be associated with higher risks of crime and violence (Hammersley, 2005).

One widespread and serious example in longitudinal research is how to manage the fact that the best predictors of most behaviours tend to be their occurrence at an earlier point in time. For example, people who used a drug at time 1 are more likely to use it at time 2 than those who did not. There are a number of possible approaches to this, none of them entirely satisfactory. One can accept the large correlations and interpret them to mean that behaviour tends to persist, but this is not a very interesting explanation of anything. One can exclude time 1 drug use from analyses predicting time 2 use. This will give more interesting results, but the problem is that whatever 'risks' predict time 2 use might be caused by time 1 use, rather than truly causing time 2 use. For instance, drug use might cause truanting at the same time, because children cannot get up in the morning, but it will look as if truanting predicts time 2 use. Or, one can make choices about where to put time 1 use in the analyses, but different choices will lead to different results.

The broader problem is that risk factors – mean tendencies and trends in survey data – are confused with causes (see Morton, 2004, 1–6). For example, truancy is a risk factor for substance use but neither a necessary nor a sufficient cause of substance use. Therefore, reducing the prevalence of truancy would have no necessary effect on the prevalence of substance use. To explain how truancy impacts substance use a causal model is required. There are a number of different possible causal models of truancy with different implications.

1 Both substance use and truancy may be markers for common underlying problems.
2 Truancy may facilitate exposure to substance use compared to sitting in class (and exposure is another risk factor).
3 Substance use may facilitate truancy because users are motivated to truant as they want to smoke, drink, etc., and are prohibited from doing so in school, and they may also find it harder to get up in the morning.

Only (2) predicts that reducing truancy might reduce substance use, and even then this depends upon the causal model of how exposure to substance use by others leads to personal substance use (see Jessor and Jessor, 1977). Model (1) predicts that reducing truancy would only make a difference if the intervention also addressed the common underlying problems, while model (3) predicts that reducing truancy might have no effect, or might increase substance use problems in school.

A second, related, problem is that aggregate 'risks' are confused with explanations for individual behaviour. Truants may include relatively few avowed abstainers. Substance use may facilitate truancy in part because substance use is a visible marker of a problematic pupil whom, informally, the school may have least interest in retaining. Thus, risk factor theories may sometimes try to use the most typical or universal factors to explain deviant activities such as substance use, which may be caused by the atypical and individual.

Table 5.2   *(continued)*

Adjusted	One form of maladjustment	Another form of maladjustment
fantasy and imagination	held to be true, hence difficulty appreciating the beliefs of others (authoritarianism is one example)	experience with real events, hence hallucinates, or has delusions, or odd beliefs
Behaves appropriately in a range of different social situations	Only functions well in a few, well-learned social situations and tends to avoid others	Behaves inappropriately sometimes, by adopting behaviours appropriate in one situation to another, or by being insufficiently flexible
Adapts to change and new social situations	Avoids new situations	Is anxious, acts out or otherwise misbehaves in new situations
Is stable in character across a range of different situations	Is excessively conformist to the current social situation – 'easily led'	Is impulsive and changeable whatever the situation – for example, inappropriately emotional

workaholics were the results not so impressive. Successful people are often driven by needs that would seem extreme or maladjusted if they were not successful. A wealthy porn star may have successfully used an unusual orientation to sexual activity that would merely seem like sexual compulsion if she had not made it a career. An academic may have a persistent fascination with a specialized area that seems obscure and uninteresting to many.

Moreover, well-adjusted people will tend to adapt their behaviours to local cultural norms. For example, if they grow up in a society that approves of violence, then they will be reasonably violent when appropriate, which may even involve murder to protect honour or avenge a wrong, but they are unlikely to be impulsively homicidal or violent for no 'good' reason. If they grow up in a society where drugs and alcohol are widely used by many people, then they will probably use them to some extent, but may be unlikely to develop severe psychosocial problems with them. If routine use is normal, then they may develop the resultant health problems, as used to happen with liver cirrhosis in wine-drinking countries. If they grow up in a deprived subculture where it is necessary to lie, cheat and sometimes steal to survive economically, then they will behave in those ways.

Furthermore, some substance use and some crime will be conducted by normal, well-adjusted people, for normal, well-adjusted reasons. However, other substance use and crime are conducted by people who are maladjusted in various ways. The actual behaviours for adjusted and maladjusted people may be almost exactly the same, but the social setting and context is very different.

Consequently, there is political debate about whether drugs and crime problems were caused by extreme social conditions, making them to some extent pardonable, or by individual pathology. Live political debates about this include whether the high rates of imprisonment among Americans of colour are the result of their low intelligence, negligent child-rearing practices and other deficiencies, or because of systematic and institutional racism that perpetuates poverty (Hagan and Foster, 2006; Manley, 2006). Another example is whether atrocities during wartime are due to systemic factors in military training and combat or to individual pathologies of military personnel. Those who wish to maintain the existing social order tend to favour individual pathology explanations of drugs and crime rather than systemic, social ones. Those who wish to challenge the existing social order tend to favour systemic, social explanations and point to ironies and inconsistencies in the rule of law: judges who are caught drink-driving and do not resign; politicians caught taking the drugs they lambast; shoplifting being disposed more harshly than pilfering; and so forth.

Nobody knows with any certainty which social conditions and what individual maladjustments are most likely to cause drug use or crime, as those activities are defined differently according to predominant social conditions. So, there is a risk of identical behaviours and social transactions being defined differently according to one or other politicized theory of the events, leading to an indefinite but futile debate over their causes. This applies even when politics judges that certain activities are absolutely wrong and never acceptable, which leads to many injustices, from the under-prescribing of opiates for pain relief to the prosecution of teachers for harassment or assault, or teachers being unable to drag a sulking pupil from beneath a table because of a policy of no physical contact. If an activity is entirely wrong, then it must be decided what constitutes that activity and what does not. If drug use is entirely wrong then what is 'non-drug use'? It is impossible to define an activity or a transaction in absolute terms without reference to the social transactions and setting where it occurs. If teachers are forbidden to touch pupils, does this apply if the pupil is breaking into the teacher's home in the middle of the night?

Individual maladjustment and social conditions both *can* cause drug use and crime and *do* cause drug use and crime, sometimes at the same time. Attempts to exclude either type of explanation are futile. What is maladjustment in some social conditions can become well adjusted in others. Levi ([1947] 1991) describes how in a Nazi concentration camp normal pro-social behaviour led rapidly to death, while ruthless theft was more successful. What haunted the survivors was often what they had done to survive as much as what was done to them.

Theorizing adulthood

Most thinking about drugs and crime assumes that the 'normal' is a steady state that involves not using drugs and not offending. In order for offending or drug use to occur, this state of normality must be perturbed somehow. Contradicting this, most surveys find that many (although not most) people have used drugs and offended, and that is only taking contemporary definitions of 'drugs' and 'crime' at face value. Research that considers wider definitions of 'substance use' and 'breaking laws and rules' (including the supposedly tolerable or trivial) suggests that most people have engaged in these activities to some extent – even if only at the level of parking offences and imbibing caffeine.

A widely held working hypothesis is that offending and substance use are not unusual among younger people. As they age and acquire more adult responsibilities, people tend to reduce these activities, or come to manage them so that they are unobtrusive, or switch to activities that are less clearly defined as 'crime' *because* they are more the activities of powerful middle-aged people. We need better information about drugs and crime among older, middle-class people, who are more capable of collectively ensuring that their activities are constructed in society as non-deviant. For example, they drink New World red wines on the patio, not tonic wine on the doorstep. The more potentially deviant the activities of middle-aged, middle-class people, the more difficult it is to find out about them. They evade drug surveys, deny use, or situate it safely as in the past, experimental and 'not really enjoyed'. They do not fiddle benefits, because they do not claim any, but they probably fiddle taxes. The moral and financial losses to the nation thereby are probably much larger than those caused by benefit frauds, but these unsavoury behaviours are contestably legal. Unsecured debt in the UK has quadrupled over the period 1993 to 2007 and mortgage debt has grown exponentially (Credit Action UK, 2007). Running up an average of £8,400 per household in credit cards and loans is not stealing, because it is a legal activity, but it makes direct shoplifting rather unnecessary, even if a large portion of the bill has gone on booze. There is no equivalent of bankruptcy for thieves, while debtors' prison has long gone.

This moves towards one well-known criminological theory: crime and drug use are generally committed by people who lack the social capital to further their own selfish ends by legal means. One form of this is 'radical theory' (Shoemaker, 1990, 228–47), which conceptualizes lack of social capital as a matter of social class. However, arguably, age itself is an important component of social stratification. But the answers to even quite simple questions about what normally happens with age rapidly become complex. For example, older people may drink less alcohol, but in recent generations who drank more in the first place this may be happening less (Gilhooly, 2005). However, widening radical theory raises the problem of why women tend to offend and use drugs less than men, despite being comparatively disadvantaged. Perhaps women manifest their difficulties more passively, including being depressed, adopting the sick role or punishing/ordering the self with an eating disorder (Busfield, 2006). Widened radical theory predicts that, as women achieve relative parity with men, they should offend and use drugs more, which appears to be happening.

Not adapting as the social, bodily and psychological environment changes with age might cause what looks like change. A lecher aged sixty may have exactly the same desires towards the same people as one aged twenty but be regarded extremely differently. Is this change – has the man *become* a dirty old man? Or is it a failure to change appropriately, and leer only at women of a decently similar age or lose libido entirely? Is fancying young women natural for men of all ages, but suppressed and managed by cultural norms? Alternatively, is it a form of perversion or arrested development? Or are these two opposing views of the same developmental processes in adulthood? A binge drinker aged thirty may have behaved the same way with alcohol every week for a decade, while his mates who drank exactly the same way aged twenty have mostly reduced their drinking. His 'problem' is that he has failed to change despite jeopardizing his health.

There is a lack of quality developmental theories of adulthood, rather than of infancy, childhood and adolescence. Psychological theories of change in adulthood are under-theorized, and the theories that we have are mostly at least thirty years old and are influenced by psychoanalysis. Important examples are Erickson's stage theory (1968) and Kohlberg's theory of moral development (1969). These theories have been criticized as being culturally biased in assuming that the ideal person is a self-actualized individual, rather than, for instance, someone who subsumes their needs in the service of other people or a greater cause, or regards the material world as illusory (e.g., Heubner and Garrod, 1993).

Erickson (1968) divided the lifespan into stages, from puberty onwards into adolescence, early adult life, midlife and old age, and postulated that each stage was associated with a different 'normative crisis' – a developmental task that needs to be accomplished for well-adjusted progress to the next stage. For example, adolescents need to form a sense of their own identity or continue in role confusion, while young adults need to form intimacy or be isolated. A difficulty with this approach and others that followed (e.g., Levinson, 1990; Bühler and Massarik, 1968) is that the adult stages are largely descriptive and it is unclear to what extent transitions are simply culturally determined, for example by the conventional ages at which people bear children or retire from work.

Sociological writing on youth tends to focus on these transitions, to show how young people's lives are structured by other factors, such as class, place and race (MacDonald et al., 2005; Hagan and Foster, 2006), or to consider youth cultures separately from adulthood. Yet, much sociology is about discourse, including how the individual is created and defined by discourse. It would be feasible to theorize how knowledge and experience cumulate in a person to create development, for, whatever the relevance of biological maturation to psychological development, older people have more experience and more learning and forgetting. The later work of the phenomenologist Maurice Merleau-Ponty (for an introduction see Reynolds, 2005) pointed in this sort of direction, implying that the study of learning was important, but hermeneutics and postmodern approaches, while influenced by phenomenology, tend to consider bodies of discourse discrete and static, if endlessly open to understanding and interpretation. Sociology and criminology would benefit from a theory of learning, indeed an appreciation of the importance of individual psychology (Moscovici, 1993).

How do children become well-adjusted adults?

To become a well-adjusted adult a child needs 'good enough parenting' and the social and cognitive skills to benefit from it (see Steinberg,

2007). It also helps if the child does not have major difficulties or disorders and if childhood does not involve major trauma of any kind. Difficulties and disorders that affect a child's social or cognitive skills are particularly challenging in terms of normal psychosocial development. Some difficulties and disorders are clearly caused by genetic and biological developmental factors. For others, this is more contentious.

There are, however, many examples of people who have overcome massive problems and become well-adjusted adults, usually because of the fortitude and determination of themselves and their parents, but sometimes because of their personal qualities and despite their parents. Overcoming major adversity can require remarkable skills rather than ones that are only 'good enough'. These include having the communication skills to seek help from adults outside the immediate family, a resultant network of social contacts, and the personal characteristics to exert self-control, notably good impulse control, intelligence and autonomy (Werner, 1995; Dishon and Connell, 2006). As parents know, it takes exhausting, repetitive work with most young children to further these characteristics and it does not take profound neglect to stifle them. More aggressive and difficult children are more likely to be delinquent and use drugs as teenagers (Brook, Whiteman and Finch, 1992).

All this implies that it is relatively easy to stray from the straight and narrow way, and easier still when life is adverse. Adjustment is an active process requiring work, not a passive condition disturbed by malevolent forces. For example, West (2006, 4) argues that the brain is inherently unstable and requires constant adjusting, like a hovering helicopter; when adjustments are inadequate, then the person can lapse into a stable, but dysfunctional, state, such as dependence.

In contrast, much research on 'risk factors' for delinquency and substance use assumes that it is normality that is stable and dependence and delinquency that are unstable. There are advantages in reversing this thinking. It is more tolerant and forgiving to recognize that it is difficult to be continually law-abiding and temperate. Additionally, explanations of maladjustment are often sought in abnormalities of the child or young adult, or their rearing or environment. This may sometimes be a mistake, when the putative 'abnormalities' are relatively common, as are substance use and delinquency. It is legitimate to seek abnormal explanations of relatively rare problems, such as ADHD, but if 20 per cent of young people offend and 40 per cent try drugs, then the proper question may be how people successfully adjust to not offend or try drugs. Part of the process of adjustment is to go to the edge of what the person finds acceptable in thought and behaviour then pull back. Edge work in contemporary societies can include some substance use and some offending. Perhaps it is the process of pulling back, rather than going over the edge, that is most in need of research and theorization.

As discussed in chapters 3 and 4, perhaps most people actually engage in transactions that in the relevant social conditions would be labelled offending, so perhaps there is no fundamental question to answer. However, developmental theory still needs to explain the persistent offender and the career criminal. With drug use, a theoretical gulf remains between explanations of use that invoke general neuropsychological mechanisms that make drugs enjoyable, reinforcing and addictive, but ought to apply to everyone, and explanations that focus on individual or social pathology. Currently, there are tenuous bridges concerning genetic differences in the impact of drugs (e.g., Caspi et al., 2005; Cichoz-Lach et al., 2007; Haile, Kosten and Kosten, 2007; Drakenberg et al., 2006), but these mostly explain why some people may develop problems when others do not, rather than being why people take drugs at all. Nobody has been able to specify a fundamental evolutionary rationale for intoxication being reinforcing. Perhaps this is a side effect of having consciousness rather than being something that is fundamentally useful. Or, perhaps consciousness and the realm beyond the material is the entire point. Certainly, those who reject the varieties of religious and paranormal experience as frauds and delusions (e.g., Dawkins, 2007) need to find an alternative explanation for intoxication seeking. 'It is fun' is not an explanation: Why is it fun?

The most plausible explanation is that substance use and intoxication are socially learned behaviours which originated as a component of religiosity (see Moscovici, 1993) but, as religion became more abstract in large, developed societies, so drug use sometimes replaced religion. Karl Marx wrote: 'Religion is the heart of a heartless world, and the soul of soulless conditions. It is the opium of the people' (http://en.wikipedia.org/wiki/Opium_of_the_People). Is opium (or alcohol) increasingly the religion of the people? Substance use and intoxication can serve three key functions of religion: the function of commune – community, sharing and bringing together; the function of transcendence – opening up another realm possibly wider, better or at least different from the everyday; and bringing heart and soul to conditions lacking these. Debates about whether experiences one has when intoxicated are valid or real apply also to debates about whether religious experiences are valid or real. In largely secular societies, drugs have the further advantage of being marketable commodities.

If this theory is correct, then it helps to explain why substance use is so contentious. Although it has long spread well beyond conventional frames of religious activity, it still involves the phenomena of commune and transcendence that people feel passionate about – hence, as with religion, widespread determination to defend the 'proper' practices and reject 'improper' and 'foreign' ones. No purely social theory of substance use can explain why it is often a solitary activity, as well as a communal one. If substance use hijacks religious functions, then solitary drug use is like solitary prayer or other religious activity. It is some attempt to achieve commune and transcendence, even on one's own. Generally, young drug users do not talk in such lofty terms. Rather they are 'having a laugh' or a 'good night' and are getting 'really out of it' or 'wasted' (Amos et al., 2004; Parker, Aldridge and Meashan, 1998).

Back, then, to a fundamental question: What is normal adult substance use or religiosity and is there any basis for judging normality other than either typicality or faith? In multicultural societies it is no longer adequate to equate normality with what one believes in. Yet, the bulk of modern social and psychological theory simply fudges the fundamental question of whether it is normal and well adjusted for an adult to be religious, or to use drugs. It makes social scientists uneasy that much accepted religious behaviour seems odd, rather than well adjusted. The devout may engage in obsessive rituals, talk to themselves, experience communications from God or others, isolate themselves, starve themselves, hurt themselves and abuse drugs in particular ways. Doing very similar things without stated religious motives, for example as a drug abuser, is positively alarming. No wonder we collectively struggle even to formulate coherent questions about normal substance use. Not that I can offer the answers. While we have some understanding of childhood and adolescence, our grasp of adult development is relatively weak.

Development of positive lifestyles

One useful alternative is to focus on assets that promote positive youth development, rather than abnormalities or deficiencies. Eccles and Gootman (2002, 74–5) summarize these assets, for American youth, under a number of headings:

- Physical development: good health habits, good health risk management skills
- Intellectual development: knowledge of essential life skills, knowledge of essential vocational skills, school success, rational habits of mind (critical thinking and reasoning skills), in-depth knowledge of more than one culture, good decision-making skills, knowledge of skills needed to navigate through multiple cultural contexts
- Psychological and emotional development: good mental health, including positive self-regard, good emotional self-regulation skills, good coping skills, good conflict resolution skills, mastery motivation and positive achievement motivation, confidence in one's personal efficacy, 'planfulness' (planning for the future and future life events), sense of personal autonomy/responsibility for self, optimism coupled with realism, coherent and positive personal and social identity, pro-social and culturally sensitive values, spirituality or a sense of a 'larger' purpose in life, strong moral character, a commitment to good use of time
- Social development: connectedness (perceived good relationships and trust with parents, peers and some other adults), sense of social place/integration (being connected and valued by larger social networks), attachment to pro-social/conventional institutions, such as school, church, non-school youth programmes, ability to navigate in multiple cultural contexts, commitment to civic engagement.

Young people strong in several of these assets are likely to prosper; few youth will have all of them. The cultural components apply to ethnic minority youth in the USA, and perhaps to those in any multicultural society. It is important that this review of community programmes to promote youth development mentions no actual behaviours as protective or risk factors, but rather goes underneath to theorize positive qualities. A youth with many of these assets might truant, offend or use drugs, but is more likely to have the assets to recover from, minimize or manage these activities in a relatively trouble-free way.

What is normal substance use and crime in adulthood?

The 'normal' law-breaking of the middle-aged probably involves fiddles, evasions, frauds, traffic violations, offences while drunk and domestic violence rather than offences generally linked to drug use. To know more, this would have to be researched more carefully. 'Normal' substance use is perhaps changing. The previous generation gap between 'traditional' substances such as alcohol and tobacco and 'drugs' is narrowing. Perhaps it is not what a person uses, but how they use. When people use in an uncontrolled or unconstrained fashion, then this increasingly tends to violate social and psychological norms and comes to look like addiction. Conversely, perhaps, normal substance use is use with constraints. Looking at the problem in this way, there are many obvious constraints on use that have been noted clinically and in research. People stop or moderate their substance use because:

1 they have explicit and active religious or other moral beliefs that prohibit use. There is a well-known relationship between religion and temperate habits, although, of course, religious adherence is fallible and temperance can fall with it.

2 people important to them are strongly opposed to use, which matters to them. The impact of systemic therapies on substance use, which among other things get users to recognize the concerns of their families, is one example. Sometimes it only matters because of extreme sanctions or the threat of them. Confrontational interventions between drinkers and their family members are an example.

3 they are concerned about the legal risks involved. This tends to be most evident when users may jeopardize their careers or family lives by detected use.

4 the substance is not readily available. Dependent people may seek it out, while non-dependent people tend to stop or reduce frequency of use.

5 the substance is unduly expensive relative to other factors. This is a predominant reason for moderating cocaine use.

6 opportunities for taking the substance are reduced by life circumstances. A work schedule with extensive travelling may prevent nights of cannabis use.

7 they have other things to do that conflict with use of that particular substance. 'Maturation' often involves responsibilities that make use more difficult. For example, child care while intoxicated or hung over can be problematic.

8 sympathetic friends to use with are not available. Moving away from a friendship network can disrupt substance use habits.

9 the substance does nothing for them. This applies to a surprising number of politicians who have tried marijuana! Seriously, some drug effects are not invariably as blatant as they are sometimes depicted to be, and they can feel ineffective to some.

10 they dislike the effects. This is well documented for alcohol, as people who cannot process one of its metabolites tend to flush and get bad hangovers. It also applies to other drugs, including cannabis, heroin, cocaine and amphetamines.

11 they like the effects too much, compared to other things. That is, they recognize a risk of immoderate use for them and therefore avoid the drug. This is often given as a reason for not taking heroin. People can use this strategy with any drug.

12 they lack the stresses and strains that lead to a desire for hedonistic, present-oriented escapism. There is a well-known link between stress and increased substance use.

13 they become jaded with consumerism/materialism. This can include becoming fed up with having to hang about drug users and dealers in order to get drugs. It can also involve rejecting the values marketed by the alcohol industry or any other relevant industry.

14 they have a personal health scare. Health scare plus minimal intervention often causes drinkers to moderate their intake. Sadly, the health problems of other people often fail to scare users.

15 they recognize immanent dependence. This phenomenon is less well researched than it should be, but it is clear that drinkers can cut back or abstain for a while as a moderation strategy, that cocaine users often take similar steps, and that some long-term heroin users adopt a strategy of carefully controlled use (not every day for example) to prevent dependence.

Most people experience some of these constraints on their substance use, hence use normally. Greatly weakened or absent constraints will be unusual and more likely in marginalized, poor and abused social groups that include some people to whom the following characteristics are likely to apply:

1 lack of moral barriers that prohibit use
2 lack of social barriers
3 disregard of the law
4 drugs endemic
5 drugs affordable relative to their pleasures and advantages
6 plenty of free time
7 little occupation
8 plenty of friends in the same situation
9 substance has 'different' effects (anything for a change)
10 substance makes positive mood more likely

11 lack of other positive activities to match drugs
12 stress and strain
13 lack of sufficient consumerism to become jaded
14 health 'scares' weakened by low expectations and low quality of life
15 less far to fall to reach dependence due to above.

While this approach does not make drugs and crime easily treatable, it at least makes them understandable. It also suggests some action points. First, young people need to be socially included. Structuring society so that young people live lives largely different and separate from adults, even under the same roof, is not a good idea. The social construction of 'youth' as intrinsically separate and as a separate cluster of market segments tends to promote activities that adults will not like, which can include drugs and crime.

Second, drugs and crime problems tend to be worst among people who have grown up poor, socially excluded and sometimes neglected, abused and traumatized. Children in these conditions need better care, although there are serious resource implications and many ethical problems with providing the care that they need. A subsidiary point is that the almost platonic ideal of the nuclear family hinders intelligent intervention when children are growing up in conditions that vary massively from that ideal. For example, in some deprived neighbourhoods grandmothers can play a key role in child rearing, but may be excluded from critical legal decisions on the grounds of parental rights, whatever the state of the parents.

Third, some degree of maladjustment including drugs and offending is not unusual as people grow up. Pathologizing it risks perpetuating the problems. We need to understand a lot more about why some people become reasonably well-adjusted adults despite challenging beginnings and others do not.

Summary

Drugs and crime are often conceptualized as problems of youth on account of developmental abnormalities. There are many risk factors that predict drug use and crime, but a causal model of development is required to intervene successfully. This is currently unclear. Such a causal model would distinguish substance use from substance use problems and dependence. The former may be normal and require no special explanation. Understanding drugs and crime in adolescence would also be helped by better theories of normal adult development, including better understanding of adult drug use and crime. The widespread assumption that 'normality' involves no drugs and no crime is idealistic and leads to the problematic assumption that drugs and crime are temporary aberrations, so interventions should return people and communities to their 'normal' drug-free, non-criminal, state; problem drug use may be a matter of a lack of constraints on use, rather than being a matter of personal or social abnormalities.

Discussion points

- Can you think of some examples of people you know whose substance use suddenly changed (for better or worse) for relatively trivial reasons?
- Do you have a drug or alcohol problem? If not, why not, and how do you know?
- If you are reading this book, you have probably been to university or are otherwise educating yourself. How has your education affected your substance use? Has it affected your use, or how much you worry about it, or both?

Further reading

Bee, H., and Boyd, D. (2005). *Lifespan development.* 4th rev. edn, London: Allyn & Bacon.

Carpenter, C., Glassner, B., Johnson, B. D., and Loughlin, J. (1988). *Kids, drugs and crime.* Lexington, MA: Lexington Books.

Eccles, J. S., and Gootman, J. A. (eds) (2002). *Community programs to promote youth development.* Washington, DC: National Academy Press.

Elliott, D. S., Huizinga, D., and Ageton, S. S. (1985). *Explaining delinquency and drug use.* London: Sage.

Gilvarry, E. (ed.) (2001). *The substance of young needs.* London: Health Advisory Service/Home Office.

Steinberg, L. D. (2007). *Adolescence.* 8th rev. edn, New York: McGraw-Hill.

6

Drugs, Crime and Contemporary Society

Drugs and crime concern societies around the world, but most research has been done in North America, Australia/New Zealand and the UK. There is also a body of relevant work in Scandinavia, particularly about alcohol. There is descriptive information about drugs and crime in many other countries and about the massive economic and political influence of the drugs trade in some producer countries (see United Nations Office on Drugs and Crime, 2006). Not enough is known about the cultures of those countries to be confident that drugs and crime are understood and dealt with universally in the ways described here (but see Goodman, Lovejoy and Sherratt, 2007).

Risk society and addiction

Drugs and crime are actually central to society because society has come to define itself as excluding drugs and crime – characterized as 'addiction'. Theoretically, this can be viewed as an extension of risk society (Beck, 1992), with drugs and the associated crimes commonly presented as large dangers to the safety of the person, the family and the community. Risk society (Beck, 1992; Adam, Beck and Van Loon, 2000) theorizes that, in contemporary society, social class and, by inference, other structural systems are breaking down. Instead, society is increasingly 'about' a direct but diffuse relationship between the individual and the collective. People are no longer systematically connected to their neighbours, their fellow trade union members, their religion, or their social caste, but rather have to forge individual positions vis-à-vis society. For good and bad, people no longer know 'their place'. Instead, they have to negotiate and choose their social identity. This liquidizing, or perhaps just weakening (Scott, 2000), of social stratification results in suspicion of the modernist enterprise, as the power structures that defined modernity are eroded. Previously technology and progress were widely viewed as solutions to the world's woes (with accidents and mistakes on the way), but now they are seen as the causes of them. Popular means of choosing identity include the construction of shared concerns, many of these being about possible dangers – risks – that are often to do with things that are new, technological or biomedical, and alien or remote from the supposed norm. Nuclear power, damage to the environment, new infectious diseases, bioengineering and electronic communications are examples of things regarded with concern. Because society is also increasingly networked across the world (Castells, 1998), many stances and identities can flourish that would have been toned down or prevented when social life was physically limited by geography. Concerns about risk, whether perhaps highly justified (global warming), or possibly barmy (health risks of fluoride), can be shared globally with like-minded people. Adam and Van Loon (2000, 2) offer five implications of risk society for social theory, which I paraphrase as follows. Risks are (1) socially constructed and therefore (2) contested. (3) No single set of knowledge practices contain, or form, risk; consequently (4) understanding risk is about mediation rather than calculation. (5) Risk is about the future, for which we nowadays should feel responsible.

Within this altered scheme, the state no longer offers, or perpetuates, social structure, but instead has come to market security as a primary function of government, often under the rubric of 'Science', or science-like practices, where experts advise on what might or could happen and what the risks are. As of 2007, in England and Wales, the aim of the Home Office is 'to protect the public and secure our future' (Home Office, 2007), whereas in 1999, 'The principal aim of the Home Office [was] to build a safe, just and tolerant society' (Home Office, 1999), with protection and security mentioned later. By 2007, justice had become the last of seven objectives, and it was only going to be 'delivered', rather than 'built', while 'tolerance' had been replaced by 'treating everyone with respect' – except presumably those who didn't deserve it, as the objectives emphasized protecting the public from violent crime, drug-related crime, terrorists, migrants and identity theft. Furthermore, the idea of 'safety' had been replaced by 'security', for one can never be safe surrounded by terrorists, migrants, violent thugs, drug users, binge drinkers and identity thieves. Risk society has penetrated widely. In the Scottish village I live in (population about 500) the council truck that sweeps the roads has 'Protection Services' on the side. In the 1970s, Scots called this service 'cleansing'.

Consequently, many kinds of harm and potential harm are being constructed as crimes (Ericson, 2006). Drugs and crime problems are regularly portrayed as so appalling that it is implicitly impossible to be *excessively* concerned about them. Any imaginable quantity of concern is scarcely enough to tackle the 'one single change' of the past thirty years that has been most harmful. This tendency is not unique to drugs and crime, and sociologists have written about the developing culture of fear (Füredi, 2006), that overemphasizes potential dangers and risks compared to the thinking of earlier generations. Not only is it impossible to be too scared, but it is inappropriate, if not immoral, to try and put the true problems in perspective.

It is a basic assumption of social anthropology that cultures define themselves by what they are not (e.g., Douglas and Wildavsky, 1983). Society wishes to claim that acceptable behaviour is not to commit crimes of the standard types discussed in chapter 3 and not to take drugs. Another, connected, assumption of social anthropology is that the format of a culture, in terms of rules, artefacts and activities, is related to the power structures of that culture. It is commonplace to lament the relationship of drugs and crime to poverty and social exclusion and it is widely assumed that poverty and social exclusion cause offending and drug problems. Social anthropology is more inclined to postulate that the activities of poor, disempowered and socially excluded people will tend to be defined as criminal and that their consumption habits will be defined as inferior or undesirable by contrast with the habits of the rich and powerful. In other words 'drugs' are what poor and disadvantaged people take. Affluent people label their ingestion practices differently.

In contemporary society, many of the habits of the less affluent are under attack. Society spent the first half of the twentieth century facilitating mass cigarette consumption, then, as the links between smoking, cancer and cardiovascular disease were discovered, more affluent Americans and Europeans began to stop smoking more quickly than less affluent ones, producing a widening class gap in smoking habits. Actually, it is not quite right to talk of the 'habits of the less affluent'. Taking a longer and wider view, these habits tend to be the same as the habits of the more affluent from some years earlier. People with less money aspire to the same things as wealthier people, but their access to those things is often limited by the relative expense of whatever is currently fashionable and desirable. As access becomes easier, wealthier people move on to new things, disdaining the older ones. Examples relevant to criminology include the British seaside, once the playground of royalty, but some sixty years on in the 1960s scene of young working-class mods and rockers fighting and a crime scare (Pearson, 1983). When mobile phones were owned by yuppies they were a status symbol. Nowadays with mass ownership by the young, they lead to bullying (Rivers, Duncan and Besag, 2007), fears about cancer (Foggo, 2007) and legislation to prevent their use while driving (Think Road Safety, 2007). Meantime, status means not needing a mobile phone, or having someone else answer it.

Society's definition of drugs

Society's definition of 'drugs' is currently in a state of flux and upheaval, because within the last 100 years or so the number of substances people can take for pleasure has widened greatly and we have become much more aware of the health dangers of the drugs that were long integrated into society. At the start of the twenty-first century, tobacco is moving towards being a 'drug' to be excluded from acceptable behaviour, while cannabis is moving away from being a drug, although movement is fitful. The illegitimate status of other drugs has fluctuated. For example, amphetamines seemed like medicines in the 1940s and 1950s, then became drugs. Cocaine was a not-so-bad drug for a while, then an even worse drug than heroin, in the form of crack anyway, and is perhaps now returning to being not quite as bad as heroin after all. MDMA (ecstasy) has been a beneficial adjunct to psychotherapy (Grob, 2000). Then it became a controlled drug but one not widely used, then as mass use has developed society has become quite confused as to whether it is a largely harmless substance taken by millions of people with very few misadventures, or an extremely dangerous substance that has killed people and may cause long-term brain damage. Exactly the same evidence about ecstasy can be used to support either opinion.

A specific exclusionary force against drugs in society is medicine's general suspicion of the consumption of psychologically active substances without medical approval. Health-care professionals' control over medicines and drugs is only just over 100 years old. Before that consumers could largely buy and consume what they wanted, although they might have to register their purchases. Doctors nowadays are trained and licensed to prescribe dangerous medicines. Reversing this, it is now self-evidently unsafe to let untrained, unlicensed patients decide what drugs to take and how, but this idea is relatively new in history. Non-concordance with medical advice, including the effective consumption of medicines, is a major problem in health care (Smith et al., 1987). However, there have been many mistakes with pre-scribed medicines that originate with medicine and the pharmaceutical industry, including inappropriate prescribing (Gallagher, Barry and O'Mahony, 2007), failing to prescribe enough of drugs thought 'dangerous' such as the opiates (Bressler, Geraci and Schaz, 1991) and adopting new drugs that turn out to be dangerous. Also, an older person may easily be on four or five medicines, even if they are in rel-atively good health for their age. Whether these different drugs inter-act and to what effects has rarely been tested. Indeed it would not be ethical to give healthy human volunteers such mixtures of drugs.

When specific drugs become popular for pleasure, medicine col-lectively rushes to document the harms that may befall users. Ecstasy and cocaine have both been treated in this fashion. In contrast, med-icine can be much more complacent about the harms that befall the users of drugs as medicines. Just one example of many is that the widely prescribed antidepressant Seroxat has been found to lead to serious problems for some users, so some fifteen years after its intro-duction it is no longer to be used for children and should not gener-ally be the antidepressant of choice (see seroxatusergroup.org.uk for information). Health-care consumers can be gullible and ill-informed, but research on health professionals' knowledge repeatedly finds that most practitioners are unable competently to evaluate the evidence for the efficacy and dangers of new medicines and instead tend to rely on manufacturers' advertising material and word of mouth, just like everyone else (Avorn, Chen and Hartley, 1982).

Emphasizing protection, it is appealing that drugs cause crime but, as discussed in earlier chapters, even if some drugs do, there is no reason why all should. However, along with the rush to document the health risks of a new drug, there is usually a parallel documentation of law-breaking by users which justifies its repression and making it illegal. Ericson (2006) describes an increasing trend to criminalize not only what is actually harmful, but what is merely suspected of being harmful, in the interests of preventing terrorism, benefits fraud and the like. The often-repeated precautionary medical and policy wisdom about drugs is that any substance with the potential to cause harm should not be used except for sanctioned medical purposes. Using potentially risky drugs for mere pleasure, or to self-medicate for worry, anxiety, pain or stress, should be criminal. This often results in entirely circular reasoning about drugs, where widespread use itself is taken to be evidence of widespread problems, justifying repression. The other main justification for repression is that drug use and drug problems have massive social costs.

Costs of drugs and crime

Class A problem drug use, predominantly heroin and cocaine with some amphetamine, has been estimated to cost England and Wales about £12 billion per year, of which about £10 billion is crime costs (Cave and Godfrey, 2005). Interestingly, the estimated non-crime costs are about £1.75 billion, which is comparable to the costs of alcohol, estimated at between £1 and £4 billion a year (Cabinet Office, 2003). For comparison, depression costs the UK over £9 billion a year (Thomas and Morris, 2003) and traffic congestion costs some £20 billion (http://eprints.ucl.ac.uk/archive/00001259/; accessed 10 April 2007). While these estimates are certainly inaccurate and the usual biases apply, it would appear that drugs cost about as much as some less demonized problems.

Hence, the polemical importance of the assumption that a large portion of drug costs are crime costs, which cannot be said of depression and can be said only in part for alcohol. Offending offends and concerns where illness does not. What is perhaps unique is the seemingly huge cost of crime by people who use drugs. Godfrey et al. (2002) estimate that there were at that time between a quarter of a million and half a million class A problem drug users in England and Wales, which means that each one costs, on average, somewhere between £34,000 and £68,000 per year, mostly in crime. Note that this best estimate varies by 100 per cent. It is even harder to estimate the numbers or costs of unobtrusive drug users. While their non-crime costs might be high, it can be surmised that they are relatively unlikely to be intensive offenders.

Crime is a problem, and drug-related crime forms a large enough proportion to make it worthwhile to try and prevent and treat drug dependence. However, this quite obvious assumption does not justify swallowing any and all claims about crime or drug-related crime. The governments of nation states have vested interests in focusing on crime and safety as big issues – protection of the public – which distract from the social and economic global forces that they cannot control. As already mentioned, crime has fallen in many places where there is concern about it, including the UK. There are far bigger problems than drugs, crime or terrorism, and some global mortality data are summarized by Jimpix (2007). That persistent criminals nowadays are often drug dependent does not mean that their offending would vanish were drugs never to have existed. Their successful rehabilitation reduces their offending, but this often involves changing lifestyle rather than simply treating drug use (see chapter 8). The scale of their offending reflects the general magnitude of their personal and social dysfunction, to which drug dependence makes a contribution of varying size. While there is a strong correlation between extent of drug use and offending, this correlation does not hold up among near-daily users. In this extreme group, the heaviest drug users are not necessarily the heaviest offenders (Hammersley et al., 1989). When drug-dependent offenders moderate or cease use, their offending reduces also (Ball, Schaffer and Nurco, 1983), but the activities are coupled within a lifestyle rather than one causing the other (Johnson et al., 1985).

If it is difficult to estimate the costs of drug dependence, it is impossible to estimate the costs of cannabis use. Whatever harms and costs are incurred, they are far more diffuse. Health disadvantages seem relatively subtle compared to those of tobacco or alcohol and consequently harder to monetarize. Furthermore, there may be benefits of cannabis use. One possible benefit is medical use to relieve symptoms of and pain caused by a variety of conditions, of which multiple sclerosis is the best established (Collin et al., 2007). Another possible, more widespread, benefit is that cannabis users might not drink as heavily as they would if they did not use, although it would be difficult to show this because cannabis users who also drink regularly tend to exhibit more signs of cannabis dependence (Barnwell, Earleywine and Gordis, 2006), so some form of careful longitudinal study would be required and then weighing the benefits of reduced drinking against the costs of cannabis use would be complex. Finally, there are indications that a generation switching away from hard drugs, specifically crack cocaine, to marijuana and alcohol reduced violent crime in the USA (Bowling, 1999).

What does crime actually cost society?

Brand and Price (2000) offer the best UK monetary estimates to date: crime costs the country about £60 billion a year, of which £19 billion is property stolen or damaged, £18 billion is emotional and physical impact on victims and £11.6 billion is criminal justice costs (other costs are relatively cheap and contribute little to their estimates). This means that, if Cave and Godfrey (2005) are correct, then problem drug users' crime accounts for about 20 per cent of all crime costs. Were drugs a simple cause of crime, they would be well worth addressing. Nonetheless, 80 per cent of costs come from crime not known to be related to problem drug users, so tackling drugs, even in the best possible scenario where prevention and treatment worked very well, would not get rid of most crime costs.

Second, it is probably safer to assume that estimates like this are ordinal indices rather than being real units of money. Notionally subtracting 'drug-related crime' from 'crime' does not produce a real figure, any more than subtracting the shortest child from the tallest one gives a medium-sized youth.

Third, as Brand and Price (2000) acknowledge, it is extremely difficult to put monetary values on the emotional and physical costs of crime (or anything else). How much does a person's fear, anger, shame or hesitancy about going out at night cost? Furthermore, can this be assigned a fixed cost at all, given that people's rated emotional reactions to being a victim are partly a function of how the questions are posed and who is asking them (Farrall et al., 1997)?

Fourth, unlike business accounts, estimates of health- and social-care costs rarely include any benefits, profits or allowable losses in the calculations. Putting this another way, how much *should* crime cost? A manufacturer knows how much manufacturing should cost to make a profit, but how much should society be willing to pay for crime and what benefits are there of crime, if any? The gross domestic product of the UK in 2000 was about £1 trillion (Officer, 2006), which means that crime in the UK cost under 7 per cent of the GDP (and crime by problem drug users about 1.5 per cent). For comparison, according to the Ministry of Defence the UK spends about 2.5 per cent of its GDP on defence. About 5 per cent is spent on education (Department for Education and Skills, 2006) and about 10 per cent on social security benefits (Department for Work and Pensions, 2007). These figures are all actual expenditure and do not include estimates of the monetary costs of various harms, which means they are under-inflated compared to the estimated costs of drugs and crime. Should drugs and crime be considered unavoidable costs, as wastage from consumer society? Under 7 per cent wastage is acceptable in some industries; in catering a third or more of food may be wasted. Is it possible to drive drugs and crime still lower in a society, or would the costs actually rise if the problems were tackled even more vigorously?

It is also feasible that crime has some benefits to the economy. Economic crimes stimulate the insurance industry, pass stolen goods on to new consumers and get victims to buy new goods (Johnson et al., 1985). Jobs are created in criminal justice, security, health and social care. As discussed in chapter 9, the illegal industries, including drugs, must also interpenetrate the legitimate economy. We do not know how much crime should cost, because the question is rarely asked.

Yet, benefits could be estimated for alcohol:

> The primary benefit of alcohol lies in the pleasure that individuals derive from consuming it. However, besides the direct benefits to consumers alcohol in itself produces wider (external) benefits for the society as a whole. These are primarily centred in alcohol's capacity to act as a catalyst in social interactions and leisure experiences. Alcohol brings people together and facilitates group interactions enhancing the capacity of individuals to relax and socialise, and hence may be seen as promoting social cohesion. (Cabinet Office, 2003, 12)

The report demurs from monetarizing these benefits, but goes on to estimate the total annual UK costs of alcohol at between £18 and £20 billion, of which £12 billion is alcohol-related crime, including road traffic offences. This is about twice the costs of problem drug use, but distributed across most of society rather than concentrated in an identifiable, stigmatized and deviant minority. Similarly, Miller et al. (2006) estimate the US crime costs of alcohol to be about twice those of drugs. Should it be possible to estimate the benefits of alcohol, similar benefits might apply to drug use; one could replace 'alcohol' with 'cannabis' or 'ecstasy' in the quote above without being very contentious.

And we should not forget the many people employed in the alcohol industry and licensed trade, the useful profits that can be gained selling drugs, and the useful tax revenue obtained from tobacco and alcohol. I cannot form an opinion about whether the personal and social benefits of alcohol, or drugs, are worth the costs, but this needs to be discussed without assuming that alcohol must be worth it and drugs not.

A final problem is that it is misleading to put justice costs into the costs of crime, because this means that the more spent 'fighting crime' the more crime seems to cost, making it impossible for criminal justice interventions to succeed in monetary terms. It also causes problems, because the costs of sincerely tackling crime could easily impede economic growth. For example, if alcohol sales were dramatically curtailed then this would probably damage city-centre night-time economies, but reduce violence. If tax levels were raised to cover the costs of enhanced social care and benefits, reducing deprivation and dysfunction, then economic competitiveness might be lost. Nor is there evidence this would reduce drugs and crime problems. If rights of detainment, search and seizure were raised to the levels that have occurred recently during peak terrorist scares, to prevent much more drug smuggling, then imports, tourism and public relations would be badly affected. The estimated costs of drugs and crime seem more like examples of risk society thinking than like unbiased exercises in economics.

Drugs and crime are sizeable social problems. But they are not society's biggest, or only, problems. A logical extension of estimating the financial costs of problems would be to try and work out what would happen if resources were spent on one problem rather than another. Unfortunately thinking about drugs and crime is often accorded a special high-profile logic of its own as if both were foreign to society. Furthermore, it is doubtful that even targeted street-level policing of drugs impacts crime (Shepard and Blackley, 2005; Lawton, Taylor and Luongo, 2005).

Why do people take drugs?

If drugs are not foreign to society, why do people take them? The answer to this question is often put in very complicated biological terms. Words such as compulsion, craving, dependency and addiction are used. Entire journal issues are devoted to discussing the mappings between these concepts and brain mechanisms. Unfortunately, answers tend to be expressed at the wrong theoretical level. The answers do not fundamentally lie at the biological level, but at the psychological level.

Teleological explanation

Put at its most simple, people take drugs because they want to, because they expect some positive or beneficial result. These expectancies include actual positive benefits to themselves, avoidance of negative effects like withdrawal symptoms, and more subtle things – for example, fitting in with their friends, not seeming to spoil the party, having a laugh and many other psychosocial happenings. So people take drugs for reasons. This form of explanation is known as a teleological explanation – explaining something from its intended consequences, not from its prior causes – which is in marked contrast to the mechanistic or reductionist explanations normally advanced for drug use. We can reframe the question of why people take drugs into a question concerning what reasons people have for taking drugs. This question becomes answerable. Indeed, because most people drink alcohol and many have tried cigarettes at one time or another, pretty much everybody knows some of the reasons why people take drugs. These are not fundamentally different from the reasons for drinking, or smoking, or taking vitamins in the hope that they will improve your health, or any other form of substance use, or indeed ingestion, which is a very wide domain of activity that might potentially include beauty products, medicines and many foods as well.

People take drugs:

1 because they enjoy the effects
2 because drugs affect their arousal or cognitive performance in ways that seem pleasurable or beneficial
3 for other instrumental reasons, including to alleviate pain, to reduce anxiety, to sleep, to stay awake, to enhance sex and to dance better
4 because it seems like the appropriate thing to do in the social setting where they are
5 because if they do not they expect unpleasant things will happen to them. For example, people believe from experience that if they do not take heroin they will have unpleasant withdrawal effects, so they seek out more heroin and take it (Johnson et al., 1985). Generally, they do this *before* withdrawal kicks in
6 as a form of escape from the problems of their everyday life
7 because mind-altering effects of drugs are, for some people, enjoyable in their own right
8 as a part of religious rituals. This may be the earliest use of drugs, although archaeological evidence cannot really distinguish debauchery from intoxicated ritual or tell whether it was naughty adolescents or priests who took the drug.

The myth of addiction

If people use drugs because of what they expect to happen, then the neurobiological effects of drugs play no necessary part in sustaining drug use. People could take things that have no specific effects at all – placebos – because they believe that they will have effects. If they expect specific strong effects from placebos then they may learn that they do not work. There is no evidence that placebos can cure physical conditions (Stewart-Williams and Podd, 2004). What placebos and expectations can do is to influence psychosocial effects, so it can be extremely difficult to decide whether or not the drug has the expected effects. Indeed, it continues to be unclear whether some substances have any genuine effects or not, ginseng being one example (Vogler, Pittler and Ernst, 1999).

Conversely, when people take drugs that have clear, strong, neurobiological effects, then those effects may not suffice to continue use. The most striking example of this is the low rate of morphine dependence and withdrawal among people prescribed morphine for acute serious pain. Once the pain is over, most people cease use without difficulty. More mundanely, many people try drugs with various strong effects, do not like them and therefore do not repeat use. This form of understanding of drug use is in marked contrast to the widespread myth (Davies, 1992; Hammersley and Reid, 2002) of drug use as being primarily about addiction and consequent crime, determined mostly by the neuropsychopharmacological properties of the drug. Sadly, simple technological fixes for drug problems are unlikely and, were they to occur, society would probably reconstruct some other form of substance use as an equivalent problem. Luckily, because society constructs drugs and crime problems, there is considerable potential for managing the problems by rethinking them. Perhaps it is for this reason that various possibilities, such as legalizing certain drugs, are often labelled 'unthinkable'. For such rethinking would undermine the caring industry managing these problems using modernist, rational, positivistic and technological methods that are, supposedly, scientific and 'true' rather than motivated by morality or the desire to make money (see Crow and Hartman, 1992; Akers, 1991; Szasz, 1974). It is also convenient to define substance problems as an addictive disease so that sufferers can be treated on health insurance (Sobell and Sobell, 2006). Rethinking would require admitting that society includes drugs and crime in a fundamental way.

If the myth is true then many other groups in society gain something. The media have a good story and politicians a safe issue. Those involved in the production and trafficking of controlled drugs may also enhance their profits by encouraging the myth and keeping their products illegal. Law enforcement also benefits as many causes of crime are poorly understood, and attempts to thwart or reduce crime can appear frustratingly unsuccessful (see Pawson and Tilley, 1997, ch. 1) in contrast to tackling drugs or alcohol.

There are also global tensions, for the major misused drugs are all produced primarily in developing countries and consumed primarily in the most developed countries (although this is changing and the USA is a major cannabis producer). Given the enormous turnover of the drugs market, substantial money must be flowing out of Europe and North America into Latin America, Africa and Asia. This possibility would concern politicians even if drugs were legal. As they are illegal, intervention in the trade is not only allowed, but also congratulated by the international community.

The pharmaceutical industry and the biotechnology research industry also have a lot to gain from the myth. If addiction is a real biological entity that is not determined by complicated psychological and social forces, then there is potential to find a simple (and highly profitable) cure, and in the meantime a programme of basic research can be funded.

Many religious and moral groups also benefit from the myth. In Judaeo-Christian and Islamic ethics, there has always been a difficulty in resolving the beliefs in individual free will and a beneficent God with the evil behaviour of people. One can dilute this problem by arguing that drugs suspend free will. One can then continue to believe that people are essentially good, but are led to do evil by drugs (Blum and associates, 1970). Many who scorn demons as superstition believe that drugs have equally odd and powerful properties.

Drug users themselves also have something to gain by endorsing the myth of drug use. Few criminals regard themselves as wicked people, and they provide rationales and justifications for their antisocial behaviour. No one likes to admit to being bad or stupid, and drugs provide a convenient explanation for actions for which one would rather not take personal responsibility (see Davies, 1992).

Last, and often most outspoken in support of the myth, are ex- and 'recovering' drug users themselves. Particularly outspoken tend to be graduates from programmes which emphasize help by other ex-users and abstinence, often with twelve-steps philosophy or some variation on it. The reason for this may be that many graduates have defined their identities in terms of their ex-addict status. In some cases they have not left drugs behind, but rather have replaced being heavily involved *with* drugs with being heavily involved *against* drugs. Successful graduates of twelve-steps programmes have had to accept their powerlessness over the addiction (Keene and Raynor, 1993; Bateson, 1971). In other words they have had to accept their permanent out-group status, for at any time they might resume their addictive behaviour.

In short, the myth is to the advantage of all concerned parties, and it is no wonder that it is so firmly believed and defended. Many defenders believe that they are defending the truth, for there is some truth to the myth. As money makes the world go round, it is particularly necessary to look critically at the roles of the substance supply industries.

The licit substance supply industries

The illegal drugs industry is often presumed criminal, wicked and associated with the vilest forms of crime, such as terrorism, armed robbery and human trafficking (e.g., Van Duyne and Levi, 2005; Naim, 2005), but the licit industries have not always been well behaved either. Sometimes, they have all had conflicts with the law and been regulated more or less heavily, and some products have been banned. The widespread peddling of ineffective and harmful patent medicines in the late nineteenth century led to regulation of the pharmaceutical industry (Boussel, Bonnemain and Bove, 1983). Despite current extensive efforts to suppress the farming of coca and opium (e.g., United Nations Office on Drugs and Crime, 2006), there is no obvious intention to prevent the farming of opium to manufacture medicines including morphine and codeine. The chewing of coca leaf is common and longstanding throughout its area of traditional cultivation in Colombia and Bolivia (Rivera et al., 2005) and might be left intact even if the manufacture of cocaine were suppressed (not that this is likely to happen successfully). Furthermore, when they have been heavily repressed, the currently licit substance industries have often been dominated by shady practices and illegal actions. The most notorious example remains the alcohol supply industry in the USA during prohibition (Behr, 1996). The origins of some reputable alcohol manufacturers lie there, when they contributed to illicit supply to the USA; likewise some Scotch whisky distillers began as bootleggers before 1823. In earlier centuries tobacco and alcohol smuggling to England from Europe was big business, as it is today.

Both the licit and illicit industries have brought benefits to many people employed by them and can enrich the areas where drugs are farmed and manufactured. The alcohol industry has repeatedly argued that in the UK the cost of alcohol cannot be raised further and that liberalization of licensing is necessary in order to support the licensed trade and the many people who work there, or in the manufacture and distribution of alcohol. Tobacco producers in the USA have made similar arguments about the need to protect the livelihoods of those working in the industry (for example, http://usgovinfo.about. com/library/weekly/aa092600a.htm; accessed 4 June 2007). The Medellin Cartel in Colombia (Strong, 1995), at one point headed by Pablo Escobar, is often held up as the epitome of a savage crime organization headed by 'Mr Big'. It nonetheless benefited the Medellin region in some ways, if completely distorting the economy and corrupting all legitimate social institutions, which were already rather weak, in the process. The profits to be made from drugs are so large that where necessary some people resort to any means, up to and including murder, to protect their trade. However, the extreme violence in Colombia related to cocaine was built on the existing traditions there of the violent and murderous resolution of social, economic and political conflicts.

The alcohol, tobacco and pharmaceutical industries in the developed world do not behave like this, nor do they need to. Nonetheless, there are parallels to be drawn between the different supply industries. These parallels illustrate some of the difficulties and dilemmas of defining 'crime' and 'drugs' and also that the definitions in wide circulation are often quite blatantly serving the interests of powerful groups in society, which include the substance-manufacturing industries themselves. Because there are obvious parallels, it is also informative to examine the activities of legitimate industries to learn about how the illegal ones may behave.

Of primary importance is that the substance supply industries share the profit motive. This motive conflicts with care of the consumer: providing products that are safe, effective and honestly priced, not marketing products that are harmful to the purse or person, and social responsibility in, for example, not selling to children. Where conflict occurs, most states and nations regulate to constrain the profit motive and most industries strain and strive against those regulations. This is no different from other industries, such as the food industry (e.g., Schlosser, 2002) or fashion (Klein, 2001). The substances industries, however, are particularly focused on supplying substances that people do not particularly need, but want a great deal; one might say that it is the 'want' that, loosely speaking, makes substances addictive. This is an unpalatable secret, which the industries exert a great deal of time and effort concealing by skilful marketing and also by offering – and being seen to offer – products that are not of this type.

Skilful marketing often includes downplaying the addictive potential of their products, and this may include playing up the addictive potential of other industries' products. Substances of dependence are the ideal consumer products because people want and need to consume them regularly. All the industries are ethical about their activities, up to a point, but willing to compromise moral or legal scruples when this seems necessary to survive in profit. None of the industries – pharmaceutical, alcohol, tobacco or illegal drugs – are so ethical that governments have never felt it necessary to regulate them in response to perceived problems.

Other consumer industries are comparatively lightly regulated, although historically regulation tends to increase more easily than decrease. Products to be ingested, which would include food, vitamins, medicines and so on, tend to have heavier regulation. In contrast, it is not, as far as I know, explicitly illegal to manufacture bookcases that can fall over, nor are there complex guidelines for preventing this. Nor is it required that the computer industry makes software that works as it should: indeed, there is much satirical writing complaining about this (some of it collected at http://homepage. eircom.net/~nobyrne/page5.htm; accessed 15 May 2007). The free market can supposedly control the quality and safety of many goods without massive intervention. Why should ingestibles be different? For most of their history, they were not. The extensive regulation of food and drugs was a response to the extensive adulteration of foods and sale of worthless medicines in the latter part of the nineteenth century, which coincided with the industrialization of their production (Boussel, Bonnemain and Bove, 1983), while the control of alcohol and tobacco began two hundred years or so earlier as an issue of taxation, before they were widely recognized as health problems.

Demand-led industrialization and commercialization

Tobacco use spread rapidly in Europe despite repression (Borio, 2007). Use continued to spread once cigarette production was industrialized. As early as 1900, 4.4 billion cigarettes were sold in the USA, while by 1923 sales had reached 73 billion. Cigarettes met with very considerable opposition. For example, by 1909 fifteen states had banned cigarettes entirely, but in 1927 Kansas was the last to repeal the ban. Lung cancer rates had already trebled.

Alcohol, in the form of naturally fermented fruit, is sought out and consumed by elephants (Siegel and Brodie, 1984) and the smell of alcohol may help primates find ripe fruit (Dudley, 2002). While occasional animal likings for cultivated human drugs, particularly marijuana, have been reported, alcohol is animals' and humans' favourite drug. By Roman times, some two thousand years ago, wine and beer were widely made (distillation was also practised) and had sophisticated distribution networks, so drinks made near the Mediterranean could end up by Hadrian's Wall in North Britain, as they do today.

From earliest mentions of alcohol, there has been awareness of drunkenness as a potential problem (in the Bible for example) but also acceptance of the drinking of alcoholic beverages as a normal dietary activity, largely unworthy of comment.

The USA imported a whole range of drinking styles, and from early on in that country's history there was disapproval of saloons and a determined and aggressive temperance movement developed (Burns, 2004). A continuing result of temperance is that, compared with European countries, the USA continues to be quite polarized about alcohol, with a high proportion of the country professing not to drink at all. This polarization led to alcohol being prohibited in the USA in 1920. Alcohol prohibition led to widespread illicit supply, with a rapid growth in organized crime, widespread corruption, and problems of unregulated premises for drinking and poor quality control of alcohol, which was sometimes even poisonous. It revealed a great national thirst for alcohol, at nearly any cost. Although these problems led to prohibition being repealed in 1933, it was not a public health disaster. The prevalence of liver disease and some other indicators of alcohol-related health problems clearly fell during prohibition and rose again afterwards (Blocker, 2006). One of the legacies of prohibition is that some contemporary alcohol companies have historical origins in bootlegging, illustrating what might happen were some other drugs to be legalized. With globalization during the twentieth century, drinking styles have tended to blur across cultures (Anderson and Baumberg, 2006). For example, in the UK more alcohol is now consumed at home than in bars, while in Mediterranean-style countries overt intoxication in bars occurs more than it used to. The thirst for alcohol remains.

The pharmaceutical industry developed across the last 130 years from a conjunction of industrialization, medicine and marketing. Up until the middle of the nineteenth century, there were few available effective medicines. Alcohol, opium preparations and cannabis were among those that actually had some effects. There was a flourishing patent medicines trade that made and sold preparations for any imaginable medical condition, making dramatic and unsubstantiated claims for efficacy. Often the medicines contained no active ingredients, or only standard ones such as alcohol or opium (Boussel, Bonnemain and Bove, 1983). Pharmacists and drug stores were also able to offer prescriptions written by medics, but they were much less tightly regulated than they are today and could also offer their own prescriptions, or make up the patient's own. Prescriptions had not usually been evaluated for efficacy, effectiveness or safety, except perhaps in the doctor's or pharmacist's own clinical experience.

As the nineteenth century changed to the twentieth century, there was a tightening of laws to prevent patent medicine (and genuine medicine) sellers from swindling the public. Simultaneously, there was a great growth in industrial chemistry and biochemistry, which has continued ever since. From its early days, the pharmaceutical industry has represented itself as a branch of medicine, as white-coated scientists working for the common good. It is not a branch of medicine, rather a highly specialized manufacturing industry that began as a branch of the chemical industry (Bioanalytical Systems, 2007, gives a convenient summary of the main companies) and has developed with and contributed to biochemistry. Great good indeed has come from pharmacology. It has led to the elimination of some diseases and the extremely successful treatment of others, including many that previously often killed people.

Marketing

It has been something of a scandal to discover that the tobacco industry knew from early on that cigarette smoking was harmful and did its best to conceal this information, as well as how highly dependence-forming tobacco was, while developing strategies for managing the fact that the number of smokers was going to decrease as the news got out (see Ling and Glantz, 2002; Feldman and Bayer, 2004). Among successful strategies were marketing alternative 'low tar' cigarettes as less unhealthy – although this turned out to be false, if it was ever sincerely believed to be true, because people smoke quicker and harder to get the nicotine they want, inhaling more tars and toxins too – and expanding into new markets, including Africa and Asia, for industrially manufactured cigarettes (De Beyer and Brigden, 2003).

As mentioned in chapter 1, in the UK the alcohol industry has a code that its advertising should not have intoxication, immoderate drinking or strength as a dominant theme, not be linked with sexual success, social success, bravado, aggressive or dangerous behaviour, not be associated with or allude to illicit drugs, not appeal to the under-eighteens or show anyone who looks under twenty-five consuming or having recently consumed alcohol. It is strange, then, that the World Health Organization believes that:

Pressures on young people to drink have increased while, at the same time, protective factors have become somewhat weaker. The sport and leisure environments, a central part of young people's social space, are strongly linked to drinking through extensive marketing practices, and this can result in unintentional injuries and violence. Youth sport and leisure environments free of alcohol and alcohol marketing could help reduce the pressure on and provide a safer social environment for young people. (WHO, 2006, 22)

Sports sponsorship is very lightly regulated across Europe (Anderson and Baumberg, 2006, 19), so it is an attractive means of promoting alcohol brands. While it is not definitively established that sports sponsorship encourages drinking among young people, having a beer brand emblazoned across the chest of an attractive, highly paid, fit and macho sports personality seems evidently counter to the UK alcohol industry's code of practice, particularly if the same young man has been 'exposed' in the press drunk on the arms of attractive young women. The alcohol industry is so keen to maintain this association between booze and sport that it recently managed to block a proposed EU-wide ban on alcohol sponsorship of sports, although it is of course 'fully behind the over-riding intention, namely addressing alcohol misuse' (European Sponsorship Association, 2006). There is also a worrying correlation between expenditure on alcohol advertising over the years and underage alcohol consumption (Institute on Alcohol Studies, 2007, 4).

There are concerns, too, about alcohol advertising's use of music and imagery that appears to draw upon drug and dance culture. Examples include lager adverts using rave imagery and running promotions in dance clubs, an anti-drug message on the back of a beer mat, with the front advertising beer, and, from New Zealand, an advert for 'the next high' which is an alcoholic energy drink (Forsyth, 2007). The latter ad shows a young woman who looks as if she is snorting the pink energy drink off a table (although the item she is holding close to her nose is not quite a tube). The alcohol industry and its advertising agencies knowingly go as close as they can to the boundaries of the relevant codes of practice and laws. Without coercion from government and health organizations, the industry does not seem to sell alcohol in an ethical fashion, which would involve 'moderate' drinking of not more than two units per day or perhaps twenty-one a week for men. Across Europe, non-abstainers consume a mean of twenty-nine units a week (Anderson and Baumberg, 2006, 3). This does not suggest the result of alcohol advertising (and it is one of the world's most heavily advertised products) is truly responsible, ethical and moderate. That the industry is officially in favour of responsible drinking does not make it a friend of public health (Wallack, 1992).

An interesting selection of historical advertisements for various drugs, including some for drugs since banned and/or found to lead to dependence, can be found at http://community.livejournal.com/vintage_ads/88173.html (accessed 26 September 2006). Pharmaceutical adverts have commonly portrayed drugs as more effective and safer than they really are. A unique wheeze of the industry is to pass much responsibility to medicine. They can sell drugs which are known to be dangerous but with choice delegated to doctors rather than end consumers.

Given the huge costs of developing new drugs, the industry has been known to massage or conceal research findings to produce favourable outcomes (Braithwaite, 1984), to bias the research agenda in its favour and focus on products that sell rather than those that effect new or better treatment (House of Commons Health Committee, 2005), to cover up or downplay drug dangers, to offload drugs banned as dangerous in more tightly regulated markets to countries where they are not regulated, and to sell products, such as vitamins, that are not scientifically credible. It has been known to use unethical marketing procedures to persuade doctors to prescribe its products (Braithwaite, 1984), to exert undue pressures to facilitate the sale of its products, and artificially to keep drugs more expensive than necessary (House of Commons Health Committee, 2005). It has also developed some of the drugs that now form the 'drug problem'. There have been repeated debates about the appropriateness of long-term prescribing of psychoactive medicines used as tranquillizers, antidepressants or sleep aids (see chapter 2). That the pharmaceutical industry is largely good does not mean that it has done no harm.

Connections to government and policy

The tobacco industry is a large industry with a lot of political influence, particularly in the USA, which is a major tobacco producer. Naturally, that influence grew as the industry's profits grew with the boom in cigarette smoking. Among the many American political figures related or otherwise linked to the industry was Harry Anslinger, the head of the Federal Bureau on Narcotics, who married into a tobacco family. Margaret Thatcher went from being UK prime minister to being a 'geopolitical consultant' for Philip Morris, at $250,000 per annum plus $250,000 contribution to her foundation (www.wikipedia.org; accessed 23 October 2006). In the USA the tobacco industry makes substantial contributions to political funds, and the current Bush administration is linked with tobacco in a number of ways (see the Democratic Party's website, at eland-slide.org, for coverage of some relevant stories).

Another important form of corruption has been the industry's various attempts to distort research findings about smoking by suppressing adverse findings and supporting academics whose views are convenient to it. Consequently most peer-reviewed journals now require statements of interest from authors, including the reporting of funding by tobacco, alcohol or pharmaceutical industries. Of course they can still cover this up. A recent high-profile example involved Roger Scruton, the well-known philosopher who was being paid a substantial retainer to publish pro-tobacco articles.

The alcohol industry has strong links to government in the UK, the USA and elsewhere. Like tobacco, alcohol is a useful source of tax revenue for government, so governments have a direct incentive to maintain sales. Additionally, the alcohol industry makes donations to politicians (e.g., Centre for Science in the Public Interest, 2007). Information from Europe is harder to come by. There can also be personal links between alcohol and government: for example, Lord Younger, of the brewing family, served in Margaret Thatcher's cabinet before going on to be chairman of the Royal Bank of Scotland (Roth, 2003) – a synergy of politics, drugs and finance that would be regarded as scandalous were a different drug and a Latin American country involved. There have been acrimonious disputes over whether the alcohol industry should be allowed to have a voice in alcohol policy and practice. Some health-care professionals consider this to be inherently corrupting, as they do engagement with the tobacco industry (e.g., Wallack, 1992). My view is that the relevant industries should have a voice, but they should not be allowed to dominate corruptly with the force of their purses, and other stakeholders should be clear that profit is the bottom line for them. As indicated earlier in this book, other stakeholders are not always altruistic and objective about substance use problems either.

According to the then UK prime minister:

A successful pharmaceutical industry is a prime example of what is needed in a successful knowledge economy. The UK's pharmaceutical industry has an outstanding tradition and has contributed very substantially to our economy and to the welfare of our citizens. . . . UK patients and people around the world have benefited from the early introduction of new and improved medicines that would not have been discovered without work undertaken in UK laboratories. (Blair, 2006)

However, this great good comes at a cost. For example, McVay (2004, 13) has compiled a table of causes of death in the USA, using various credible sources. About 32,000 hospitalized patients die each year from adverse reactions to prescribed drugs. This compares with 17,000 dying from illicit drug use. While far more people are given medication in hospital than use illicit drugs, this is hardly the common image of the relative scale of the problems. It is also of concern that the pharmaceutical industry has huge influence on medicine, partly because of its financial muscle (House of Commons Health Committee, 2005). This includes funding large-scale drugs research to its own agenda and buying the favours of doctors with various inducements, from free post-it notes bearing product logos to lavish training events in exotic locations with golf courses.

In short, the licit substance supply industries are motivated by profit, have sometimes shady or downright illicit pasts, and are not above dubious practices in the present. This has led to tight regulation, which means that they often behave.

Illegal drugs

For our purposes, the drugs supply industry did not get going until the 1960s, although it is worth mentioning the opium wars (1834–43 and 1856–60, when England wanted to supply opium to China, whether the Chinese wanted opium or not (see http://en.wikipedia.org/wiki/Opium_wars; accessed 11 May 2007). That links to the production of the opium poppy, because opium and its extracts are, to this day, valuable medicines. Before the 1960s, despite various attempts to generate panics about drugs such as cocaine, heroin and marijuana, use seems to have been restricted to more bohemian groups like musicians, or to places where the drugs were grown, and there does not seem to have been a complicated supply industry. Popular demand began to increase globally in the 1960s and increased steadily until the 1990s. It now shows signs of stabilizing or even decreasing slightly, but at high levels compared to those of the 1960s. In the early days drug supply seems to have been relatively unsophisticated. Essentially someone would go and obtain, or make, some drug and sell it in a comparatively small-scale way. This is surmised mostly from anecdote and biographical accounts, not quality research. Rumour in the late 1970s had it that one or two amphetamine factories were supplying most of the UK, for example. A person might go to North Africa and smuggle back cannabis resin, having got funds from a collective to do so, who then sold the drug and shared the profits, as well as the cheap hash. Although individuals were sometimes making large amounts of money this way – up to hundreds of thousands of pounds at today's prices – the supply industry was not heavily industrialized or globalized and the consumers were stimulating the industry, sometimes by setting up supply themselves, rather than the industry being self-motivated.

All this changed gradually. The RSA (2007, 38–50) report provides a useful summary of the main facts. Key influences on the change included the heroin epidemic in the USA in the 1970s, which probably increased and professionalized global trafficking methods, followed by the cocaine epidemic, which brought South American interests into the picture and further toughened and professionalized the industry. The professionalization of supply probably spread then to Europe and elsewhere. Although the industry is estimated now to be one of the world's largest (Castells, 1998), it is not in the shape of one big hierarchical organization, but is a loose network of people and organizations where no single part or person is irreplaceable. The network probably configures in different ways from deal to deal, according to what is necessary. Not all that much is known about the industry, and some knowledge comes from supply-prevention sources whose interest it is to make their enemy seem as large and dangerous as possible. Nonetheless the following can be surmised.

Drug supply has globalized in that it is willing and able to move drugs and the products needed to make them around the world as required, and can supply products grown or made anywhere to anywhere else where there is a demand. This is no different from many legitimate industries these days, but it is an impressive feat for an entirely covert operation. Given the network nature of drug supply (Castells, 1998; RSA, 2007), media and police descriptions of parts of the system belonging to specific ethnic groups or countries are probably no more accurate than calling a London newspaper 'Scottish' because the editor was born in Scotland, except insofar as kinship ties facilitate security in an illicit business.

While violence and the threat of violence are a part of the drugs trade, even in Colombia the extremely violent Medellin Cartel was less successful than the less violent and more secretive Cali Cartel, who may have successfully gone 'legitimate' (Strong, 1995). Incentives other than violence are widely used too, the most important being money itself. The supply industry collectively has enough money to buy its way out of much trouble, but how it uses this money is unknown. To an extent, violence is a distraction from the problem of corruption, which is probably much more serious.

The drugs industry is intertwined with other illegal industries and activities and has also interpenetrated legitimate activities in ways that can only be guessed at. The use of drugs money for criminal and terrorist ends is well publicized, but in Scotland alone I am aware of a number of cases of successful legitimate entrepreneurs who acquired their start-up money by dealing in drugs or, should I say, discovered a flair for business and went legitimate. The financial industry must be laden with drugs money, as the number of discovered cases of money laundering is relatively low and the profits of the world's largest industry cannot all be buried in the ground.

If drug suppliers influence governments, what do they achieve?

Many among the public would prefer that drugs were less heavily regulated, or more easily available (Runciman, 1999), although few favour complete deregulation or legalization. This may apply also to street-level sellers. What about drug suppliers? Presumably they would prefer that their activities were not a high priority and were even ignored. In addictions, we are so focused on the relatively huge amount of money that goes into supply reduction work – police, customs, intelligence agencies, military action and so on – that we forget that the costs of this are trivial compared with the profits of the drugs trade. The USA spent $7.2 billion on supply reduction work in 2004 from a total of $11.7 billion on drugs work of all kinds (Office of the President of the USA, 2004). This is by far the largest expenditure globally. The illicit drugs industry is much larger, at least $45 billion and perhaps as much as $280 billion (Thoumi, 2005), although the whole matter is a guessing game distorted by the covert nature of the industry, sometimes wild estimates from limited information and the huge price differential between the farm gate and a retail price on the street. In a true war, victory tends to go to the side with the best resources (Smith, 2006), by which index the drug suppliers are winning by a good margin. So, they are getting the result that they want in the face of sometimes spectacular but largely ineffective opposition. There are also weird and perhaps somewhat irrelevant stories about the involvement of intelligence agencies such as the CIA in drug supplying. One website (www.ciadrugs.com) is devoted to stories and books about alleged CIA activity in this area.

Whatever lobbyists for drug suppliers there are would be wise to lobby for more supply-side spending and as little work to reduce demand as possible. They can do this understanding that there is no political will to invest enough in supply reduction to make any real difference. In contrast, demand reduction work is dangerously cheap and can succeed, so serious investment in it is to be discouraged (less than $2 billion per annum in the USA, under $5 per head of population). It supposedly 'sends the wrong signals' by encouraging discussion of drug use, or accepting that it will occur to some extent. Even the most optimistic estimates of the impact of supply reduction activity do not think that it has a significant effect on supply (see RSA, 2007), although opium production may have fallen (United Nations Office on Drugs and Crime, 2006a). There are occasional, local exceptions where prices rocket and availability is greatly reduced (e.g., Donnelly, Weatherburn and Chilvers, 2004). Legalizing drugs would, however, have consistent financial implications for the industry, which would probably be heavily taxed like the tobacco and alcohol industries, would be required to meet health and safety legislation for both employees and consumers, would not be allowed to adulterate products whenever convenient, and would probably be held responsible for the harms caused to consumers. Drug suppliers will be striving to keep their vested interests illegal and unregulated.

For the illicit drugs industry to thrive, it has to corrupt legitimate economic institutions. Vast illegal profits are useless if they cannot be spent. At the extreme, some propose that the US national debit is substantially propped up by drugs money laundered by US banks, which constitutes a sort of under-the-table tax on the rest of the world (http://narcodollars.potmail.org; accessed 10 April 2007). While the reasoning on this website seems quite logical, there are the usual problems of lack of concrete evidence and no sound foundation for estimating the actual sums of money involved. There is also a question of whether corruption happens deliberately and systemically as a form of conspiracy or whether it happens commonly but often on a relatively modest scale, simply because money laundering is an attractive source of revenue. It is logically obvious that the enormous profits of drug trafficking have to go somewhere. Even the most ostentatious trafficker cannot simply blow it all on bling, and wise traffickers should buy influential friends if they can. Trafficking jeopardizes the legitimate governments of many producer and shipper countries (e.g., Engvall, 2006).

It benefits the drugs industry's profitability that it remains illegal and unregulated, whereas it is in our societies' interests to regulate it in order to minimize the harms caused. It is a fantasy to believe that cannabis, amphetamines, heroin, cocaine, ecstasy, LSD and all the other drugs, including those not yet invented, can be driven away by regulation and control (see RSA, 2007). The fantasy is a recurrent one in history, having been applied in Europe over the past 500 years to alcohol, tobacco, tea and coffee (Barr, 1995) before being applied to other drugs during the twentieth century. The demand for drugs is such that supply will be provided at any cost that can be passed on to the consumer. Compared to some other goods, drug commodities are relatively price inelastic, but, like other goods, when they are dearer fewer people seem to use them and fewer try them, although quality data are rarely available and elasticity varies somewhat for different substances (Rhodes et al., 2000). So raised industry costs can be tolerated. Indeed, were drugs to be legalized, the prices should be controlled via taxation. Refusing to regulate a huge, hugely profitable industry is not a policy that should be sustained much longer. If it is, it makes one wonder about the hidden political and economic power the drugs industry exerts, as yet largely unchecked.

Summary

Drugs and crime fit into society, but primarily as activities to be problematized, rejected and excluded. This applies also to the illicit drugs industry. The reasons for substance use are not mysterious, but there is considerable appeal in society for drugs and crime as major sources of risk and fear. This appeal can be understood by a variety of mechanisms that make drugs and crime socially functional, but this is an underdeveloped area of study that is contentious among those who favour more biological, reductionist explanations. Sometimes it goes along with a simplistic morality that defines certain activities as absolutely bad, without considering what else they are related to. Eradicating drugs and leaving alcohol seems unlikely. There is also need for debate about how little drugs and crime is enough to be tolerable, and this debate should include consideration of better regulation of the illicit drugs industry.

Discussion points

- Interventions often begin because a problem has peaked, then it often reduces again, or concern wanes, so the intervention

sort of seems to have worked. How could policy intervene in a better way?
- How would one go about regulating the illicit drugs industry?
- Why is it widely claimed that drugs are the biggest social problem of our time?

Further reading

Adams, J. (1995). *Risk*. London: Routledge.
Beck, U. (1992). *Risk society: towards a new modernity*. London: Sage.
Füredi, F. (1997). *Culture of fear: risk-taking and the morality of low expectation*. London: Cassell.

7

Prevention

In 2002, the Association of St Petersburg Waxworks Museums created a touring exhibition illustrating the dangers of drugs. Harking back to carnival traditions, the exhibitors had ammonia on hand to revive anyone who fainted at such horrors as an image of the wasted lead singer with Queen, allegedly 'close to death from drugs', and other images that were equally casual about letting accuracy interfere with a dramatic tableau (Freddy Mercury, whatever his substance use, probably acquired AIDS via unprotected sex with men). This is a striking recent example of the use of fear messages to try to deter people from taking drugs. The waxworks focused on the health and social problems caused by drugs, rather than on the criminal mayhem they allegedly cause. Perhaps twenty-first-century Russian criminal mayhem is caused by other things. Also, there was no mention of alcohol, despite Russia's very prevalent, longstanding and often fatal problems with alcohol (Nicholson et al., 2005).

There is a long history of fear messages about drugs, some even more exaggerated than the above, and they remain popular with people who do not use drugs. Unfortunately, the effectiveness of fear messages is limited and complex to predict (Ruiter, Abraham and Kok, 2001). It is easy to instil fears that support what people already believe, but when fear messages go against what people want to do then their impact can be more complicated.

Many campaigns against crime also attempt to instil fear – of being caught, for example. However, some mass-media campaigns – whether against benefits fraud, theft from cars, cocaine or drinking too much – appear to be aimed more at impressing the public that something is being done than at effecting change. When the government or other public agencies are really advertising themselves, then fear messages can be given free rein and will appeal to the majority who are opposed to the activity.

For a fear message to change behaviour, the following steps are required. The person:

1 understands the message
2 relates the message to their own behaviour
3 considers the source of the message to be legitimate and credible
4 accepts the message as true
5 believes that changing their behaviour would reduce their fear, or the consequences of the behaviour that causes the fear
6 considers the fear to override other reasons for continuing the behaviour
7 believes that they are capable of changing their behaviour.

Looking at each of these in turn will tell us a lot about the difficulties of educational approaches to prevention, so this chapter will deal with these points before turning to other approaches.

Understanding the message

In Scotland during the mid-1980s, a series of posters with the slogan 'Heroin Really Screws You Up' included one of a male model lightly adorned with spots. Although he was supposed to look 'screwed up', some female heroin users found him attractive and put the poster up on their walls. In our postmodern, image-centred world, almost any statement, picture or video clip is ambiguous and, to make things worse, what is bad can be good. Audiences consume fear, and there is a risk that the most shocking messages might also be the most entertaining, as with horror films. So putting benefit cheats in the spotlight or threatening them with computer surveillance may frighten them, or it may make them feel that they are participating in a virtual reality SF film, which gives an enjoyable frisson to what they had previously thought were tedious activities of claiming benefit and working in a low-paid job. Similarly, fear messages about drugs often try to convey the idea that drugs have strong, dangerous effects. Unfortunately, some people are attracted to drugs for those very reasons. Hallucinogens that do not make you hallucinate and stimulants that do not make your heart pound are of poor quality. So in warning about 'danger' there is a risk of promoting drugs as 'strong', hence 'good'.

A final difficulty with relating fear messages to oneself is that fear can induce cognitive dissonance, with the person feeling conflict about a thought or action. They may enjoy it but feel it to be harmful, or believe it is good but feel it to be frightening or unpleasant. Fear-mongers hope that cognitive dissonance will lead to behaviour change. Often, it leads to ignoring or rejecting the message instead. Smokers include some who reduce their cognitive dissonance over smoking by minimizing the dangers of tobacco. Fear can lead people to avoid the fear-provoking situation rather than changing behaviour. If the doctor gives you frightening messages about your vices, don't go to the doctor. The fear-inducing content of the messages may make it even more likely that people will reject the relevance of the message.

Considering the source of the message to be legitimate and credible

As already mentioned, exaggerated fear messages may jeopardize the credibility of any source. However, there are more fundamental problems concerning who has the right to be an authoritative source on drugs and crime. A white van that parks in Glasgow's West End bears the sticker 'Don't steal, the government hates the competition.' Powerful people and organizations can be complacent about the general acceptance of their authority and can sometimes issue guidance and legislation without considering whether they will be regarded as credible. Often, their guidance on drugs and crime is seen as motivated, because it is – principally as a non-contentious vote winner. Moreover, how can the anti-drug pronouncements of politicians be seen as credible when the alcohol and tobacco industries have helped to fund and support so many of them? How can doctors' warnings about drug abuse be taken seriously when they routinely over-prescribe for psychological problems? If police officers or prison staff are themselves violent or corrupt, then why should their anti-crime statements be taken seriously?

One example is that there is currently a backlash against cannabis in the UK, with allegations of its increased potency and its recent depenalization being blamed for an increase in mental health problems and cannabis dependence (This is London, 2007). Decades of exaggerated anti-cannabis propaganda are at least equally to blame for an excessively blasé approach to cannabis today, as users reasonably consider health-care professionals and policy makers to have cried 'wolf' too often.

Accepting the message as true

Warnings and fear messages are often phrased as simple, straightfor-ward messages that are supposed to be applied in all situations. Unfortunately, often this also gives the impression that they express general truths, when they don't. Even drugs that have bad effects do not seem bad in every situation.

Jessor and Jessor (1977) wrote a theory of adolescent drug use that outlines how people's attitudes change as they are exposed to drugs and then try drugs themselves. The theory probably applies to adults and to other negatively viewed activities as well. Before any exposure to alcohol, tobacco or drugs, children have strongly negative attitudes to them. At this point they mainly have their parents' substance use to view. Taking tobacco smoking as a common example, although the processes are similar for other drugs, children initially regard tobacco smoking as very bad and very dangerous, and believe that they will never smoke. They are often strongly opposed to their parents smoking and readily list the reasons why people should not smoke. As they age and some of their peers begin to try smoking, young people are confronted with more contradictory information. Some of their peers enjoy it, and it seems to be fun in a naughty sort of way. Perhaps most importantly, they begin to see evidence that smoking is not immediately harmful to everyone, particularly as the serious harms of tobacco are mainly to do with getting fatal diseases in adulthood, and young people find it difficult to imagine their indi-vidual mortality. In the face of this personal evidence, attitudes to tobacco begin to become less negative. Then, once their attitudes have softened, some people try tobacco. The key point is that attitudes change first, as a consequence of personal exposure to drugs, then drug trying occurs. Simple fear messages, even if true, have difficulty countering such processes and when fear messages are exaggerated, or do not differentiate among substances and behaviours, then they will seem false to the people that they are aimed at.

The 'truth' about drug use, and probably about adolescent offending too, is that the relevant activities are often ones that people do because at the time they seem like a good idea. Often people initi-ate a new form of substance use or a new type of offending with some trepidation – acting *despite* fear, not because they ignorantly lack fear. So a heroin smoker may try injecting very aware of the dangers of unhygienic injecting practices and anxious that injecting may be more addictive than smoking. They manage these fears by ensuring that they only use sterile works and by intending to inject no more often than they previously smoked. Some people manage to control heroin injecting by such measures; others find that use escalates too easily into dependence and that standards of hygiene slip too meantime.

Drug users and criminals do not differ fundamentally from other people engaged in other behaviours. People make choices, act according to what seems acceptable at the time, and attempt to manage the risks as best they can. Drug use and offending are among common behaviours where the risks are well known. People also buy houses that may acquire negative equity, eat food that is bad for them, speed along motorways monitored by cameras, and lose their tempers and are rude to people in ways that have unpleasant repercussions. All these behaviours occur without the person intending the harmful effects to occur; indeed, they may believe they will not occur and they may be able to cite the statistical unlikelihood of harm occurring. Why should they be one of the rare but unfortunate ecstasy takers who dies of hyperthermia?

As people decide how to behave through their lives, they are only rarely confronted with absolute truths or choices which they can make with certainty. Currently, there is a widespread pretence that different drugs can be ranked by their dangerousness, as if heroin were always more dangerous than alcohol. As discussed in chapter 2, this is not realistic. As the Royal Society commission proposes (RSA, 2007), the focus should be on consequences rather than substances.

Believing that changing one's behaviour would reduce one's fear

A key finding across several areas of health promotion is that young people have difficulty imagining their personal mortality or morbidity. Young smokers tend to believe that they can quit at will (Eiser et al., 1989). Similarly, young drinkers may see thirty as 'old' and fail to grasp the seriousness of developing life-threatening conditions in their thirties rather than their seventies. Drug users tend to define drug problems and addiction as belonging to 'other types' of user. It appears to have been less researched, but young criminals in interviews can show a similar disregard for the future. They believe that they are unlikely to be caught – which can be true relative to the number of offences they commit – that they will be able to stop offending at the point when they face the adult sentencing system, and that they will not build up to a prison sentence that they will have difficulty serving. From bravado and experience, they may consider a few weeks or even a few months in prison as manageable and a sign of criminal honour. Such attitudes are often labelled 'impulsivity', and the conventional understanding of impulsivity was discussed in chapter 4.

Another way of looking at impulsivity is to propose that people often behave in ways cued by their immediate psychological, social and physical environment, without engaging in detailed deliberate thought about the consequences of their actions (e.g., Tiffany, 1990; Everitt, Dickinson and Robbins, 2001). People vary in their propensity for spontaneous processing, but all people are influenced by it sometimes. In everyday language, sometimes even wise people behave stupidly. The sexual peccadilloes of senior politicians are an example. It is therefore important not to pathologize 'impulsivity' too hastily. Behaviours that occur spontaneously will be resistant to change by fear messages. Environmental psychology also emphasizes the impact of the environment and social setting on people's behaviour. Settings that facilitate substance use may cause substance use simply in the absence of strong intentions not to use. For example, if cigarettes are available at a dinner party, a surprising number of ex-smokers will smoke later on in the evening once the wine has flowed. Indeed, people with strong abstinence intentions often elect to avoid settings conducive to use, whether a bar with cheap drinks where everyone drinks fast standing up, a heroin shooting gallery, or the neighbourhood and friends with whom they used to use.

Considering the fear to override other reasons for continuing the behaviour

Using drugs and committing crime are not activities or transactions that occur in isolation. For example, someone fiddling benefits may be more worried or fearful of how they are going to make money if they do not fiddle than they are about fiddling. Not fiddling, they may believe that they will have to resort to even more illegal activities, live in abject poverty or take an appalling job which they may be incapable of holding down. A drinker may find it unlikely that they can face life without alcohol. A drug user may express great willingness to stop using in theory, but fail to see how this can be accomplished in practice while they are homeless and sleeping rough. This is one reason that more sophisticated prevention initiatives tend to focus on holistic lifestyle improvements rather than single issues. Activities such as smoking, excessive drinking, drug use, antisocial behaviour, petty offending and not enjoying or taking school seriously tend to go together. Isolating one of these issues can be unrealistic. Young people should worry about tobacco smoking, but they may consider it an essential component of cannabis use, which is an integral part of their social life (Amos et al., 2004).

Some prevention programmes emphasize positive life activities instead of substance use, often sport or outdoor activities. A fundamental of behaviour change is that it is easier to replace the undesired behaviour with another behaviour than it is simply to cease. Unfortunately, substance use is compatible with a very wide range of other behaviour, and it is not easy to replace intoxication with something else. Drugs and sport often *do* mix. As for drugs and the arts . . .

Believing that one is capable of changing one's behaviour

Among the people who may have difficulty accepting that they can change their behaviour are addicts and so-called career criminals – who may call themselves, or even get tattooed with, such phrases as 'born to be bad'. Often, people who apply such labels to themselves do so because in their experience their misbehaviours have persisted despite repeated good intentions to stop or moderate. As will be discussed in chapter 8, addicts and career criminals represent a residue of people who, for some reasons, have been unable to moderate their behaviours by themselves. Being unable to quit or moderate is *the definition* of a problem, or the symptoms of one, not the explanation of it. Were it the explanation, then most persistent teenage criminals would not stop (Elliott, Huizinga and Ageton, 1985; Carpenter et al., 1988), heavy drinkers would be unable to return to controlled drinking (Heather and Robertson, 1981), most tobacco smokers would not be able to quit unaided (see West, 2006) and heavy cocaine or heroin users would be unable to quit unaided (see Ditton and Hammersley, 1996). Our perception of the difficulties of behaviour change is distorted by widely broadcast information about the perils and problems of addiction and criminality, while those who manage their problems unaided are comparatively unobtrusive and of less immediate interest to professionals. People with persistent problems may reject fear messages about the harm they are doing by denying their truth, or by avoiding those who bring the messages. Alternatively, they may verbally endorse the fear messages but seem incapable of acting on them. Services commonly see clients who swear that they really want to quit drinking, drugs or smoking, but

never seem able to do so for more than a few hours or days, sometimes despite truly awful harm to themselves.

What are the outcomes of prevention?

An advantage of simplistic thinking about drugs and crime is that
prevention's outcomes sound straightforward. People, especially
young people, should not take drugs or commit crimes. As we have
seen, substance use and law-breaking are not unusual activities.
Consequently, hyper-focus on certain substances and certain activities is unrealistic and hypocritical, while trying to prevent all substance use, or all activities that can be interpreted as law-breaking, is
unachievable. Often, prevention work has targets set according to
changes in officially recorded outcomes, which are inaccurate records
of behaviour and easily moulded by changes in definition and record-
ing. Official targets have gravitas and are relevant to the practitioners
involved, but may be irrelevant to the people whose activities are supposed to be influenced by the preventative work, because few of the
relevant events are detected and those that are detected appear to be
random at best and subject to systematic prejudice at worst. For
example, if black pupils are searched for marijuana much more frequently than white pupils, then there will appear, officially, to be more
use of marijuana among black children. This will not be how the
children see it, and their actual use of marijuana may continue
uninfluenced by search policies, which they will see as an arbitrary
hassle rather than a disincentive.

To genuinely prevent certain activities, rather than their official statistics, it is necessary to be clear about what the desired outcomes are
to be. Many prevention programmes fudge this for political reasons.
It is often seen as ideologically unacceptable to tolerate *any* drug use
or *any* delinquency by teenagers, despite evidence that about 20 per
cent of young people are delinquent at some point and much drug use
and delinquency reduces and resolves naturally (Elliott, Huizinga and
Ageton, 1985). Societies currently lack clarity about what substance
use patterns they want and approve of, or at least tolerate. Where
alcohol advertising is allowed, and while tobacco continues to adver-
tise indirectly via sports sponsorship and clothing brands, society does
not truly seem opposed to substance use. Use of cannabis is probably
no worse (or better) than use of alcohol or tobacco (Runciman,
1999). Dangers of other drugs depend rather on patterns of use. Is
ecstasy once a week more dangerous than alcohol every day? Such

comparative risks are difficult to compute and, even when the relevant epidemiology has been done properly, users may find it difficult to relate to or understand. Behind this difficulty in setting clear outcomes lies major uncertainty about the nature of normal or acceptable substance use by adults.

Currently, tobacco smoking is an undesirable adult outcome, and few adult smokers would actively wish their children to smoke. However, tobacco continues to be widely available and widely experimented with below the legal age of purchase (e.g., Sarvela et al., 1999). There may be intent to phase cigarettes out, but meanwhile smoking is often children's first opportunity to experiment with bad adult behaviour: it often comes before alcohol, before other drugs, before crime and before sex (Jessor and Jessor, 1977; Elliott, Huizinga and Ageton, 1985). Being completely opposed to smoking yet making it widely available, hence functionally available to children, sends a message that harmful, bad things are there to be tried.

Moderate alcohol use is the desired adult outcome in many countries, although some countries, such as Sweden and Norway, take the harder line that the desired outcome is as little use as possible, preferably none. Some countries ban alcohol altogether. Tight controls or a complete ban do prevent alcohol-related harms, but work best when the culture is not inclined to drinking. The alcohol industry meanwhile does its best to market alcoholic drinks as modern, sophisticated, Westernized beverages that signify material success. Where there is a national thirst for alcohol, there are continual tensions between many people wanting to drink as much as possible without harming themselves and medical understanding that the less they drink the better. The alcohol industry adds pressure and promotes a view that moderate alcohol use is normal and harmless. This view is a myth. It has been estimated that the 20 per cent who are the heaviest drinkers consume 80 per cent of the alcohol (Raistrick, Hodgson and Ritson, 1999), which is a mirror of the heroin market, on a much larger scale. Furthermore the typical younger drinker drinks more than what is medically acceptable (e.g., Measham, 1996), so there are at least two different definitions of 'moderate alcohol use'. One would involve drinking a small number of drinks per day and having drink-free days. The other involves not being an alcoholic, indeed exercising restraint and perhaps not getting 'too' drunk, but having bouts of heavy drinking (Hammersley and Ditton, 2006; Measham, 1996). Across Europe, the per capita consumption of alcohol exceeds the medical definition of moderation (Anderson and Baumberg, 2006), which suggests that the public are confused. Perhaps the concept of a 'safe limit' for drinking has backfired and drinkers are treating it as an allowance, rather than as a maximum. Also, if there can be safe drinking, then logically there can be safe drug use, if it is controlled and kept to low levels. Unfortunately, society has demurred from setting any standards by which to define such a low level.

A key starting point of prevention is to set sensible objectives for it. There needs to be society-wide debate, but meanwhile here are some tentative objectives that may be achievable: (1) slow the development of substance use; (2) prevent harmful patterns of substance use; (3) prevent criminal engagement through substance use. Most drugs prevention to date has focused on the first and second of these.

Slowing the development of substance use

Many existing drug prevention programmes are hindered by the hope that young people will not try drugs at all, or at worst will only 'experiment' with them. This often creates a credibility gap, as even the non-using recipients of programmes are usually aware of normal peers whose use exceeds this and does not seem harmful. The credibility gap is also widened by the need either to ignore alcohol and tobacco or to finesse the problem that much adult alcohol and tobacco use is palpably excessive and dangerous, compared to some patterns of drug use. There is therefore a risk that prevention work will either be rejected as lacking credibility or will better inform potential users, making them more likely to use. Probably the biggest programme in the world is DARE (Drug Abuse Resistance Education: www.dare.com, from which all unattributed quotes are taken) which is:

> a drug abuse prevention education program designed to equip elementary, middle and high school children with knowledge about drug abuse, the consequences of abuse, and skills for resisting peer pressure to experiment with drugs, alcohol and tobacco. Based on the premise that prevention is the only long-term answer to drug abuse, the program includes all 50 states and 53 countries. The D.A.R.E. program is taught in over 75% of the nation's school districts, creating a positive atmosphere for students to interact with uniformed law enforcement officers. This unique program uses uniformed law enforcement officers to teach a formal curriculum to students in a classroom setting.

The trouble is that DARE is ineffective (Hanson, 2007), although stakeholders like it and believe that the children have benefited. It is probably ineffective because: (1) despite their best intentions, police officers usually make as good educators as I would a uniformed law enforcement officer; (2) 'drug resistance' involves a 'Strong "NO USE" message', which is unrealistic; (3) DARE's primary mission 'is to provide children with the information and skills they need to live drug-and-violence-free lives.' Yet: 'Your message to your child must be simple and clear-cut: Drinking beer, wine, or distilled spirits is only for grownups who drink responsibly.' This is inconsistent with a no-use message for drugs and finesses the major problems of alcohol-related violence and children's wide exposure to occasional drunkenness, which commonly includes some aggression, such as coerced sex (e.g., Lodico, Gruber and DiClemente, 1996). (4) DARE is often delivered to children too young to have yet been exposed to peer use and to have formed consequent curiosity about drugs (see Jessor and Jessor, 1977).

The alternative would be programmes that accepted that substance use is a personal choice, that were realistic about the risks, dangers and benefits of use, and that offered reasonable guidelines about what patterns of use, at what ages, were less risky, or even acceptable. Currently, such guidelines are lacking. In more drug-liberal conditions such as the UK, there tend to be two sets of guidelines. One 'official' set based on abstinence and unlikely moderation – no more than two drinks a day, no drugs at all – and another unofficial set covertly promoted by sensible practitioners – cannabis is OK if not used too heavily or every day, don't get too drunk, be careful trying other drugs, avoid heroin and cocaine. At what age should this be, however? Telling people that they should not use drugs at all, rather than not yet, means that, if tempted, they may as well use now and that they may as well use dangerous drugs as well as safer ones.

Alternatives that take on some of these problems and have evidence of efficacy exist. For example the Life Skills Training Program

> . . . promotes healthy alternatives to risky behavior through activities designed to:
>
> • Teach students the necessary skills to resist social (peer) pressures to smoke, drink, and use drugs
> • Help students to develop greater self-esteem and self-confidence
> • Enable students to effectively cope with anxiety
> • Increase their knowledge of the immediate consequences of substance abuse
> • Enhance cognitive and behavioral competency to reduce and prevent a variety of health risk behaviors.
>
> (lifeskillstraining.com)

Another educational approach that is effective is project ALERT (projectalert.com), which assumes that young people consider some forms of substance use to be socially positive. Consequently, ALERT focuses on addressing young people's motives for use. It also focuses on common substances – alcohol, tobacco, cannabis, inhalants – rather than rarer ones, which makes candid discussion easier, uses slightly older peers as positive models, rather than uniformed police officers, and makes students take an active part in the programme.

Interventions with families can also be effective in preventing or reducing substance use by children (see chapter 8). These vary from interventions that have children consider parents' viewpoints on drugs, through those involving parents and children, to long-term intensive interventions in the family home. It is not easy to generalize across such a variety of systemic interventions, but two key points are that involving the family makes young people more likely to engage with drug services and that redressing systemic issues, such as poor communication within the family, can prevent or reduce substance use problems.

Other forms of community intervention not particularly focused on drugs, but rather on improving young people's psychological, social and practical functioning, may also reduce substance use (Eccles and Gootman, 2002). Possibilities vary from clubs and extra-curricular activities, such as the Scouts or Guides, to interventions focusing more tightly on improving young people's self-esteem, coping or pre-paredness for adulthood, to those concentrating on drug use or offending. It would be premature to be confident that such interventions have a specific and measurable impact on substance use, and the problems of measuring 'improvement' apply, but there are sound the-oretical and practical reasons for hoping that such work, with a wider scope, is superior to interventions that simply dissuade from drugs. Furthermore, interventions tightly focused on drugs may have no spin-off benefits when they are unsuccessful, while community inter-ventions may improve young people's functioning, which logically should reduce the likelihood of drug problems, if not drug use.

There is also potential for delaying and slowing substance use by altering relevant social norms. Young people tend to overestimate the extent that their peers engage in these behaviours. Correcting these exaggerated beliefs can shift norms and reduce substance use, although there can be resistance to such attempts (Granfield, 2005). It might be feasible to do something similar with crime. One difficulty with mass campaigns against drugs or binge drinking is that they dis-seminate widely the idea that these are common activities. Even if it is not possible to provide correct norms, it is counter-productive for the media and policy makers to exaggerate the prevalence of drug use, binge drinking, violence or other crime. This probably raises norms, with the result that heavier users believe that their behaviour is unexceptional.

It may be important to delay the age of first use of substances because, the younger a person starts, the more likely they are to develop problems later and the more likely they are to escalate to more serious forms of use (e.g., Hingson, Heeren and Winter, 2006). Early use may be a sign of problems deserving early intervention. Use of some drugs may have particularly adverse effects on immature nervous systems, although, as discussed in chapter 5, this should not be assumed from correlational evidence. Also, the earlier a person starts a habit, the more practice they get at it. For example, a young person who began smoking daily aged ten will have smoked 36,500 cigarettes by age twenty at the rate of ten per day – twice as many as someone who began at sixteen. Someone who drinks alcohol twice a week from the age of ten will have had nearly a thousand 'practices' at drinking by the time they reach the legal age for drinking. Such practice has implications both for kicking the habit and for the build-up of physiological tolerance to the substance.

One possible way of delaying age of use is to make substances less available to younger people. The most intensively studied example of this was the raising of drinking ages in many US states from eighteen to twenty-one. This appeared to reduce the number of road traffic accidents involving eighteen- to twenty-year-olds and decrease reported alcohol intake in this age group (Wagenaar and Toomey, 2002). Perhaps a downside is the making of drinking by teenagers illegal, driving it underground and perhaps rendering drugs a more tempting alternative, although there is scant evidence that this occurs. Whether such initiatives are a good idea or not, they are only feasible when access to a substance can be regulated. Access to illegal drugs is completely unregulated, denying society the use of such measures to prevent people using them too young. It is possible that delaying onset of legal drugs might have knock-on effects in delaying illegal ones, but this has not been demonstrated.

Preventing harmful patterns of substance use

This is difficult because it requires hitting a shifting target. Much substance use that is entirely unremarkable in contemporary society is extremely harmful. While the media remain obsessed with addiction and violent crime, tobacco smoking and heavy drinking eventually help kill many people and drugs are a leading cause of mortality among younger people (who do not die very often). Alcoholics and other addicts can be extremely damaging to themselves and those around them, but they are in a minority. In this context, in order to prevent harmful patterns of use there would have to be agreement about what those patterns were. It is also important that prevention work does not simply wash its hands of people who stray beyond harmless use.

Moderate alcohol consumption is widely considered relatively harmless, as long as intake does not exceed about two drinks per day, does not occur every day and does not begin too young. Similar standards should probably be applied to cannabis. Beyond these somewhat saintly lower limits, harmlessness rapidly becomes a minefield of opinion, anxiety, claim and counter-claim. One commission (RSA, 2007) seems tempted towards the view that moderate use of any drug is relatively harmless, which is rational. Unfortunately, few long-term substance users adhere to moderate use at all times. Some are generally moderate but have lapses or binges, commonly at the weekend. Some go through longer periods of immoderate use, for example when unhappy or stressed. Some find that moderate use creeps up to immoderate use over months or years, and this can happen more than once in a lifetime. There are also measurement problems and reporting biases, as discussed in chapter 2. Additionally, many moderate users try drugs other than alcohol and cannabis, which may be of more concern, whether this concern is scientifically justified or not. For example, a moderate heroin user might inject twice a day, three days a week (Shewan and Dalgarno, 2005). Rightly or wrongly, this activity is not viewed with the equanimity accorded alcohol or cannabis taken that occasionally.

Over the next decades societies will probably work out more functional rules about acceptable, dangerous and problematic use of drugs, as they have for alcohol. The following are probably bad things to be avoided: daily use, use from waking to sleep, intoxication to severe cognitive impairment, very heavy use, use abnormally young, use in ways that can have very dangerous immediate consequences. We still need to quantify the qualitative words such as 'severe', 'abnormally', and so on.

A dilemma is that people commonly use drugs in ways that pose immediate dangers at relatively low probability – such as the dangers of accidents – and that pose more probable dangers to their health in the far future. At first thought this might be due to ignorance or irrationality, but it may simply characterize the ways in which people make decisions about risk (Slovic, 2000; Adams, 1995). Someone who 'rationally' considered all low-probability immediate risks as well as all high-probability long-term risks before acting would probably appear to be suffering from a neurotic mental illness and would struggle to leave the house, manage everyday life around the home, or eat a normal diet, never mind taking drugs or alcohol. Unfortunately, if it is rational to avoid drugs or alcohol, it is also rational to avoid innumerable things shown to pose risks, including high-fat food, food with manufactured additives, food low in vitamins and fibre, caffeine, many medicines, household cleaning products, sitting too long, working on computers, watching TV, using mobile phones, road transport, long working hours, stress, marriage, divorce, having children and not having children. Once one considers social and global risks as well as personal ones, the list becomes longer and excludes most of modern life, from cheap clothing made in sweatshops, to anything transported a long distance, to electricity generated with coal, oil or gas (e.g., Bauman, 2006; Castells, 1998). Harking back to a pre-industrial pastoral bliss is no good either, because without modern medicines and comforts (many highly risky) life was 'nasty, brutish and short' (Hobbes, 1660).

It is unclear whether it is rational to live an ascetic life entirely oriented to health at the expense of all pleasures and comforts. Even if such a life is morally superior in some sense, most people clearly seek pleasure and comforts regularly, to the extent of their resources and abilities. Part of the future debate about the safeties and dangers of drugs will probably involve reconsideration of the nature of health and wellbeing, particularly mental health and wellbeing. Perhaps the truly mentally healthy person should have no need for drugs or other comforts and pleasures. Or is this unusual asceticism an indicator of abnormality? Why is a longer, less hedonistic life preferable to a shorter, more hedonistic one? Quite puritanical religious values still underlie much of the debate about drugs. These values have their attractions for many people, but they are profoundly incompatible with the contemporary consumer societies in which many people live. There is also a fundamental moral problem that it is widely held to be acceptable to pray or practise self-improvement for personal benefit, whether material, mental or physical, but unacceptable to take drugs or be a glutton to feel better; the ends clearly do not justify the means in this case, or there is something false about drug-enhanced living. Unfortunately, many people seem to find it easier to manage life when it includes intoxicants than when it does not. We should learn to be more forgiving about drug use and other unhealthy behaviour.

Preventing criminal engagement through substance use

The most obvious way of doing this is to weaken the links between substance supply and the rest of the criminal economy by tolerating or decriminalizing supply and possession. Let us set aside this political hot iron until chapter 9. Meanwhile, how can substance users be dissuaded from criminal engagement? In reality, there are now about twice as many young people who will admit to drug use as will admit to offending, while most offending is relatively trivial and most of it ceases spontaneously. So the problem may be overstated. When substance use leads to criminal engagement, it often does so through liaison with drug dealers. Becoming a street-level dealer may support a person's own use, may benefit the friends they supply or purchase for, and may be lucrative (Johnson, 1973), but it also carries risks of becoming exposed to other criminal activities. Norms about crime may be raised, other lucrative possibilities may be learned, and there may be direct pressure to offend in other ways, for instance to repay money owed for drugs bought on credit, then consumed, lost or stolen. With the increasing professionalization of drugs supply, dealing–crime links may perhaps be weakening for users. For example, if phone orders and home delivery have become more common (RSA, 2007), then users need not necessarily be exposed to anyone except the drug courier at their front door.

An advantage of regulating drug supply would be to reduce its links to criminality. A black market would likely continue – for example, there is substantial smuggling of alcohol and tobacco from the continent to the UK because of price differentials – but this would be at a reduced level. By tolerating and regulating the supply of cannabis in some areas, the Netherlands appears to have had some success in reducing the criminalization of users without increasing use (Reinarman, Cohen and Kaal, 2004; Van Solinge, 1999). This would seem less likely to work for heroin or cocaine because of the complexity of drugs–crime links (see chapter 4). However, whether serious offenders with multiple problems are truly made worse by drug dependence, rather than some alternative expensive and unsavoury habit, is a moot point.

Minimizing delinquency

As discussed in chapters 3 to 5, offending is partly a matter of definition. One could minimize delinquency by encouraging more lenient standards, or maximize it by encouraging more strict ones.

This rarely happens deliberately, but standards about crime and delinquency vary as a function of politics, religion and attitudes, which in turn influence the perception and definition of these problems. This applies even in rigorous definitions. For example, several US surveys define minor theft as being of something with a value of at least $5. Were this definition never to be revised, after years of inflation this 'objective' definition could lead to a substantial increase in the seeming prevalence of minor theft. Although usually stated as absolute acts, most instances of offending in reality are specified relative to current cultural norms, and this applies even to unpalatable transactions where zero tolerance is laudable. How much coercion is acceptable in courtship and when does it become 'stalking', coerced sex or rape? Can a person truly assess the impact of their coercive, or persuasive, actions or words on another? Is getting someone drunk a legitimate sexual warm-up strategy, or 'drink spiking'? Most people can intuit the extremes of what is currently acceptable and unacceptable, but the boundary is where many offences occur and is much harder to define. Feeding a sixteen-year-old half a bottle of wine might indeed begin date rape, where it would merely be a romantic prelude to sex for a more seasoned drinker. Yet, what actually went on at the time might be almost indistinguishable except perhaps for the wobbliness of the participants.

Some readers will be irritated by this dogged relativism. Suspending it by assuming it is possible to keep norms constant, what might reduce delinquency? Interestingly, between 1997 and 2005, as crime fell in the UK, child poverty also fell, although poverty among single adults rose (Joseph Rowntree Foundation, 2005). So far, nobody seems to have suggested that there might be a link, perhaps because criminologists are rarely comfortable tackling poverty and those studying poverty often object to labelling the poor as criminals. Tackling poverty might reduce children's stress and deprivation and make it less likely that they act out by offending, more likely that they feel conventional mores deserve some respect, and less likely that they feel a need to prosper by delinquent means. This general approach could reduce delinquency, however it was currently defined. Crimes are rarely correlated with affluence.

Some forms of systemic intervention also appear to reduce offending among other problematic activities. Such interventions typically involve working closely and intensively with the young person and their family. For example, this can involve a key worker working in the family home and being on call twenty-four hours. This leads to high per case costs, which restricts its use to cases where the benefits are likely to be considerable – for instance, to families whose members are problem cases across a wide range of local health and social-care services.

Summary

'Prevention is better than cure' – better perhaps, but much harder in the cases of drugs and crime. Both intoxication and transgressions of rules and laws are commonplace. A good prevention initiative needs to consider what its intended outcomes are, and nationwide abstinence is unlikely. It also needs to communicate information in ways that the audience will respond to. This is often hindered by political and moral constraints on the kinds of messages that 'should be' acceptable. Generally, balanced, empowering interventions that place drugs and crime in a lifestyles context seem most promising.

Discussion points

- Drugs education is now part of children's schooling. What do teachers need to do to make the difference between good drugs education sessions and bad ones?
- Why do people like getting intoxicated?
- What message would you promote to reduce student drug use?

Further reading

Adams, J. (1995). *Risk*. London: Routledge.

Dunn, C., Deroo, L., and Rivara, F. P. (2001). The use of brief interventions adapted from motivational interviewing across behavioral domains: a systematic review. *Addiction*, 96(12): 1725–42.

Eccles, J. S., and Gootman, J. A. (eds) (2002). *Community programs to promote youth development*. Washington, DC: National Academy Press.

Raistrick, D., Hodgson, R., and Ritson, B. (1999). *Tackling alcohol together: the basis for a UK alcohol policy*. London: Free Association Books.

www.lifebytes.gov.uk

8

Treatment of Drug Dependence

Happily, I know of no adequately evaluated treatment for drug dependence that has managed to reduce substance use while failing to reduce the associated offending. Furthermore, coerced treatment is no less effective than treatment that is self-referred (Stevens et al., 2005). Treatment rarely eliminates either activity for everyone.

What is substance dependence or addiction?

Over the past hundred years or so a highly influential myth has evolved which assumes that addicted substance use is qualitatively different from non-addicted substance use. Consequently, addicts lack adequate control over their substance use or other related misbehaviours. Over the past thirty-five years, the concept of 'dependence' has become used more widely than 'addiction'. 'Dependence' was designed to acknowledge the diversity and complexity of the syndrome or disorder, including diversity in the extent to which people lost control, and to make fewer assumptions about there being a biologically distinct state underlying it (Edwards and Gross, 1976). Nonetheless, theoretical controversy remains over whether 'dependence' is a distinct syndrome or a descriptive summary of what can happen when someone uses drugs or alcohol heavily for a long time (Hasin et al., 1997; Finagarette, 1988; Hammersley and Reid, 2002). The form and outcomes of dependence can be complex and varied. Indeed, it may be more helpful to consider 'dependence' as a process rather than a state (Mullen and Hammersley, 2006). Here, 'addiction' will refer to theory that regards it as a state with some biological underpinning and 'dependence' as something more descriptive, diffuse and elusive.

The addiction view has been predominant in the USA because it fits well with the twelve-steps self-help movement that began there, though compared with other countries the twelve-steps philosophy in the USA is also highly influential in the area of treatment that has to be paid for (Sobell and Sobell, 2006). Because most treatment in the USA is paid for via private medical insurance, there is a lot of money to be made treating addiction. It is also simpler for insurers to cover, and so to treat, a distinct condition like 'addiction' than to tackle the complexities of paying for help with complicated but subtle social and psychological difficulties. Relatively speaking, in other countries addiction services tend to run on a shoestring. The USA is also dominant in research and influential national bodies such as the National Institute on Drug Abuse officially endorse the view of addiction as a brain disease. This helps to support an enormous biomedical research programme that hopes to find treatments and cures for addictions.

The aim of treatment, under this philosophy, is abstinence (as discussed in chapter 2, what 'abstinence' means in practice can be ambiguous), because in the long term moderating or controlling substance use is held to be nigh impossible for anyone who is truly addicted. It is also widely held that repeated and protracted use of alcohol or a drug runs a serious risk of addiction developing. Surveys tend to find that about one in ten long-term users show some signs of dependence. This applies to heroin (Hall et al., 2000), cocaine (Kraus et al., 2007), alcohol (Falk, Yi and Hiller-Sturmhofel, 2006) and marijuana (Stinson et al., 2006). A higher proportion of long-term users are dependent on tobacco, but this is still socially somewhat easier. Other than for tobacco, that leaves approximately nine out of ten long-term users who are not showing signs of dependence. Inverting this 'fact', it is likely that psychiatry and psychology collectively set the level of problems judged to be 'dependent' at about the level that one in ten users experience. Changing the criteria would change this number; there is no magic cut-off point, and diagnosing 'dependence' involves judging qualities such as 'severity' of problems. This is less contentious for alcohol or marijuana than it is for heroin (Shewan and Dalgarno, 2005) or cocaine (Ditton and Hammersley, 1996). Also, as discussed in chapter 5, thinking of addiction as an all-or-nothing state clouds the fact that over their lifespan a person may use substances in many different ways, including periods of dependence, abstinence, heavy use and more moderate use. Even people who have been dependent at one time did not necessarily reach that state via ever-increasing use. Having been dependent at some time, people can have outcomes other than continuous addiction or abstinence (maybe with an occasional relapse). Other outcomes can include extended periods of controlled use, varied periods of diverse forms of drug use, and extended periods of abstinence interspersed with brief periods of very heavy use.

The USA commercial treatment industry (e.g., www.cenaps.com; www.bettyfordcenter.com) generally endorses abstinence; however, many of their treatment techniques borrow from cognitive behavioural therapy and similar interventions not ideologically wedded to abstinence. For example, CENAPS includes sensible advice for avoiding relapse (Gorski, 2000). Unfortunately, despite the substantial costs of treatment, outcome data for these methods are not made public, if they are even obtained. Furthermore, an outcome of failing to comply with treatment, by continuing to use drugs or alcohol, can be discharge, which conveniently disposes of clients who are not responsive to the methods. This is the more worrying because of the high costs sometimes involved. For example, the Betty Ford Center charges $23,000 for thirty days' residential treatment.

Another problem with the twelve-steps/addiction approaches to substance use problems is that some people promote a number of ideas that have not received empirical support. It is difficult to cite references for these ideas because of the lay, practice-oriented and often anonymous nature of the relevant movements, but below I reference the evidence against them.

- *Addicts are unable to return to controlled drinking (or, by analogy drug use).* Yet, some can, even those who were highly dependent (Heather and Robertson, 1981).
- *It is easier to treat people with more problems, who are at their lowest point, 'hitting bottom', than those with fewer.* In reality outcomes are better for people with the fewest problems (Kampmann et al., 2004; Gottheil, McLellan and Druley, 1992). For example, heavy drinkers with good social support and employment can often reduce drinking or quit with a brief intervention (Miller and Rollnick, 1991). Waiting until they are unemployed, homeless street drinkers with no social support is a bad idea.
- *Harm reduction measures are counter-productive because they encourage continued use and delay the required 'hitting bottom'.* In reality, harm reduction measures can reduce morbidity and mortality, making eventual improvement, rather than death, possible (Ritter and Cameron, 2006).
- *Only twelve-steps or Minnesota model-style treatment can genuinely treat addiction.* In objective evaluations it usually fares as well, but

no better, than alternative treatment approaches (e.g., Allen et al., 1999; Orford, 2001). It seems likely that the main effect of treatment lies in generic aspects of the therapeutic relationship between therapist and client, including a genuine warmth and interpersonal regard (Orford, 2001; Jarvis et al., 2005), rather than in the theory and philosophy underlying treatment methods.

- *Only a counsellor who has been addicted him- or herself can effectively treat an addict.* When ex-addicts have been compared with non-addicts, if anything the non-addicts are better as therapists (De Angelis and Ross, 1978).
- *Group work with other addicts is an essential component of treatment.* Rather surprisingly, despite its popularity, the specific efficacy of group work for addictions has been little evaluated. Programmes including group work such as Minnesota model treatment can be effective, but it is unclear that the group sharing experiences, feelings and problems is always helpful. There are many anecdotes of instances where groups are counter-productive. For example, addicts reminisce about substance use and relapse, or form a dysfunctional but shared view of their problems, or collude to con the therapist (Weppner, 1981). Effective and informed guidance is probably important to ensure that the group develops in productive ways.
- *Treatment can lead to abstinence for a majority of clients.* No treatment can do this unless it cheats on its outcome statistics. Sadly, for any given treatment episode, less than a third of clients will still be abstinent twelve months later. Higher success rates are usually the result of (1) selective intake to treatment that, for instance, only includes people who have already stopped successfully, (2) ignoring people who drop out, (3) ignoring people who are hard to follow up and (4) not measuring outcome rigorously or for long enough (Miller and Sanchez-Craig, 1996).
- *Treatment involving substitute prescribing, or the prescribing of psychotropic medicines, merely propagates chemical dependency.* In Don Simpson's case (see chapter 2), and in many others, this is indeed true. However, the specific use of particular medicines can be beneficial, including using oral methadone instead of injected heroin, antidepressants instead of alcohol and drugs, specific medicine to manage attention-deficit disorder rather than self-medication with cocaine or amphetamines, and antipsychotic medication rather than deadening psychotic symptoms with alcohol and marijuana. Only if the sole acceptable outcome of treatment is abstinence from everything do these interventions fail, but this is

circular reasoning. It is generally acceptable to medicate to redress 'abnormalities' in physiology, even when the abnormalities are artificially induced, as when organ transplant recipients must take immunosuppressant drugs. If addiction were a brain disease, then logically it would be acceptable to redress it chemically. However, more on methadone below.

This is not the place to review general treatments for substance dependence, but a number of key points should be noted.

- Substance dependence is very treatable compared with some other mental health problems. In well-conducted and objective follow-ups, about 20 per cent to 30 per cent of people treated remain improved – using less or not at all – twelve months later (Orford, 2001). That 70 per cent or more of people do not improve is only considered failure if it is based on unrealistic expectations.
- Furthermore, the majority of people who begin to show signs of dependence manage their problem, usually unaided, and return to controlled substance use of some kind (Biernacki, 1986; Webb et al., 2007; Granfield and Cloud, 1999).
- People may exhibit many different patterns of use and be more controlled at some times than at others. There are trajectories other than a lifetime of moderation or abstinence or a gradual downwards path into addiction (Ditton and Hammersley, 1996; Mullen and Hammersley, 2006).
- This means that treatment centres (and the self-help movements) see a residue of people who for various reasons have found it impossible to control their use unaided.
- When different treatments for dependence have been compared, then the quality of the therapeutic relationship between counsellor and client seems to matter more than the philosophy or methodology of treatment (Jarvis et al., 2005). There do not appear to be marked differences between treatments depending upon what outcomes are specified. The same treatments lead to abstinence, improvement and other benefits, whether or not the philosophy of the intervention approves of outcomes other than abstinence (Allen et al., 1999).
- What does appear to matter is the length of treatment. Treatments that last a few weeks or less appear to be less successful in the long term than treatments that last for a period of months (Orford, 2001). It is not clear that the intensity of treatment matters as much as its length, so intense daily residential treatment is not necessarily

superior to less frequent non-residential treatment that lasts longer; psychological change takes time.

- Successful reduction or cessation of substance problems tends to be associated with major changes in lifestyle. These can be internally driven; the person changes their life on purpose. Other changes can come from outside, facilitating reduced substance use. Many people find heavy substance use incompatible with parental responsibilities, for example. It is hard to sort out substance abuse in isolation from lifestyle. For people who offend, sorting out dependence without also sorting out offending is highly unlikely.

- People who have struggled with dependence (rather than easily quitting or moderating unaided) often talk of it being 'their time' to stop when they finally succeed. What makes it 'their time' seems to be a highly personal thing involving the costs of continued use outweighing the benefits and the benefits of stopping also outweighing the costs of stopping (Mullen and Hammersley, 2006). For some people, relatively minor costs and benefits make it 'their time'. For others, huge costs are not enough. For example, the great soccer player George Best was unable to moderate his drinking permanently despite a liver transplant (http://en.wikipedia.org/wiki/George_Best). When a person's 'time' seems mysterious, then perhaps it is because the problem has not been looked at completely. Too often, treatment explores the costs and benefits of using, but neglects the costs and benefits of not using. The majority in our society feel that life is nicer when it includes intoxication sometimes.

- Dependence is a systemic problem, rather than only being a property of an individual addict with a clear-cut biological problem. Many successful interventions involve systemic work considering family, social networks, community and employment, whether this is formally defined as systemic therapy or not. However, because there is insufficient research on such factors (but see, for example, Webb et al., 2007; Velleman, 2006; McKeganey and Barnard, 1992; Johnson et al., 1985; Bourgois, 1995; Alasuutan, 1992), we have only limited understanding of how systemic factors help create and sustain addiction. Researching and theorizing systemic factors is difficult because sociologists and ethnographers, who are often best at this kind of research, are not always interested in interventions.

States and processes

There is a widespread false assumption implicit in a lot of writing about drugs and crime, which is that offending and drug problems are abnormalities, and consequently the result of treatment, intervention or rehabilitation is that the person 'returns to normal', as if their problems had never existed. The assumption is that a normal state is temporarily disrupted by an abnormal one. Generally, drugs and crime problems are extended, chronic problems across the lifespan. There is no 'normal' to which to return because the problems are formative parts of people's life histories. Effective treatment must be about a process of change, not about returning from an abnormal state to a normal one.

Among the processes of change required are methods of managing a person's social and psychological status as a former drug user or former offender. Even if the person is completely rehabilitated and functions at every level as if drugs and crime were not relevant to them, the life by which they arrived at this place was different from the life of someone who has never offended or acquired a drug problem. They have different experiences, different skills, different social networks – who view them differently – and different strengths and weaknesses, and they are exposed to different dangers. For example, a former heroin-using shoplifter may be unable to go into the local town centre without being hassled by the police. Consequently, their everyday lives can be different and they are likely to behave differently under stress or when experiencing life difficulties. One common occurrence is to 'relapse' – return to old habits and behaviours. One, of many, reasons for relapse can be continued suspicions about drug use from family members, with resultant arguments, leading the ex-user to feel frustrated and angry and that they might as well use. A 'normal social drinker' might react to minor setbacks in life by drinking too much and brooding or complaining to friends; the equivalent behaviours for someone who has formerly had a drug or alcohol problem can be disastrous.

The twelve-steps self-help movements, among other philosophies, have always been aware of the lifespan nature of problems. They emphasize that a person should continue through the processes of recovery, accept their status as an addict – never as an 'ex-addict' who can safely return to substance use – and examine and learn from their dysfunctional life history in order to manage without substance abuse. This is achieved partly by accepting that they are powerless over the problem, in that they cannot control, combat or contain it, as well as by finding other ways of coping, or indeed avoiding stress in the first place.

This is in marked contrast to another view that was popular up until the late 1980s, which was that the key to successful treatment was to detoxify the addict, getting both the drugs or alcohol and the need for them out of their system. Once detoxified, supposedly, the addict would be back to normal. This simple state view of addiction has been found untenable. Detoxification is only the first step in a long process of change. Sadly, this applies even to the most modern forms of detoxification, which may involve sedation or anaesthesia and substitute prescribing to alleviate withdrawal symptoms.

As discussed in chapters 1 to 3 of this book, while it makes some sense to conceptualize drug dependence as a condition of the person, it is less clear that 'being a criminal' is a state or condition of the person. Rather it is a stereotyped description of a person who has been found to be engaged in certain sorts of transactions. Perhaps in consequence, the desirable outcomes of interventions for offending sometimes seem incoherent and contradictory. There are five main types of outcome for interventions against crime.

1 *Punishment*: The offender should suffer in proportion to the wrongs they have committed, for example by an appropriate prison sentence. Also, people should not be punished for offences they have not committed.

2 *Deterrence*: The intervention should discourage others from offending, for example by making them afraid. This requires that interventions are not misapplied to non-offenders, or to a biased sample of people who offend. For, when this happens then the deterrent link cannot be learned because it seems arbitrary. This is a key reason for ensuring that policing is perceived to be fair and just and that specific ethnic or social groupings are not singled out.

3 *Prevention*: The offender should be prevented from further offending, for example by being incarcerated. But people who will not offend further – including those innocent in the first place – should not be subject to prevention, if nothing else because it is expensive.

4 *Rehabilitation*: The offender should be less likely to offend after the intervention than before it. For example, after an anger management programme they no longer become violent when they get angry. What 'less likely to offend' means in practice is enormously complicated.

5 *Restoration*: The intervention should sort out the social damage and wrongs created by the offence. For example, the victim should not remain fearful of repeat victimization. While restoration may be possible for the victim, if the offence was an acute isolated incident,

as already discussed, going back to the pre-offending state may not be possible for the offender.

Interventions against drug problems appear to be less enthusiastic about punishment and restoration as legitimate objectives, although twelve-steps recovery includes acknowledging and putting right wrongs. They do try to deter other people from problem use, to prevent the user continuing problem use and to rehabilitate users so that they are functional, non-addicted members of society.

Drug problems and drug abuse

As well as being 'addicted' or 'dependent', many users can be classified as 'abusers' of drug or alcohol. In a nutshell, this means that they do not fit criteria for dependence, but they have experienced significant problems related to their substance use and have persisted with use nonetheless. Both the DSM-IV-R (American Psychiatric Association, 1994) and the ICD-10 (WHO, 2007) contain diagnostic criteria for abuse. Simply talking of 'drug or alcohol problems' is also sometimes necessary, applying better, for instance, to people whose use may jeopardize their health in the future but is not a problem in the present. This would include the large number of people who binge drink (more than eight units of alcohol per session) on a regular basis.

If dependence is not a distinct biological state, but a descriptive syndrome, then these precise definitions are not so important in deciding treatment. Fortunately, the best-evidenced treatments, including cognitive behavioural therapy, motivational interviewing and systemic therapies, take an individual approach to formulating the client's problems and developing a treatment plan. Moreover, the activities that actually occur in drugs agencies often address problems wider than substance use (Hammersley, Reid and Minkes, 2006).

Outcomes for treatment of substance problems

For the reasons outlined above, abstinence is not the only acceptable outcome of treatment. Even for people with very serious problems, where abstinence would clearly be the ideal, other treatment outcomes are worthwhile. These include:

- better mental health
- better physical health
- lower mortality
- better social and emotional functioning
- less offending
- less problematic and disruptive behaviour for others
- more stable lifestyle
- substance use less predominant in the person's life
- substance use in more appropriate ways
- reduced quantity and frequency of use
- not forgetting abstinence.

Many practitioners have become wary of abstinence as the fundamental objective of treatment, not because it is wrong – indeed it is often highly desirable – but because it diverts thought and effort away from other worthwhile objectives that may be more immediately achievable and can be necessary stepping stones to abstinence.

Generic properties of efficacious treatment

Efficacious treatments are those that have been shown to be capable of working, which does not mean that they will always be effective, with every client, with every counsellor and in every situation. For drug and alcohol problems, such treatments have a number of general characteristics. First, they involve the basic principles of effective counselling, which requires a successful interpersonal relationship between counsellor and client that includes warmth, effective communication and mutual positive regard (Jarvis et al., 2005). Second, for more intractable problems they are relatively long-term (Orford, 2001), although brief interventions, sometimes only one or two sessions, suffice for people who can easily change their behaviour given initial prompting (Dunn, Deroo and Rivara, 2001). For example, many young cannabis users moderate their use if they come to recognize that it is important to do so, as can many heavy-drinking middle-aged men (Saitz et al., 2007). Third, efficacious treatments are wide and flexible in defining useful outcomes and working towards these, rather than relying only on more ambitious outcomes such as abstinence or cessation of offending. Wider outcomes include changes that cause less harm and stabilize and improve the person's life. For example, homeless people might be helped with housing. Fourth, they focus on facilitating change in the client, rather than on analysing the past, seeking explanations as to why the client developed their problems, or letting the client express their feelings, although all these activities can be important for change. Finally, they focus on empowering the client to cope with difficult situations where they are likely to 'relapse': 'Quitting smoking is easy, I've done it hundreds of times' (Mark Twain; www.famousquotes.com).

In this work, counsellors tend to consider and address the following: (1) the client's motivation for change and engagement with treatment; (2) the situations and thought processes that lead to and sustain substance use; (3) helping the client set achievable goals for treatment; (4) reducing the harm of any continued substance use and the related behaviours; (5) addressing the client's physical and mental health needs, as well as their addictive behaviours; (6) considering and involving family, friends and other sources of social support in treatment as appropriate; (7) improving lifestyle and social functioning, which includes modifying offending, antisocial, selfish and irresponsible behaviour.

Denial or ambivalence?

It is widely held that people with alcohol or drug problems are often 'in denial' (Paredes, 1974). This means that a person denies to counsellors, family or friends, and perhaps to themselves (although it is hard to divine what people really think), that there is a problem, or downplays the extent of their substance use, or denies the health and other problems they may acquire in the future, or denies the strength of the links between other problems that they have experienced and their substance use. For example, they drive perfectly well full of alcohol, they have done this many times, but they just had the misfortune to be stopped by the police.

These behaviours were believed to be the consequence of a Freudian defence mechanism, of 'denial', that needed to be confronted or broken through before effective treatment could be accomplished. For example, some interventions make use of confrontations with family to tackle 'denial'. Tackling denial head on can be counterproductive, as it can damage the therapeutic relationship or even cause the client to abandon treatment. On the other hand, waiting until the denial stage is over and the person 'hits bottom' is not recommended either. Also, while these behaviours definitely can occur, there are a complex set of psychological processes and reasons underlying denial that do not conform to a unitary defence mechanism that can be confronted and broken (Howard et al., 2002). Rinn et al. (2002) also suggest that cognitive deficits may hinder alcoholics' appreciation of the harms of their drinking. It may be more useful to accept that people are often, even always, ambivalent about their substance use (Orford, 2001; Shaffer and Simoneau, 2001), and this needs to be accepted and addressed during treatment. For example, many people who have quit remain partial to the effects of their favourite drugs. I have spoken to a number of ex-heroin users who privately admitted that they would resume use were heroin to be pure, cheap, legal and not socially stigmatized. Some forms of treatment, including motivational interviewing and cognitive behavioural therapy, explicitly address ambivalence. I suspect that other successful forms implicitly address similar problems, using different discourse.

Some widely used and often effective treatments

Brief interventions

Brief interventions typically occur over one session, occasionally two or more. They usually involve postulating that the client's substance use appears to be causing them harm, or will cause harm in the future, getting them to reflect on this and recommending some action, such as reducing or quitting the relevant substance use. They often also involve addressing client motivation (see below). Brief interventions are cheap and easy to provide and can lead to a significant minority of recipients (about 10 per cent) modifying their behaviour (see Moyer and Finney, 2004; McCambridge and Strang, 2003; Heather and Richmond, 1992; Lang, Engelander and Brooke, 2000). They have been most widely evaluated for alcohol, are often offered by generic practitioners rather than by specialists, and are most useful for forms of substance use that rarely require more intensive treatment, such as non-dependent cannabis use or ecstasy use. They are unsuitable for people with more serious problems (Saitz et al., 2007).

Cognitive behavioural therapy (CBT)

If not the Rolls-Royce of psychological interventions, certainly the reliable Ford fleet car, CBT is widely used for mental health problems of all kinds, including substance abuse (Beck et al., 1993). Among its advantages is a strong evidence base, because treatment involves setting clear objectives that can easily be evaluated. Also, it has been successfully applied to complex problems, including psychotic symptoms (Morrison et al., 2004), personality disorders (Young, 1999) and substance misuse in people with other severe mental health problems (Graham, 2004).

CBT is most often employed in individual therapy, although couple and systemic therapy can also make use of its techniques. Its principles can also be used in group work to some extent, although this may limit the capacity to tailor individual formulations and goals. Offending behaviour programmes often utilize CBT techniques (e.g., Home Office, 2003), although more intensive work is suggested for seriously drug-dependent offenders. This form of work can reduce reoffending by some 14 per cent (Friendship et al., 2003).

CBT makes the basic assumption that many mental health problems, including problems of addiction, are caused and sustained by dysfunctional beliefs (cognitions). Specific situations (antecedents) trigger these beliefs, which lead to problematic consequences. For example, many people with substance use problems use drugs or alcohol to manage anxiety or low mood; experiencing anxiety triggers beliefs such as 'feeling bad is unbearable', 'if I do not use drugs I will be unable to cope', 'I am useless and might as well get high', leading to drug use. Such dysfunctional beliefs are often exaggerated, distorted or otherwise unrealistic. Furthermore, people often act on their beliefs rather than testing their reality. For instance, the drug user may be able to cope without drugs or alcohol, but has not actually tested this for years. Underlying these types of dysfunctional beliefs are deeper core beliefs or schemata. One schema that often underlies drug use is that feeling bad is not a normal part of life but is unacceptable, or is evidence that the person is worthless or unable to cope. Therapy addresses the reality of the dysfunctional beliefs and attempts to replace them with more functional beliefs by getting clients to look critically at their realism and to conduct behavioural experiments to see whether the beliefs are accurate: What happens if you do not get high after a quarrel with your spouse? What happens if you go to a party and do not drink? Do 'normal' people really never feel bad? As therapy progresses, schemata will also be addressed. For substance use problems, there are two additional difficulties to consider. First, that as problems develop, substance abuse itself can become the antecedent for dysfunctional thoughts, leading to further substance use. Second, the effects of many drugs include impairing or blocking cognitive processes, so while intoxicated people may be incapable of fully appreciating the reality of their situation and many instead operate on schemata and stereotype: 'party, party, party' because the alternative feels too frightening to face up to.

There is also a growing body of research on the cognitions of substance users and on the outcome expectancies (what people expect to happen as a result) of alcohol, and, by analogy, drugs. People have both positive and negative expectancies for use and for stopping use (Jones, Corbin and Fromme, 2001). These appear to be weighed up and influence decisions to use, or to stop using. However, as discussed above, triggers for specific use episodes may be more rapid and less influenced by conscious reasoning.

Another developing line of research is to explore the cognitive biases of users (e.g., Bearre et al., 2007; Field, Mogg and Bradley, 2004; Everitt, Dickinson and Robbins, 2001; Cox, Fadardi and Pothos, 2006). It appears that users learn to be more sensitive to external cues, thoughts and reminders of drugs or alcohol. This is not surprising, as heavy users have generally much more practice with use, in a wider variety of conditions. A number of experimental procedures are being explored that might desensitize users to such cues, perhaps making use, or relapse, less likely.

Motivational interviewing

The subtitle of the classic text by Miller and Rollnick reads: 'Preparing people to change addictive behavior'. This entails providing *Advice*, removing *Barriers*, providing *Choice*, reducing *Desirability*, practising *Empathy*, providing *Feedback*, clarifying *Goals* and active *Helping* (Miller and Rollnick, 1991, 20). It is not confrontational and it regards people's difficulties in changing as due to ambivalence rather than denial or resistance. It also focuses on empowering the client to discover the means to change themselves, rather than imposing a fixed set of rules on them. Thus, it has a lot in common with CBT. It is effective for a wide range of behaviours, not just alcohol or drugs (Rubak et al., 2005) and is often used in brief interventions (Dunn, Deroo and Rivara, 2001). Burke, Arkowitz and Menchola (2003) concluded that motivational interviewing was effective in improving alcohol intake, drug use, diet and exercise, but not smoking or HIV-risk behaviours. It has also been applied to sex offenders (Laws, 1999) and could perhaps be appropriate for other forms of persistent offending.

Therapeutic communities and Minnesota model treatment

This section attempts to make some generalizations about therapeutic communities for people with substance problems and treatments based on twelve-steps principles, sometimes called 'Minnesota Model' treatment (Cook, 1988a, 1988b). This is difficult because communities vary, some being more democratic in how they operate, others more hierarchical (Lees, Manning and Rawlings, 2004; Vandevelde et al., 2004). They also vary in their specific philosophies, although most aim for abstinence and are connected to twelve-steps principles. Also, given the network nature of twelve-steps organizations, interpretation of twelve-steps philosophy and the resultant practices vary quite widely. Furthermore, communities have changed over the years, have become more sophisticated and have incorporated techniques from other forms of treatment. The notorious severity of Synanon is no more. Also, therapeutic communities nowadays accept a wider range of clients than they would have done, with growing markets in adolescents and in marijuana users. Whether adolescent marijuana users generally need a six-week residential intervention, rather than a briefer, less disruptive and cheaper treatment, is another question. Therapeutic communities exist in prison and are effective there (Vandevelde et al., 2004). Minnesota model treatment is effective for substance-dependent adolescents, particularly if they complete the programme (Winters et al., 2000), subject to the problems of bias and of diagnosing dependence in the under-eighteens (see below). Twelve-steps treatment is as effective for dependent alcohol drinkers as motivational interviewing or CBT (Allen et al., 1999), which surprised many when data came out from project MATCH, the largest evaluation of psychological interventions to date. Twelve-steps interventions emphasize that the person is powerless over their addiction and that they need to abstain and surrender to a higher power to allow them to do so, rather than continuing to try and control their addiction (Bateson, 1971). They also emphasize that the person should face up to the consequences of their addiction and make restitution where they can.

Twelve-steps treatment and therapeutic communities tend to be focused on abstinence. Consequently, they tend to discharge or exclude people who continue, or resume, drug or alcohol use. Conversely, those who successfully complete a programme are those who can manage to remain abstinent for a period of weeks or months. This is quite a demanding minimum requirement, and it is likely that anyone who could remain abstinent for, say, three months, whether treated or not, would have a good outcome. Thus, without careful comparison groups, the success rates of such programmes are often exaggerated. Another potential difficulty with residential treatment is that it can be somewhat distanced from the person's everyday life, where the substance use problems occurred. Return to that life can lead to relapse unless continuing support is in place. That 'support' nowadays sometimes looks rather like motivational interviewing or CBT. Nonetheless, there is evidence that such programmes can be effective.

Psychodynamic approaches

Psychodynamic and psychoanalytic practitioners frequently see clients who have problems with substance use, but this approach has yet to be adequately evaluated for such problems. This is in part because these forms of practice do not necessarily regard outcomes such as 'abstinence', 'reduced consumption' or 'less offending' to be the main goals of therapy. Furthermore psychodynamic theories tend to postulate that substance use problems are symptoms of underlying psychopathology, rather than being causes of problems in their own right. For example De Paula (2004) considers drug abuse to involve, in neo-Freudian terms, a symbiotic object relationship (dependence on external objects) with narcissistic functioning, pleasure without object and omnipotently controlled need. In one way this is simply a reformulation of 'dependence' into specific theoretical terms. More profoundly, this theorization suggests that, for many dependent people, were it not one thing, it would be another; if not drugs, then alcohol or another non-substance 'pleasure without object'. It is odd that little research has been directed to this approach, because psychodynamic principles underlie the twelve-steps movement, therapeutic communities, many everyday drugs counselling practices and group work. Moreover, while the treatment approaches described above can reduce drug use and offending, there are often other prominent problems to address, such as deficient parenting, trauma and poor conventional socialization. Some understanding of how a person's past affects their present psychological functioning would be beneficial here.

Systemic interventions

Family therapy is widely used to treat adolescent substance abuse, with some evidence of effectiveness. It does not appear to have been evaluated much for adult clients, although textbooks exist (Kaufman and Kaufman, 1991; Stanton and Todd, 1982), and family members can often be involved in treatment of adult clients. With children, under the aegis of 'family work', interventions have varied from brief family skills training (Spoth, Redmond and Shin, 2001) to full systemic sessions with multiple therapists (e.g., Liddle and Dakof, 1995). In their systematic review, Elliott et al. (2003) identify thirteen different family interventions, which is almost as many as studies of their effectiveness. Family-based interventions have also been used effectively for drugs prevention (e.g., Ennett et al., 2001). Williams and Chang (2003) concluded that family therapy was superior to other forms of outpatient treatment for adolescents, while Liddle and Dakof (1995) review the evidence that 'family-based treatment' to use their preferred phrase, is effective for adolescent substance use problems. They helpfully classify such treatments as: (1) more behavioural, skills-based interventions such as behaviour contracting, parenting skills or communication skills training; (2) structural and strategic interventions aimed at altering family dynamics in constructive ways; (3) multisystemic interventions that address the adolescent's social systems in and beyond the family.

'Family' therapy does not necessarily involve the full participation of all the members of the client's family or social system. Not all young substance users have families or networks of people who would readily attend therapy. Family therapy can simply mean looking at family and systemic issues with the individual client, particularly getting them to consider and explore other people's points of view (Carr, 2000). Family-based therapy increases both uptake of treatment (Santisteban et al., 1996; Szapocznik et al., 1998) and retention in treatment (see Liddle and Dakof, 1995, 228–9). Put in commonsense terms, children stay in treatment out of concern for their parents. It also leads to reductions in drug use. Liddle and Dakof (1995) review a range of studies where 40 to 80 per cent of clients were drug-free at the end of treatment. However, most of these involved small samples and few followed clients up beyond the end of treatment. These success rates are considerably higher than the 'honest' abstinence rates one would expect for adult substance dependence treatment.

Industry standard one-to-one counselling

Drugs counselling is not a highly regulated area of professional practice. People whose clients are drug or alcohol users can be highly qualified and experienced psychiatrists, clinical psychologists, psychotherapists, social workers or psychiatric nurses. They can also be modestly qualified, with first degrees in related subjects, only vocationally qualified, with something like a diploma in counselling, or simply volunteers or low-paid workers with a basic in-house training. For this reason, it is useful to consider what usually happens in drugs counselling, at least in the UK. This section is based on work evaluating drug services for the Youth Justice Board (Hammersley et al., 2004).The evidence from talking to numerous drug workers over the years is that this portrait seems representative of the UK scene.

Services generally offer some of the following: assessment, counselling (which might include any of the following as elements), advice and information, harm reduction and preventative work, motivational interviewing, one-to-one solution-focused work, relapse prevention, various other forms of psychological therapy, notably cognitive behavioural work, and anger or anxiety management programmes, as well as befriending, mentoring and advocacy, referral to leisure or educational activity programmes, alternative health therapies, referral to other agencies for treatment, family support, training for professionals and drugs education.

Services tend to be client centred, with positive regard for the client. Rapport is seen as very important, which involves ensuring that the client is comfortable with the setting of counselling, being aware of the potential gaps between counsellor and client, being nonjudgemental even about difficult behaviours, and ensuring that the client's right to privacy and confidentiality is respected.

While they are aware of many treatment options and good practices such as thorough assessment, service providers nonetheless put clients first. If a worker is concerned that a particular procedure could jeopardize the counsellor–client relationship, then often the procedure is truncated or avoided. It is extremely difficult to deliver standardized treatment packages under these conditions. These realistic difficulties contrast markedly with a quasi-medical model of consent that assumes that clients, having agreed to treatment, should comply with the requirements of treatment as specified by the counsellor and service. The quasi-medical model is presumed in most large-scale outcome evaluations.

The implication of this is that one should exercise caution in assuming that a specific treatment is delivered in a 'pure' form on the ground. Person-to-person working is the core of all treatment and requires flexibility. Even abstinence-oriented treatment may be more flexible about defining 'relapse' or 'use' in practice than in policy. For example, if the consequences of proven use would be serious, practitioners may tacitly collude with clients and not ask, or test, at moments of crisis.

Substitute prescribing

Once upon a time, alcoholics hospitalized for medical problems were prescribed alcohol. Nowadays this would rarely be good practice. In the societies this book is mostly about, alcohol is cheap and easy to get, so there is no need to improve drinkers' functioning by maintaining them on prescribed ethanol. Whether there is a need to improve the functioning of other people dependent on other drugs is a controversial question.

Opiate dependence is widely treated by the provision of a substitute opiate. Generally, this is methadone or, more recently, buprenorphine. Compared to heroin, both are relatively mild and long-lasting synthetic opiates which do not produce such an intense hit and do not need to be consumed so many times a day to avert withdrawal. This form of substitute prescribing is primarily palliative, the intent being to replace a very harmful dependence with a less harmful form and to maintain the person on this until they are ready to quit, minimizing the damage meantime. A difficulty can be that people simply stay on their substitute drugs, topping up with others from time to time (Preble and Miller, 1967; McKeganey et al., 2006). Another widely used form of substitute drug is nicotine replacement therapy via gum, patch or spray. Similar debates apply about whether this is true 'treatment' or simply substituting one addiction for another – or whether it even matters. Society is less sanguine about methadone, although, as discussed in earlier chapters, there is not a completely logical rationale for this.

A more controversial form of substitute prescribing is to replace street drugs with prescriptions of pharmaceutically pure ones; heroin users prescribed heroin, amphetamine users prescribed amphetamine and cocaine users prescribed cocaine. This is effective in reducing use of street drugs and in reducing offending and, while heroin prescribing is more expensive than methadone, it reduces offending more (Dijkgraaf et al., 2005). However, it obviously does not promote abstinence, or even necessarily reduction in substance use. Another major problem is that a system of prescribing street drugs is even more prone to abuse than prescribing less popular alternatives. 'Conning the croaker' has a long history (Burroughs, 1977), and people getting scripts can either top up with street drugs or sell the drugs on at a profit. Does it matter if some people are prescribed heroin or another drug indefinitely? Or is there a risk of creating a two-tier system of 'worthy', stable, better functioning addicts and 'unworthy', chaotic, dysfunctional addicts? Should this happen, does it matter? The underlying issue is whether being dependent on a drug is intrinsically bad, or whether it is only the adverse effects of dependence that are bad, in which case, were these to be minimized to almost nothing, then there is no genuine problem.

Another form of substitute prescribing can be of drugs that block or hinder the use of the drugs of dependence. Examples include Antabuse (Disulfiram), which causes nausea if alcohol is drunk, slow administration of naloxone via a depot, to block the effects of opiates, and, currently, a large-scale clinical trial of a vaccine of TA-CD (from Xenova Group plc) which produces anti-cocaine antibodies, rendering cocaine less active. A difficulty with this approach is that with sufficient determination a user can overcome the problems or blockade, by consuming even more of the drug or ignoring the nausea. People already motivated to quit may not need such drugs and people poorly motivated may not benefit.

All substitute prescribing should occur in a context where the clients' substance use is monitored carefully and they receive counselling (See Seivewright, 1999). Lapses can be dangerous and lead to misuse of the prescribed drugs along with street drugs, or to their being sold on. The UK General Medical Council's largest ever case of misconduct involved prescribing problems at one of the UK's foremost private drug clinics (Dyer, 2006). It is probably best to regard substitute precribing as (1) an incentive to maintain service contact with problem drug users, where that contact is used to attempt to prepare them to change and (2) a palliative until change occurs. Whether substitute drugs should be given to people with no sincere desire to change is a moral dilemma, distorted by the illegal status of drugs.

Co-morbidity

Offenders have much higher rates of mental health problems than the general population (Fagan, 2005; Siegel and Williams, 2003; Fazel and Danesh, 2002). This appears to be a generic finding including, as well as substance use problems (Fazel, Bains and Doll, 2006), depression, anxiety, psychosis, schizophrenia, personality disorders, specific learning difficulties, eating disorders, post-traumatic stress disorder, and physical and sexual abuse. People with substance abuse problems are also more likely to have other mental health problems (Conway et al., 2006; Jane-Llopis and Matytsina, 2006). Additionally, sometimes substance use that would not be a problem for others causes difficulties for people suffering from some mental health conditions. For example, heavy alcohol intake can be linked to binge eating and bulimia nervosa (Stewart et al., 2006; Duncan et al., 2006). Cannabis use can incline schizophrenics to cease taking their anti-psychotic medication (Linzen et al., 2003).

Thus, in reality the same people are often being treated for different problems under different labels and by different teams of professionals. If one broadens the concept of a case from a person to an entire family, then often a relatively small number of families in an area provide a large proportion of the work for a wide range of professionals. Furthermore, one person with problems in a family can cause yet more problems. For example, having a child with ADHD is difficult and stressful for parents (Barkley 2006, 195–8), which can worsen parental substance use and cause marital conflict, which in turn may reduce the effectiveness of the parenting of other children in the family, in turn meaning that several of the children use drugs and offend, including those who started off problem-free.

Because substance use (and abuse) is widespread, it becomes intertwined with many other problems. It can be complicated to determine the extent to which one problem, perhaps the presenting problem, is contributed to by another. For example, many young offenders use drugs and many use in excess of sensible norms. If they were assessed appropriately for substance abuse at intake to youth justice, then a large proportion of them might be referred for specialized interventions.

Treatment for the under-sixteens

Intervening with younger clients is not the same as with older ones. Several comprehensive reviews of evaluations of substance use treatments for young people exist (Dakof, Tejeda and Liddle, 2001; Deas and Thomas, 2001; Elliott et al., 2003; Liddle and Dakof, 1995; Lowman, 2004: Titus et al., 2001; Williams and Chang, 2003), a number of large multi-site trials are currently underway (Dennis et al., 2002; Tims et al., 2002) and there have been calls for improvements in young people's services (Gilvarry, 2001). Hammersley, Reid and Minkes (2006) note the following problems. Working with children (the under-sixteens) raises systemic and ethical issues that complicate both intervention and evaluation. These include children's concerns about parents overreacting to substance use, a generation gap in attitudes to substance use, and duties of care and risk assessment resulting in adults having to break children's confidentiality, harming the therapeutic relationship. Assessing or diagnosing substance use problems in the under-eighteens is problematic and often neglects the systemic aspects of pathways to treatment. This includes adult concerns about age-normative substance use coercing the child into treatment, appropriate adult concerns about substance use clashing with the child's view of it as normal or harmless and the difficulties of telling these apart. It is also difficult to firmly diagnose dependence or abuse among younger people, and a vaguer label of 'problems' may be appropriate (Newcomb, 1995). Defining realistic and acceptable long-term outcomes for substance use in this age group is problematic. As discussed previously, substance use generally increases as people age into young adulthood. Much policy has difficulty in facing up to this reality, so practitioners may find themselves obliged to pursue unlikely objectives such as abstinence and to 'treat' problems that they do not believe require treatment, but are preconditions of a criminal justice order or ending school exclusion. In consequence of these difficulties, operating, auditing and evaluating a substance problems service for children requires flexibility and sensitivity of practice.

More on costs

A considerable effort in applied economics has been expended to put financial values upon the costs of interventions and match these to the costs of drugs and crime if no intervention is provided. These figures are always approximations and require some contentious reasoning, such as putting a financial cost on a year lived at a specific level of quality of life (and indeed numerating quality of life in the first place). On such measures, drug problems and crime turn out to be expensive enough to justify most interventions. As discussed in chapter 6, a person who uses class A drugs and offends intensively can cost upwards of £35,000 per year in crime costs and other social costs. Methadone maintenance treatment, with support, costs about £8,500 (Dijkgraaf et al., 2005), and this leads to a reduction in but not an elimination of criminality. Psychological interventions without substitute prescribing may cost less.

The US Federal Bureau of Prisons estimate a national annual cost of $23,000 per prisoner (Newsletter of the Federal Courts, 2004). In the UK it is about £25,000 (Hansard, 2005). In Sweden costs are much higher, at €91,000 (Johansson, 1998), illustrating that relatively humane prison systems are more expensive. Other disposals can cost much less than prison. Referral orders for young offenders in the UK, where the young person is referred to an appropriate intervention for their problems, cost an average of over £630 per person (PSSRU, 2003). The effectiveness of such disposals remains to be seen, but they are certainly inexpensive.

More intensive interventions cost more. In California, the 8 per cent solution (Schumacher and Kurz, 2000), which intervened intensively with the most serious juvenile offenders, cost about $1.4 million per annum for about 100 youth and their families ($14,000 per case). In the UK, one integrated supervision project for persistent young offenders cost over £7,000 per successful completion (NCH, 2002). At the intensive end of interventions, projects providing intensive family support for families at risk of receiving an antisocial behaviour order (ASBO) cost about £30,000 per completed case (NCH, 2006). This is a cost comparable to prison, but the report estimates that failing to intervene can cost over £245,000 if a family loses its tenancy, children are taken into care and so on. Such interventions are for families with severe problems. Unfortunately, clear outcome data are not available for these NCH projects.

All these interventions cost large amounts of money compared to the incomes of people who are often disadvantaged and unemployed, and in some countries have reduced benefit entitlements because they are young and single. The thought has crossed my mind that, were they to be paid a stipend of the order of £10,000 per annum on the condition that they sorted themselves out, took drugs less and offended less, this might be as effective as paying for complex interventions that left them poor, if hopefully wiser. Sadly, societies that like spending money on punitive disposals such as prison tend to dislike spending money on welfare, even when it may be the cheaper option. One effective component of treatment is to give dependent people vouchers (for goods or services) to stay drug-free (Plebani Lussier et al., 2006).

Drugs treatment and criminal justice

Effective treatments for drug problems, the high prevalence of drugs problems among arrestees and convicts, and the relatively affordable costs involved tempt criminal justice systems to treat drug and alcohol dependence. The mostly widely mentioned concerns are that coercing people into treatment may be unethical and may lead to insincere engagement, purely to duck more punitive disposals. Fortunately, when compulsory and voluntary treatment have been compared, the outcomes of both are often equivalent (Stevens, Trace and Bewley-Taylor, 2005) and indeed many who attend 'voluntary' treatment are under some form of coercion, for example from family or workplace (Orford, 2001). Drug courts and other methods of compelling drug-dependent people to obtain treatment as well as or instead of punishment appear to work (e.g., Logan et al., 2004). A number of difficulties remain.

If drug-dependent offenders deserve somewhat compassionate treatment, what about those who have other treatable problems, which is arguably the majority of them? It seems inequitable to divert addicts through drug courts while incarcerating their peers who are traumatized, depressed, or have learning difficulties, personality disorders, alcoholism or other serious psychological difficulties. While justice services do their best, rarely are similar resources put into these less high-profile problems.

Relatively substantial resources are put into drug treatments in the political hope that this will reduce crime. It often reduces individual offending rates, but rehabilitated drug-dependent criminals tend to be replaced by others – hence the potential importance of prevention, were it to be coherently targeted. There is a risk that drug treatment resources will vanish, particularly if regional crime rates were to rise again anyway.

Another problem is that there is a very high prevalence of substance abuse and dependence among offenders. Were all those eligible referred to treatment, drugs services in most places would be overwhelmed. There is a risk of 'stack 'em high and treat 'em cheap' programmes developing, which may be more profitable than successful.

From the arrestee's perspective, sometimes treatment is a preferable option to another disposal, such as prison. In other conditions, it can seem like an additional punishment, particularly if the person perceives their offence to be relatively commonplace or minor. A shoplifter, or drugged driver, may consider repeated compulsory attendance at a relevant programme considerably more onerous than a fine. This means that it can be in offenders' interest to manipulate strategically their presentation of drug problems to the system, as best they can. There can be a risk of compulsory treatment being biased to the most naïve and the most cynical offenders, missing many in the middle.

An appealing solution is drug testing, but this poses several problems. Some drugs are far easier to detect for longer than others, and testing may deter users from cannabis and attract them to opiates or cocaine. Tests are only as accurate as the laboratories processing them. The stand-alone kits in wide use are problematic because they only show presence/absence data, which depend upon some threshold of the presence of specific chemicals. It is commercially safer to make tests that are not oversensitive – nobody gets upset at false negatives – for exceeding a specific threshold may be due to the ingestion (or contamination) of small quantities of a substance very recently or of massive quantities long ago (e.g., Vandevenne, Vandenbussche and Verstraete, 2000). Some drug users are capable of ingesting quantities of drugs that would be fatal to a naïve user, which may show positive test results far longer than is predicted. While testing is useful in the context of a planned treatment programme, using the results punitively or to discharge someone from the programme is potentially problematic.

Criminal justice is a good place to locate and sometimes rehabilitate drug-dependent people, but results are only as good as the quality of the treatment programme. Simplistic, excessively brief or rigid treatment will not work quasi-compulsorily any more than voluntarily. Indeed, offenders often have complex problems that require skilled intervention. There is often a low ceiling on expenditure to rehabilitate criminals, which sometimes results in second-rate or overstretched services. Professionals can also be glad to refer difficult cases to 'the specialists', passing on the problem without having to care about the solution. For instance, criminal justice professionals can sometimes think of 'treatment' as if it were a uniformly effective, scientifically based set of practices, when it isn't.

Summary

Treatment for substance dependence and substance-related problems can be effective, and when it is it usually reduces any offending also. It needs to be long-term, usually requires one-to-one counselling, possibly among other interventions, and needs to work towards considerable changes in lifestyle, including changes in client thinking. More successful treatment appears to empower clients to change, rather than imposing change upon them or offering a generic plan for change. Substitute prescribing is more useful in the context of an agreed plan for change than when it is simply used as a palliative holding procedure. The costs of effective treatment are easily outbalanced by the crime and health costs of a continuing criminal substance user. There is therefore no justification for continuing treatments that are probably ineffective, even if they are shorter, easier or cheaper.

Discussion points

- What are the advantages and disadvantages of compulsory drug testing at work?
- Why is counselling for criminals often politically unacceptable?
- Most effective treatments are cheap enough to be cost-effective. So how should we choose between them?

Further reading

Ghodse, H. (2002). *Drugs and addictive behaviour: a guide to treatment.* Cambridge: Cambridge University Press.

Gossop, M., Marsden, J., Stewart, D., and Kidd, T. (2003). The National Treatment Outcome Research Study (NTORS): 4–5 year follow-up results. *Addiction*, 98: 291–303.

Jarvis, T. J., Tebbutt, J., Mattick, R. P., and Shand, F. (2005). *Treatment approaches for alcohol and drug dependence.* Chichester: Wiley.

Lightfoot, L. O. (2000). *Programming for offenders with substance abuse and dependence problems.* Ottawa: Correctional Service of Canada. www.csc-scc.gc.ca/text/rsrch/compendium/2000/chap_14_e.shtml; accessed 23 May 2007.

Miller, W. R., and Heather, N. (1998). *Treating addictive behaviors.* New York: Plenum.

Perry, A., Coulton, S., Glanville, J., Godfrey, C., Lunn, J., McDougall, C., and Neale, Z. (2005). *Interventions for drug-using offenders in the courts, secure establishments and the community.* Cochrane Database of Systematic Reviews (3): Art. No. CD005193 2006.

Seivewright, N. (2000). *Community treatment of drug misuse: more than methadone.* Cambridge: Cambridge University Press.

Taxman, F. S., Perdoni, M. L., and Harrison, L. D. (2007). Drug treatment services for adult offenders: the state of the state. *Journal of Substance Abuse Treatment*, 32(3): 239–54.

9
The Futures of Drugs and Crime

So far this book has looked at how to think about and understand drugs and crime. This final chapter will examine some emerging trends, which will probably affect how we think about them in the future.

Coping with the evidence

Evidence-based practice? Borrowing Gandhi's comment on Western civilization: 'I think it would be a good idea.' It is only occasionally criticized (Freshwater and Rolfe, 2004; Berk and Janet, 1999; Clarke, 1999; Tanenbaum, 2005), yet it is far from clear what it is, or whether it improves things. Evidence-based practice originated in medicine (Guyatt, 1992), but it is now also widely applied to social and educational problems. Many social scientists are suspicious of it because it imports scientific methods inappropriately into the understanding of people and societies and because the researchers and practitioners who use those methods can fail to appreciate the extent to which knowledge and the means of acquiring it are themselves socially constructed. This covers many of the problems discussed earlier in this book, including definitional problems, lack of easily measured and unbiased outcomes and reflexivity, where altered attention to problems transforms both the relevant behaviours and our understandings of them. For example, students today are sometimes surprised to discover that 'stress', nowadays a mandatory component of the aspirational lifestyle, only entered academic psychological understanding in the 1960s and exploded into popular consciousness some twenty years later.

A lucid alternative to formulaic evidence-based practice can be found in Pawson and Tilley (1997). They propose that evaluations need to consider the context of the intervention, the theoretical mechanism by which it might have an effect, what the outcome should be, theoretically, and how it will be measured, in practice. Through their lens, multiple-site randomized controlled trials may sometimes deal with outcome, but they can fail to consider context or theoretical mechanism adequately. Different contexts can affect whether a theoretically sound intervention will work. A straightforward case is that, if the intervention requires special technical skills that are better in some places than others, then this may make a difference. For example, some drug-testing laboratories may have sloppy procedures, making it more possible to muddle or contaminate specimens. Such problems may be ironed out for biological and medical interventions, but it can be extremely difficult to control context for more psychosocial interventions. For example, the quality of substance use services for young offenders depends upon the quality of the inter-service partnership arrangements (Minkes, Hammersley and Raynor, 2005).

There is also always a problem of the incompleteness of the evidence upon which practice could be based. Adams (1995) offers a witty and devastating critique of attempting to weigh up the risks of anything on the basis of evidence that is extremely incomplete and biased, particularly when the behaviour that contributes to the 'evidence' may change as a result of applying the evidence. Although incomplete, evidence can also be overwhelming. For example, the addiction, alcohol and drugs journals listed on Web of Science published 48,938 articles between 1970 and 2007, at a rate of 830 per annum in 1980 and 3,970 in 2006. Of the total, only 524 articles have the words crime, offending or delinquency in their titles. One can be confident that most of the remaining 48,000 articles will be irrelevant, but that some will not be, and that relevant work will be published elsewhere too. Choosing what evidence to read taxes the most diligent and experienced academic, and it is not at all clear to me how a modern 'scientist-practitioner' has any hope of keeping up at all, given that most of their working day is taken up with practice rather than reading. Hence there has arisen a genre of reviews and meta-analyses, but these can be theoretically banal and overly rigid in their adherence to 'scientific' standards of evidence that are detached from the reality of practice. There is a serious problem of readers being able to pick and choose whatever 'evidence' fits their existing prejudices.

Also, criminology often fails to collect or consider any evidence at all except that gathered by practitioners according to their prejudices of the moment, which are often remarkably traditional and durable in the face of contradictory evidence. The individual source of the statistics may easily be the weakest link:

> Harold Cox tells a story of his life as a young man in India. He quoted some statistics to a Judge, an Englishman, and a very good fellow. His friend said, Cox, when you are a bit older, you will not quote Indian statistics with that assurance. The Government are very keen on amassing statistics – they collect them, add them, raise them to the nth power, take the cube root and prepare wonderful diagrams. But what you must never forget is that every one of those figures comes in the first instance from the *chowty dar* [chowkidar] (village watchman), who just puts down what he damn pleases. (Stamp, 1929, 258–9)

Nowadays, in place of the chowty dar we have the police officer, the social worker, the school teachers, the youth justice worker and the community psychiatric team, not forgetting the store security team, the CCTV operatives and the fieldworkers conducting surveys door to door or on the telephone. It matters what these people choose to record as crime, or drug use. Paperwork and procedures can restrict their choices, but they cannot eliminate choice or prevent errors of omission and fabrication. Chowty dars may not have had performance targets, but these only serve to motivate further fiddling of the data (Levitt and Dubner, 2005, 19–51). There are two fundamental methods for adjusting statistics about drugs and crime at street level: if one wishes to highlight a particular problem then it is easy to find lots of examples of it. If one does not wish there to be a problem then it is easy to fail to spot appropriate cases. For example, I have had doctors awkwardly ask me about my alcohol intake during health screenings: 'Alcohol. About how much do you drink a week?' I hesitate. 'Not more than twenty-one units?' 'No.' 'Good.' Other doctors more patiently elicit a detailed answer.

Evidence-based practice in one sense simply replicates the scientific method for practice. Scientific methods involve observation and openness to modification of ideas, rather than dogmatism and assuming that specific authorities are correct. There is a need to evolve methods to understand and evaluate drugs and crime practices that are scientific in this general sense, rather than simply mimicking science with the latest statistical or meta-analysis methods. A particularly worrying form of mimicry is when key repeated cross-sectional surveys fail to evolve their questions as understanding develops, purely to ensure comparability with earlier waves of the survey. Collecting precisely the same fatuous data again and again is not science, even if it permits policy makers to point to charts and multi-variate statistical analyses where drugs or crime rates rise and fall, supposedly according to some of their policies.

In the future, there could be more open-ended funding of research related to drugs and crime problems on a scale appropriate to the supposed political magnitude of these problems, rather than mostly biological studies of drugs. Alternatively, more and more 'research' may be so closely specified by political concerns that it finds nothing out except that current policies are good and that current practices reflect money well spent.

Surviving practice

For these reasons, it is unwise to be to assured about the evidence on drugs and crime and what will work to reduce them. Indeed, over my twenty-two years in the field, progress has consisted primarily of it becoming widely accepted that drug problems are here to stay, rather than being temporary epidemics or moral aberrations that will be resolved soon. This has meant that there is more permanence and professionalism in the agencies that deal with these problems. As discussed earlier, it is not clear that drugs add much anyway to the oceans of alcohol consumed around the world, assuming these are very similar sorts of problem. There is a fair amount of knowledge about how to treat a drug-dependent criminal. There is a gap in knowledge about how to prevent the formation of new people with these problems, because there has been too much focus on completely preventing crime and drugs instead, which is impossible.

Informed thinking (e.g., RSA, 2007) is moving towards a view that what is required is, first, to identify the true harms of drugs and crime, avoiding exaggeration of 'wicked' transgressions and minimization of 'normal' ones; second, to try to discover which of these harms are primarily products of the ways in which drugs and crime are currently conceptualized and tackled – for example, imprisonment often increases or fails to decrease reoffending (Kuziemoko and Levitt, 2004; Doob and Webster, 2003), even if it temporarily incapacitates offenders (Marvell and Moody, 1994); third, to develop practices that minimize or treat the true harms of drugs and crime. We remain far from being able to identify these. For instance, is dependence intrinsically harmful, or is it only the financial and social by-products of dependence that are harmful? There is a need for clear theory about drugs and crime which can inform intervention. Evidence-based medicine flourishes when such understandings are available – in infection control for example – and flounders when they are not. In the absence of clear theory, policy and practice often lurch from one concern or crisis to another. Much effective practice continues despite new initiatives, new evidence and new requirements. Most successful treatments of drugs or crime involve, in some way, working effectively with people. This art has a widening range of techniques, but no magic bullet cure that can be administered, for example, by practitioners who lack the time, skill, or interest to 'work with people' properly.

It would be enormously useful if most practitioners could reflect on their practice and learn from both positive and negative outcomes. Too often, they are required to believe that negative outcomes represent failures that may be punished, and hence tend to be covered up. Too often, their evolving practices are repeatedly disrupted by new policies and initiatives that are clumsily 'evidence-based' and which are insensitive to the nuances of practice. To survive repeated policy changes, often coupled with repeated managerial restructuring, many practitioners show token adherence to whatever the current policy crazes are, complete their obligatory statistical returns accordingly, and covertly continue business as usual.

Outcomes

It is extremely difficult to assess the outcome of psychological and social interventions. Hoped-for changes often taken months, even years or decades, and there is rarely the funding or political will to support evaluations of the appropriate length and scope. The fundamental principles of change (see also Adams, 1995) are as follows. (1) Interventions are generally introduced because things are perceived to have got worse, so often begin just after a problem has peaked. (2) Things that have got worse tend to improve again, and unless controls are used that improvement tends to be attributed to the intervention. (3) The use of appropriate controls and adjustments is complex and often causes disagreements that allow people to interpret data according to their own biases. (4) Change is influenced more by incomprehensible fluctuation and extraneous factors than by intervention. Among these factors are relevant changes to policy, practice and data-gathering during the period when outcomes are to be assessed, including deliberate changes in response to the evaluation. None of this makes it easy to demonstrate that change has truly occurred or that it can safely be attributed to the intervention. There is also a risk that, by the time true outcomes are established, political interest in the issue has waned.

In the absence of genuinely scientific outcome studies, which would usually be complex, protracted, expensive and considered, much evaluation work is crude and is often abused as propaganda to support various moral and political agendas.

Attitudes

Writing about food, in a manner that applies also to drugs, Tannahill (1988, 348) commented:

> Before the 1960s there were many among the silent majority in the Western world who canalized their ordinary human need to feel superior into what had for centuries been a socially acceptable (if less than admirable) intolerance of homosexuals, Jews, people who ate garlic or dyed their hair, Catholics, blacks, old clothes, four-letter words, promiscuity, pacifism . . . and so on. Then, at one blow, all these faithful old prejudices became unrespectable, and those who had held them were deprived of an outlet for their need to disapprove.
>
> The next generation, however, with the same need and no traditional focus for it, was saved by the American evangelical tradition and the new obsession with diet and health.

'Criminals' have never been liked and are nowadays treated rather better than when they were disfigured, transported or killed for relatively minor theft. The disapproval of drugs may turn out to be temporary – like the banning of cigarettes when they were first mass marketed – and may already be being supplanted by disapproval of 'terrorism', which at first glance seems more reasonable, until one considers that it involves disapproval and distrust of entire religious and ethnic groups – as in the bad old days.

People's common love of inebriation will never be particularly laudable, but it seems unlikely to vanish. It could be that societies will gradually accommodate some or all of the drugs that now cause great concern. Alternatively, we could settle down with some of the drugs and lose interest in others. Cannabis is used very widely already and is most likely to become integrated, despite concerns about psychosis. Awful and true warnings about the health risks of cigarettes and alcohol have not diminished their popular use in the past. On past form, drugs will become more integrated into society as generations who take them more for granted age into positions of power. The previous generation of politicians did not use drugs at all (with a few exceptions), the present generation inhaled but did not enjoy it. In twenty years time will politicians have injected but not enjoyed it? It is also probable that, however bad contemporary drugs are, currently unimaginable things that initially seem even worse will be developed with biotechnology and information technology.

Tackling drugs and crime

Drugs and crime are linked in three basic ways, but links are not the same as causes. First, some forms of drug use are linked with acquisitive crime, both to obtain money to buy drugs and because the people attracted to certain forms of drug use tend also to be criminal. The reasons for this are complex and only very rarely boil down to simple causes amenable to mechanistic interventions. Many links are connected to relative poverty. An implication is that measures to reduce income differentials in a society might reduce drugs and crime problems; however, this would be at the expense of tax and fiscal policies that would probably be unpopular. There is also a question as to whether drugs and crime problems are an unavoidable residue in a relatively free society.

Second, some forms of drug use are linked with crime and disorder under some conditions. Alcohol is the most notorious drug here, but other drugs can also lead to disorder and violent crime – amphetamines and cocaine for example. If drugs were to become even more widespread, it is quite feasible that yet other drugs would become linked to violence and disorder. The drugs–disorder and drugs–violence links are not understood very well, perhaps because research has tended to focus on finding or rebutting some form of mechanistic neuropsychological drugs–violence connection. Measures that discourage extreme intoxication can reduce violence and disorder.

The third connection between drugs and crime is the globalization of the illicit drugs supply industry. This industry is currently by definition criminal and, not having recourse to legal means to police itself, is also liable to be violent and criminal in ways other than simply in the supply of drugs. It also penetrates and corrupts legitimate institutions, probably to a much larger extent than is currently known. So far, attempts to destroy the industry have failed and there is no plausible scenario where they would succeed. The industry needs to be regulated in ways more similar to those of alcohol, tobacco and pharmaceuticals. This would require depenalizing laws for at least some of the widely use illicit drugs.

It is not clear that it is possible to eliminate drugs or, thinking about licit substances too, what this would actually mean. Were alcohol only available under conditions of lavish supply at a cost people would pay (not necessarily cheap), then alcohol–crime links would probably replace current drugs–crime links. Temperance likes to present itself as the natural state of humankind, but it is a relatively modern movement that began as a reaction to widespread habitual drunkenness. At least in relatively affluent societies, with continued social inequalities and stress, widespread habitual drunkenness (and by analogy drug use) appears common. It can be damped down, but not eliminated.

Even successful reductions in drug supply tend only to be temporary and can backfire. For example, in the UK 'Operation Keymer' in summer 2006 involved raids on a large number of indoor cannabis farms, temporarily limiting supply. However, suppliers sourced cannabis from elsewhere, probably importing it, and some of it was found to contain microscopic glass particles that might damage smokers' lungs (UKCIA, 2007). Recent reviews of drugs and crime have been uniformly pessimistic about the utility of reducing drug supply in any reasonable or cost-effective way (RSA, 2007; Stevens et al., 2005). Reported reduction in supply tends either to be temporary, at the expense of something else, or based on biased and self-seeking estimates by agencies trying to justify their existence. Genuine temperance seems unlikely. Perhaps limiting the supply of some things would be easier if the supply of others were regulated or permitted. For example, would it be better if local cannabis farmers who are not connected to organized crime (see Potter and Dann, 2005) were encouraged to supply pure weed of known strength and content? They could at least not be discouraged by being tautologously labelled 'organized crime' and closed down.

It is therefore important to have a serious think about what steps might be taken to remove, sever or reduce the links between people who are drug dependent and offending to ensure that drug use occurred in ways that did not lead to theft, violence and disorder and to prevent the criminalization of the world's largest industry. This leads on to some action points.

There are five major things that a society can do to tackle drugs and crime. It could (1) reduce social inequalities, (2) discourage harmful patterns of substance use, (3) regulate the illicit drugs industry, (4) increase tolerance and accommodation of drugs and crime. This would include recognizing that these activities are often signs of serious personal and social problems, rather than wickedness that should be punished. (5) Finally, society could accept that 'drugs' and 'crime' are boundary activities that define normal social behaviour. Wherever they are laid, there will always be activity at the boundaries. If these problems were more often framed in this relativistic way, then it would become feasible to try and rearrange the boundaries to minimize drugs–crime links.

Reducing inequality

There is potential in tackling the social and economic inequalities that create people who have little to lose by taking drugs or committing crimes and often much to gain by doing both. Drug use is in part a response to the direct stress of being deprived and disadvantaged in society. It is also a response to the stress of the many life problems and difficulties that can go with being deprived and disadvantaged in society. Additionally, more deprived and disadvantaged people have more need to break the law in order not only to steal or obtain stolen goods, or buy stolen goods, but also to negotiate successfully through a complicated system of controls that govern benefits and taxation. These controls disproportionately impact people with less money and less of the social capital that would ease their progress through the system. Poorer, less articulate and less educated people are put in a position where they have to lie and cheat in order to better themselves, or even get their fair access to services. They often have more of a struggle on their hands and are more willing to break the law. If inequalities were to be reduced it is conceivable that crime would also be reduced.

The reduction of social inequalities is rarely considered to be the remit of the professionals who work with drugs and crime. In societies that have major social inequalities and where drugs are prohibited and consequently unregulated, it is questionable whether other forms of intervention can have any serious impact on drugs–crime links. It may be possible to vary the shape and form of the problems, including containing them to some extent, but it is unlikely that they will be substantially reduced or eliminated. This conclusion may be defeatist, but it was the conclusion that led to the repeal of alcohol prohibition in the USA (Behr, 1996). How to reduce inequality is outside both my expertise and the remit of this book.

Discouraging harmful patterns of use

Other than completely preventing drug use, this is the main objective of current policy and practice. Using alcohol as an example, it is clearly possible to change drinking patterns and attitudes over a period of years by health promotion and health education, combined with intelligent legislation. Examples include the less positive attitudes to and less engagement in drink-driving and the reduction in the per capita consumption of alcohol in the wine-drinking countries of Europe (from a very high starting point; Anderson and Baumberg, 2006). However, not all changes are for the better. There has been a considerable and harmful increase in alcohol intake in the UK over the past thirty years, back up to the historical levels that existed before the First World War. This has occurred behind a concerted drive against drugs which has perhaps overly normalized getting drunk, which is perceived as wrong, but preferable to drugs. The role of industry is also problematic as it is tempted to promote high levels of consumption of its product (whichever drug that is), if ideally without too much harm.

There needs to be more understanding of how to identify and minimize patterns of drug use that lead to dependence. Simplistic views of some drugs as addictive and others as not have hindered understanding here and, for example, allowed an increase in cannabis combined with alcohol-related problems among the young. This might have been reduced had cannabis not become falsely contrasted with 'dangerous' drugs, implying that liberal use was acceptable. There is a need to discover the difference between excessive drug use as a temporary response to life difficulties and excessive use that develops into a more chronic problem. Other mental health problems, such as depression, face similar difficulties of differentiation in diagnosis and treatment.

Regulation

This point is hard to face up to. The illicit drugs industry needs to be regulated. It is completely unacceptable that the world's largest industry is subject to no regulations of health and safety for its employees or its customers. Regulating the industry would involve at least partially legalizing some aspects of it. Governments are happy to work with other 'morally repugnant' industries, notably the armaments industry, if they consider it to be for the public good and for the good of the national purse. The war on drugs needs amnesty. As with some real wars, the only people who benefit from the continuing drugs war are those directing and profiting from the active combatants. The civilians in whose name the war is allegedly being fought are victims, as are the foot soldiers. As long as the industry is not regulated it remains completely illegal and there will be strong drugs–crime links.

Some key problems with regulation include:

- Which drugs should be regulated?
- Who would be licensed to supply and sell them?
- What mechanisms would be used to ensure that drugs were sold only in relatively safe forms, rather than in forms that are too strong, too cheap, or too easy to consume at will?
- How should drugs be taxed?
- What age limits should be set on drug use and should these vary from substance to substance?
- More legal availability might increase use or make patterns of use more chronic, although the depenalization of marijuana does not appear to have had this effect (e.g., Donnelly, Hall and Christie, 1995). More use would probably cause more health problems. Who will pay for this?

Tolerance

The prohibition of (some) drugs and strong anti-crime stances tend to be linked to fantasies that a society can exist without drugs or crime. A utopia might result in no substance problems and no note-worthy crime, if a utopia were created. Utopia might do this by ensuring that all its inhabitants were either well adjusted, or received whatever help they needed to become well adjusted in a timely and appropriate fashion. At the time of writing, utopian thinking in the USA and the UK is facilitating some markedly dystopian laws to prevent drugs and crime, or to more or less forcibly rehabilitate or control those involved. Examples include being able to seize the assets of suspected drug dealers, forcing young drug users' parents to undergo parenting programmes, and compulsorily referring all young people identified as having drug problems to treatment. On the other hand, it is defeatist to suppose that this is already the best society that can be achieved and that drugs and crime are just unfortunate side effects of the free market.

Tolerance of drugs and crime involves uncertainty, which is often scientific, usually reasonable and occasionally evidence-based. It is unwise and inhumane to be complacent about socially accepted activities and critical and rejecting of unaccepted ones. It is counter-factual to pretend that intoxication and illegal or immoral activities are not widespread. It is unrealistic to claim that any feasible counter-measures will eliminate intoxication or crime, although many steps might make the balance more tolerable. There is a need for more hesitancy about bold moves to sort things out, for many have been tried and most have failed. Change for drugs and crime occurs over decades rather than years and tends to have multi-modal causes, insofar as it has understood causes at all.

It would be preferable that policy and practice against drugs and crime took a lead on defining boundaries, rather than staying cautiously behind social change. There are some issues that need to be constantly debated and renegotiated rather than old-fashioned standards being simultaneously asserted and flouted. The following are some issues that need to be addressed.

1 Are the consequences of social inequality on the relatively poor worth the benefits to the relatively affluent? If they are, then we should be kinder to those less fortunate than ourselves, rather than punitive. If they are not, then we should reduce inequalities.
2 Is justice blind to social inequalities, or does it systematically victimize the people with least social capital? It is easy to point to other countries where there is very little justice, but this should not create complacency about justice in our countries.
3 In psychotherapeutic terms, punishment is almost universally ineffective and the personal desire to punish others is usually due to poor personal adjustment of some kind. Why are people's most maladjusted desires allowed to shape policy on drugs and crime?
4 What should contemporary social norms be for the use of intoxicants? Complete abstinence is unrealistic, as is complete tolerance. Without an understanding of what kind of substance use we approve of in adults, it is very difficult to socialize and educate children in the appropriate direction. Liberal boozing, widespread consumption of medicines and complete repression of 'drugs' looks increasingly unrealistic and hypocritical.

Conclusions

Kind words butter no parsnips. We also need to base practice in the contemporary world rather than in a world that might be. Even if there is no functional alternative to the global free market with rampant consumerism, network society, risk society and the poverty gap, in the narrow domain of drugs and crime it is still possible to tackle and define these problems in a more rational and open-minded way.

Policies and practices should consider alcohol and tobacco along with drugs. Drug–crime links should not be limited to worries about heroin and cocaine. It may not be feasible to dissuade young people from substance misuse in societies that keenly promote alcohol and the use of other psychoactive substances and medicines. The awkward issue of whether crime is the necessary boundary of free enterprise needs airing.

Society's sometimes self-congratulatory detestation of drugs and crime perhaps emphasizes the wrong problems. Keeping the public safe from drug addicts, terrorists, organized crime, etc., diverts attention from the global harms that may destroy society. The day I completed the second draft of this book, 'the Clean Development Mechanism (CDM), which is supposed to offset greenhouse gases emitted in the developed world by selling carbon credits from elsewhere, [was] contaminated by gross incompetence, rule-breaking and possibly fraud' (Davies, 2007). In fifty years, the 'drug decades' may be the topic of nostalgia.

Discussion points

- Are drugs and crime largely products of social inequalities? If so, given that social systems based on equality have failed, how should society handle drugs and crime?
- Is there really a common human need for prejudice against others, including control and punishment of their behaviour?
- If cannabis was fully legal, then at what age should people be permitted to smoke it?
- Do political concerns about drugs and crime simply reflect widespread social concerns about these problems, or are the problems hyped up to serve the interests of the powerful and affluent?

Further reading

Adams, J. (1995). *Risk*. London: Routledge.

Ericson, R. (2006). *Crime in an insecure world*. Cambridge: Polity.

Freshwater, D., and Rolfe, G. (2004). *Deconstructing evidence based practice*. Abingdon: Routledge.

RSA (2007). *Drugs – facing facts: the report of the RSA commission on illegal drugs, communities and public policy*. London: Royal Society for the Encouragement of Arts, Manufactures and Commerce.

Stevens, A., Trace, M., and Bewley-Taylor, D. (2005). *Reducing drug-related crime: an overview of the global evidence*. London: Beckley Foundation.

Runciman, R. (ed.) (1999). *Drugs and the law: report of the independent inquiry into the Misuse of Drugs Act 1971*. London: Police Foundation. www.druglibrary.org/schaffer/Library/studies/runciman/default.htm; accessed 31 May 2007.

References

Adam, B., and Van Loon, J. (2000). Introduction. In B. Adam, U. Beck and J. Van Loon (eds), *The risk society and beyond: critical issues for social theory*. London: Sage, pp. 1–31.

Adam, B., Beck, U., and Van Loon, J. (eds) (2000). *The risk society and beyond: critical issues for social theory*. London: Sage.

Adams, J. (1995). *Risk*. London: Routledge.

Adler, R. B., and Towne, N. (1993). *Looking out/looking in*. 7th edn, Fort Worth: Harcourt Brace.

Agar, M. (1973). *Ripping and running: a formal ethnography of urban heroin addicts*. New York: Seminar Press.

Akers, R. L. (1991). Addiction: the troublesome concept. *Journal of Drug Issues*, 21: 777–93.

Alasuutan, P. (1992). *A cultural theory of alcoholism*. New York: State University of New York Press.

Alcohol Concern (2004). *Alcohol Concern factsheet: advertising alcohol*. www.alcoholconcern.org.uk/files/20040506_085240_Advertising%20fact sheet%20April%202004.pdf; accessed 16 November 2005.

Allen, J. P., Mattson, M. E., Miller, W. R., Tonigan, J. S., Connors, G. J., Rychtarik, R. G., Randall, C. L., Anton, R. F., Kadden, R. M., Litt, M., Cooney, N. L., DiClemente, C. C., Carbonari, J., Zweben, A., Longabaugh, R. H., Stout, R., Donovan, D., Babor, T. F., DelBoca, F. K., Rounsaville, B., Carroll, K., and Wirtz, P. W. (1999). Summary of Project MATCH. *Addiction*, 94(1): 31–4.

Alliance against Urban 4x4s (2005). *The Safety Myth*. www.stopurban4x4s. org.uk/safety.htm; accessed 18 April 2007.

American Psychiatric Association (1994). *DSM-IV-TR: diagnostic and statistical manual of mental disorders*. Washington, DC: American Psychiatric Association.

Amos, A., Wiltshire, S., Bostock, Y., Haw, S., and McNeill, A. (2004). 'You can't go without a fag . . . you need it for your hash' – a qualitative exploration of smoking, cannabis and young people. *Addiction*, 99(1): 77–81.

Anderson, P., and Baumberg, B. (2006). *Alcohol in Europe: a public health perspective*. Brussels: European Commission. http://ec.europa.eu/health-eu/news_alcoholineurope_en.htm; accessed 15 May 2007.

Anderson, T., and Levy, J. A (2003). 'Marginality among older injectors in today's illicit drug culture: assessing the impact of ageing'. *Addiction*, 98: 761–70.

Archer, J. (1988). *The behavioural biology of aggression*. Cambridge: Cambridge University Press.

Armstrong, D. (2004). A risky business? Research, policy, governmentality and youth offending. *Youth Justice*, 4: 100–17.

Australian Transport Safety Bureau (2002). *Driveway deaths: fatalities of young children in Australia as a result of low speed motor vehicle impacts*. Canberra, Australian Transport Safety Bureau. www.atsb.gov.au/publications/2002/driveway_deaths.aspx; accessed 18 April 2007.

Avorn, J., Chen, M., and Hartley, R. (1982). Scientific versus commercial sources of influence on the prescribing behavior of physicians. *American Journal of Medicine*, 73(1): 4–8.

Ball, J. C., Shaffer, J. W., and Nurco, D. N. (1983). The day-to-day criminality of heroin addicts in Baltimore: a study in the continuity of offence rates. *Drug and Alcohol Dependence*, 12(2): 119–42.

Barkley, R. A. (2006). *Attention-deficit hyperactivity disorder: a handbook for diagnosis and treatment*. 3rd edn, New York: Guilford Press.

Barnwell, S. V. S., Earleywine, M., and Gordis, E. B. (2006). Confirming alcohol-moderated links between cannabis use and dependence in a national sample. *Addictive Behaviors*, 31(9): 1695–9.

Baron, S. W. (2006). Street youth, strain theory, and crime. *Journal of Criminal Justice*, 34(2): 209–23.

Barr, A. (1995). *Drink: an informal social history*. London: Bantam Press.

Bass, U. F., Brown, B. S., and Dupont, R. L. (1972). Use of heroin by an offender population: report over time. *Corrective Psychiatry and Journal of Social Therapy*, 18(4): 24–30.

Bateson, G. (1971). The cybernetics of self: a theory of alcoholism. *Psychiatry*, 34: 1–18.

Bauman, Z. (2006). *Liquid fear*. Cambridge: Polity.

Bean, P. (1971). Social aspects of drug abuse: study of London drug offenders. *Journal of Criminal Law, Criminology and Police Studies*, 62(1): 80–6.

Bean, P. (2004). *Drugs and crime*. 2nd edn, Cullompton, Devon: Willan.

Bearre, L., Sturt, P., Bruce, G., and Jones, B. T. (2007). Heroin-related attentional bias and monthly frequency of heroin use are positively associated in attenders of a harm reduction service. *Addictive Behaviors*, 32(4): 784–92.

Beck, A. T., Wright, F. D., Newman, C. F., and Liese, B. S. (1993) *Cognitive therapy of substance abuse*. New York: Guilford Press.

Beck, U. (1992). *Risk society: towards a new modernity*. London: Sage.

Becker, H. (1953). Becoming a marihuana user. *American Journal of Sociology*, 59: 235–42.

Beckett, K., Nyrop, K., Pfingst, L., and Bowen, M. (2005). Drug use, drug possession arrests, and the question of race: lessons from Seattle. *Social Problems*, 52(3): 419–41.

Bee, H., and Boyd, D. (2005). *Lifespan development*. 4th rev. edn, London: Allyn & Bacon.

Behr, E. (1996). *Prohibition: thirteen years that changed America*. New York: Arcade.

Bennett, T., and Holloway, K. (2005a). *Understanding drugs, alcohol and crime*. London: McGraw-Hill.

Bennett, T., and Holloway, K. (2005b). Disaggregating the relationship between drug misuse and crime. *Australian and New Zealand Journal of Criminology*, 38: 102–21.

Bennetto, J. (2007). Police accused of brutality after officer beat woman during arrest at nightclub. *The Independent*, 8 March. http://news.independent.co.uk/uk/crime/article2338652.ece

Berk, M., and Janet, M. L. (1999). Evidence-based psychiatric practice: doctrine or trap? *Journal of Evaluation in Clinical Practice*, 5(2): 149–52.

Bhaskar, R. (1997). *A realist theory of science*. London: Verso.

Biernacki, P. (1986). *Pathways from addiction: recovery without treatment*. Philadelphia: Temple University Press.

Bioanalytical Systems (2007). *The pharmaceutical industry*. www.bioanalytical.com/info/calendar/99/index.htm; accessed 15 May 2007.

Blair, T. (2006). Foreword to *Pharmaceutical Industry Competitiveness Task Force*. www.advisorybodies.doh.gov.uk/pictf/index.htm; accessed 15 May 2007.

Blocker, J. S. (2006). Did prohibition really work? Alcohol prohibition as a public health innovation. *American Journal of Public Health*, 96(2): 233–43.

Blum, R. H., et al. (1970). *Society and drugs: social and cultural observations*. San Francisco: Jossey-Bass, ch. 11.

Blunkett, D. (2002). Foreword to *Updated drug strategy*. London: Crown Office.

Borio, G. (2007). *The tobacco timeline*. www.tobacco.org/History/Tobacco_History.html; accessed 10 October 2007.

Bourgois, P. (1995). *In search of respect: selling crack in El Barrio*. Cambridge: Cambridge University Press.

Boussel, P., Bonnemain, H., and Bove, R. (1983). *History of pharmacy and the pharmaceutical industry*. Paris: Asklepios.

Bowlby, J. ([1963] 1997). *Attachment and loss*. London: Pimlico.

Bowling, B. (1999). The rise and fall of New York murder: zero tolerance or crack's decline? *British Journal of Criminology*, 39: 531–54.

Braithwaite, J. (1984). *Corporate crime in the pharmaceutical industry*. London: Routledge & Kegan Paul.

Branch, C. W. (1997). *Clinical interventions with gang adolescents and their families*. Boulder, CO: Westview Press.

Brand, S., and Price, R. (2000). *The economic and social costs of crime.* Home Office Research Study 217. London: Home Office.

Bressler, L. R., Geraci, M. C., and Schatz, B. S. (1991). Misperceptions and inadequate pain management in cancer patients. *DIPC – The Annals of Pharmacotherapy*, 25(11): 1225–30.

Bright, S., and Boy George (1995). *Take it like a man: the autobiography of Boy George.* London: Pan.

Brook, J. S., Whiteman, M. M., and Finch, S. (1992). Childhood aggression, adolescent delinquency and drug-use: a longitudinal study. *Journal of Genetic Psychology*, 153(4): 369–83.

Brotchie, J., Finch, E., Marsden, J., and Waller, G. (2003). Impulsiveness and psychopathology among substance-abusing offenders on Drug Treatment and Testing Orders. *Journal of Forensic Psychiatry and Psychology*, 14(2): 266–79.

Bühler, C., and Massarik, F. (eds) (1968). *The course of human development.* New York: Springer.

Burke, B. L., Arkowitz, H., and Menchola, M. (2003). The efficacy of motivational interviewing: a meta-analysis of controlled clinical trials. *Journal of Consulting and Clinical Psychology*, 71(5): 843–61.

Burnham, G., Lafta, R., Doocy, S., and Roberts, L. (2006). Mortality after the 2003 invasion of Iraq: a cross-sectional cluster sample survey. *The Lancet*, 368(9545): 1421–8.

Burns, E. (2004). *The spirits of America: a social history of alcohol.* Philadelphia: Temple University Press.

Burr, A. (1987). Chasing the dragon: heroin misuse, delinquency and crime in the context of South London culture. *British Journal of Criminology*, 27(4): 333–57.

Burroughs, W. S. (1977). *Junky.* Harmondsworth: Penguin.

Busfield, J. (2006). Men, women and madness: understanding gender and mental disorder. London: Palgrave.

Cabinet Office (2003). *Alcohol misuse: how much does it cost?* www.pm. gov.uk/files/pdf/econ.pdf#search=%22economic%20and%20social%20c osts%20of%20alcohol%22; accessed 10 October 2006.

Carpenter, C., Glassner, B., Johnson, B. D., and Loughlin, J. (1988). *Kids, drugs and crime.* Lexington, MA: Lexington Books.

Carr, A. (1999). *The handbook of child and adolescent clinical psychology.* London: Routledge.

Carr, A. (2000). *Family therapy: concepts, process and practice.* Chichester: Wiley.

Carroll, A., Hemingway, F., Bower, J., Ashman, A., Houghton, S., and Durkin, K. (2006). Impulsivity in juvenile delinquency: differences among early-onset, late-onset, and non-offenders. *Journal of Youth and Adolescence*, 35(4): 519–29.

Caspi, A., Moffitt, T. E., Cannon, M., McClay, J., Murray, R., Harrington, H., et al. (2005). Moderation of the effect of adolescent-onset cannabis use on adult psychosis by a functional polymorphism in the catechol-O-methyltransferase gene: longitudinal evidence of a gene x environment interaction. *Biological Psychiatry*, 57(10): 1117–27.

Castells, M. (1996) *The rise of the network society*. Oxford: Blackwell.

Castells, M. (1998). *End of millennium*. Oxford: Blackwell.

Castells, M. (2002). *The internet galaxy: reflections on the internet, business and society*. Oxford: Oxford University Press.

Cave, J., and Godfrey, C. (2005). *Economics of addiction and drugs*. www. foresight.gov.uk/Previous_Projects/Brain_Science_Addiction_and_Drugs/ Reports_and_Publications/ScienceReviews/Economics.pdf; accessed 10 October 2006.

Centre for Science in the Public Interest (2007). Under the influence: a compilation of alcoholic-beverage industry political contributions to members of the appropriations committee of the U.S. House of Representatives, 1997–1999. Washington, DC: Centre for Science in the Public Interest.

Chambraud, C. (2005). Révélations sur le transit via l'Europe de prisonniers aux mains des services secrets américains. Des pays européens accusés de collusion avec la CIA. www.lemonde.fr/cgi-bin/ACHATS/acheter.cgi? offre=ARCHIVESandtype_item=ART_ARCH_30Jandobjet_id=923466

Chamlin, M. B., and Cochrane, J. K. (2005). Ascribed economic inequality and homicide among modern societies: toward the development of a cross-national theory. *Homicide Studies*, 9(1): 3–29.

Cichoz-Lach, H., Partycka, J., Nesina, I., Celinski, K., Slomka, M., and Wojcierowski, J. (2007). Alcohol dehydrogenase and aldehyde dehydrogenase gene polymorphism in alcohol liver cirrhosis and alcohol chronic pancreatitis among Polish individuals. *Scandinavian Journal of Gastroenterology*, 42(4): 493–8.

Clarke, J. B. (1999). Evidence-based practice: a retrograde step? The importance of pluralism in evidence generation for the practice of health care. *Journal of Clinical Nursing*, 8(1): 89–94.

Cloward, R. A., and Ohlin, L. E. (1961). *Delinquency and opportunity: a theory of delinquent gangs*. London: Routledge & Kegan Paul.

Coalition for Juvenile Justice (2006). *What are the implications of adolescent brain development for juvenile justice?* Washington, DC: Coalition for Juvenile Justice.

Cochran, S. D., Ackerman, D., Mays, V. M., and Ross, M. W. (2004). Prevalence of non-medical drug use and dependence among homosexually active men and women in the US population. *Addiction*, 99(8): 989–98.

Cohen, C., and Regan, T. (2001). *The animal rights debate*. New York: Rowman & Littlefield.

Cohen, J., Cohen, P., West, S. G., and Aiken, L. S. (2002). *Applied multiple regression/correlation analysis for the behavioral sciences*. New York: Erlbaum.

Cohen, S. (1988). *Against criminology*. New Brunswick, NJ: Transaction.

Collin, C., Davies, P., Mutiboko, I. K., and Ratcliffe, S. (2007). Randomized controlled trial of cannabis-based medicine in spasticity caused by multiple sclerosis. *European Journal of Neurology*, 14(3): 290–6.

Conway, K. P., Compton, W., Stinson, F. S., and Grant, B. F. (2006). Lifetime comorbidity of DSM-IV mood and anxiety disorders and specific drug use disorders: results from the national epidemiologic survey on alcohol and related conditions. *Journal of Clinical Psychiatry*, 67(2): 247–57.

Cook, C. C. H. (1988a). The Minnesota model in the management of drug and alcohol dependency: miracle, method or myth, 1: The philosophy and the program. *British Journal of Addiction*, 83(6): 625–34.

Cook, C. C. H. (1988b). The Minnesota model in the management of drug and alcohol dependency: miracle, method or myth, 2: Evidence and conclusions. *British Journal of Addiction*, 83(7): 735–48.

Cooke, D. J., Michie, C., Hart, S. D., and Clark, D. A. (2004). Reconstructing psychopathy: clarifying the significance of anti-social and socially deviant behavior in the diagnosis of psychopathic personality disorder. *Journal of Personality Disorders*, 18(4): 337–57.

Costa, P. T., and McCrae, R. R. (1997). Stability and change in personality assessment: the revised NEO personality inventory in the year 2000. *Journal of Personality Assessment*, 68(1): 86–94.

Cox, W. M., Fadardi, J. S., and Pothos, E. M. (2006). The addiction-stroop test: theoretical considerations and procedural recommendations. *Psychological Bulletin*, 132(3): 443–76.

Credit Action UK (2007). *Debt facts and figures*. www.creditaction. org.uk/debtstats.htm; accessed 19 April 2007.

Crow, S. M., and Hartman, S. J. (1992). Drugs in the workplace – overstating the problems and the cures. *Journal of Drug Issues*, 22: 923–37.

Curtis, R. (1998). The improbable transformation of inner-city neighborhoods: crime, violence, drugs, and youth in the 1990s. *Journal of Criminal Law and Criminology*, 88(4): 1233–76.

Dakof, G. A., Tejeda, M., and Liddle, H. A. (2001). Predictors of engagement in adolescent drug abuse treatment. *Journal of the American Academy of Child and Adolescent Psychiatry*, 40: 274–81.

Dalgarno, P., and Shewan, D. (2005). Reducing the risks of drug use: the case for set and setting. *Addiction Research and Theory*, 13: 259–65.

Dalla-Dea, H. R. F., de Miceli, D., and Formigoni, M. L. O. S. (2003). Effects of identification and usefulness of the lie scale of the drug use screening inventory in the assessment of adolescent drug use. *Drug and Alcohol Dependence*, 72: 215–23.

Davies, J. B. (1992). *The myth of addiction*. Reading, MA: Harwood Academic.

Davies, J. B. (1997). *Drugspeak*. Reading, MA: Harwood Academic.

Davies, N. (2007). Abuse and incompetence in fight against global warming. *The Guardian*, 2 June, p. 1. http://environment.guardian.co.uk/ climatechange/story/0,,2093835,00.html

Dawkins, R. (2007). *The God delusion*. London: Black Swan.

De Angelis, G. G., and Ross, E. (1978). Comparison of treatment effectiveness of non-addict and ex-addict professionals in an adolescent treatment program. *Drug and Alcohol Dependence*, 3(5): 319–29.

De Beyer, J., and Brigden, L. W. (eds) (2003). *Tobacco control policy: strategies, successes and setbacks*. New York: World Bank.

De Paula, R. S. (2004). What can we learn from psychoanalysis and prospective studies about chemically dependent patients? *International Journal of Psychoanalysis*, 85(2): 467–87.

De Winne, R., and Johnson, R. W. (1976). Extraversion–introversion: personality characteristics of drug-abusers. *Journal of Clinical Psychology*, 32: 744–6.

Deas, D., and Thomas, S. E. (2001). An overview of controlled studies of adolescent substance abuse treatment. *American Journal on Addictions*, 12: 178–89.

Dennis, M., Titus, J. C., Diamond, G., Donaldson, J., Godley, S. H., Tims, F. M., et al., and the CYT Steering Committee (2002). The Cannabis Youth Treatment (CYT) experiment: rationale, study design and analysis plans. *Addiction*, 97(1): 16–34.

Denton, B., and O'Malley, P. (1999). Gender, trust and business – women drug dealers in the illicit economy. *British Journal of Criminology*, 39: 513–30.

Department for Education and Skills (2005). *Trends in education and skills*. www.dfes.gov.uk/trends/index.cfm?fuseaction=home.showChartandcid=5andiid=34andchid=147; accessed 16 November 2005.

Department for Education and Skills (2006). *Total education spending as a proportion of GDP*. www.dfes.gov.uk/rsgateway/DB/TIM/m002002/edspendrev2006.pdf; accessed 23 April 2007.

Department for Work and Pensions (2007). *Social security benefit expenditure: by recipient group, 2001/02: Social Trends 33*. www.statistics.gov.uk/STATBASE/ssdataset.asp?vlnk=6474; accessed 23 April 2007.

Dignan, J. (2004). *Understanding victims and restorative justice*. Maidenhead: Open University Press.

Dijkgraaf, M. G. W., van der Zanden, B. P., De Borgie, C. A. J. M., Blanken, P., Van Ree, J. M., and van den Brink, W. (2005). Cost utility analysis of co-prescribed heroin compared with methadone maintenance treatment in heroin addicts in two randomised trials. *British Medical Journal*, 330: 1297.

Dishon, T., and Connell, A. (2006). Adolescents' resilience as a self-regulatory process: promising themes for linking intervention with developmental science. *Annals of the New York Academy of Science*, 1094: 125–38.

Ditton, J. (1979) *Part-time crime: an ethnography of fiddling and pilferage*. London: Macmillan.

Ditton, J., and Hammersley, R. (1996). *A very greedy drug: cocaine in context*. Reading, MA: Harwood Academic.

Donnelly, N., Hall, W., and Christie, P. (1995). The effects of partial decriminalisation of cannabis use in South Australia, 1985 to 1993. *Australian Journal of Public Health*, 19(3): 281–7.

Donnelly, N., Weatherburn, D., and Chilvers, M. (2004). The impact of the Australian heroin shortage on robbery in NSW. *Crime and Justice Statistics Bureau Brief*, March, New South Wales Bureau of Crime Statistics and Research.

Donohew, R. L., Hoyle, R. H., Clayton, R. R., Skinner, W. F., Colon, S. E., and Rice, R. E. (1999). Sensation seeking and drug use by adolescents and their friends: models for marijuana and alcohol. *Journal of Studies on Alcohol*, 60(5): 622–31.

Donohue, J. J., and Levitt, S. D. (2001). The impact of legalized abortion on crime. *Quarterly Journal of Economics*, 116(2): 379–420.

Doob, A. N., and Webster, C. M. (2003). Sentence severity and crime: accepting the null hypothesis. In M. Tonry (ed.), *Crime and justice: a review of research*, 30: pp. 143–95.

Douglas, M., and Wildavsky, A. (1983). *Risk and culture: an essay on the selection of technological and environmental dangers*. San Francisco: University of California Press.

Dowling, K., Storr, C. L., and Chilcoat, H. D. (2006). Potential influences on initiation and persistence of extramedical prescription pain reliever use in the US population. *Clinical Journal of Pain*, 22(9): 776–83.

Drakenberg, K., Nikoshkov, A., Horvath, M. C., Fagergren, P., Gharibyan, A., Saarelainen, K., Rahman, S., Nylander, I., Bakalkin, G., Rajs, J., Keller, E., and Hurd, Y. L. (2006). Mu opioid receptor A118G polymorphism in association with striatal opioid neuropeptide gene expression in heroin abusers. *Proceedings of the National Academy of Sciences of the United States of America*, 103: 7883–8.

Drucker, E., and Clear, A. (1999). Harm reduction in the home of the war on drugs: methadone and needle exchange in the USA. *Drug and Alcohol Review*, 18(1): 103–12.

Dudley, R. (2002). Evolutionary origins of human alcoholism in primate frugivory. *Quarterly Review of Biology*, 75(1): 3–15.

Duncan, A. E., Neuman, R. J., Kramer, J. R., Kuperman, S., Hesselbrock, V. M., and Bucholz, K. K. (2006). Lifetime psychiatric comorbidity of alcohol dependence and bulimia nervosa in women. *Drug and Alcohol Dependence*, 84(1): 122–32.

Dunn, C., Deroo, L., and Rivara, F. P. (2001). The use of brief interventions adapted from motivational interviewing across behavioral domains: a systematic review. *Addiction*, 96(12): 1725–42.

Dyer, O. (2006). GMC finds three doctors guilty of irresponsible prescribing to addicts. *British Medical Journal*, 332: 747.

Eades, C. (2006). Young people and knife carrying: What to do? *Criminal Justice Matters*, 231: 10–13.

Eccles, J. S., and Gootman, J. A. (eds) (2002). *Community programs to promote youth development*. Washington, DC: National Academy Press.

Edwards, G., and Gross, M. M. (1976). Alcohol dependence: provisional description of a clinical syndrome. *British Medical Journal*, 295: 1058–61.

Eiser, J. R., Eiser, C., Gammage, P., and Morgan, M. (1989). Health locus of control and health beliefs in relation to adolescent smoking. *British Journal of Addiction*, 84(9): 1059–65.

Elliott, D. S., Huizinga, D., and Ageton, S. S. (1985). *Explaining delinquency and drug use*. London: Sage.

Elliott, L., Orr, L., Watson, L., and Jackson, A. (2003). *Drug treatment services for young people: a systematic review of effectiveness and the legal framework*. Edinburgh: Scottish Executive Effective Interventions Unit.

Engvall, J. (2006). The state under siege: the drug trade and organised crime in Tajikistan. *Europe–Asia Studies*, 58(6): 827–54.

Ennett, S. T., Bauman, K. E., Pemberton, M., et al. (2001). Mediation in a family-directed program for prevention of adolescent tobacco and alcohol use. *Preventative Medicine*, 33(4): 333–46.

Erickson, E. (1968). *Identity, youth and crisis*. London: Faber & Faber.

Ericson, R. (2006). *Crime in an insecure world*. Cambridge: Polity.

Ermisch, J., and Francesconi, M. (2001). *The effects of parents' employment on children's lives*. London: Joseph Rowntree Foundation, Family Policy Studies Centre.

European Sponsorship Association (2006). *ESA helps head off alcohol sponsorship ban*. www.sponsorship.org/esaPressDetail.asp?id=172; accessed 15 May 2007.

Evans, E. P. (1987). *The criminal prosecution and capital punishment of animals: the lost history of Europe's animal trials*. London: Faber & Faber.

Everitt, B. J., Dickinson, A., and Robbins, T. W. (2001). The neuropsychological basis of addictive behaviour. *Brain Research Reviews*, 36(2–3) SI: 129–38.

Fagan, A. A. (2005). The relationship between adolescent physical abuse and criminal offending: support for an enduring and generalized cycle of violence. *Journal of Family Violence*, 20(5): 279–90.

Falk, D. E., Yi, H. Y., and Hiller-Sturmhofel, S. (2006). An epidemiologic analysis of co-occurring alcohol and tobacco use and disorders – findings from the National Epidemiologic Survey on Alcohol and Related Conditions. *Alcohol Health and Research*, 29(3): 162–71.

Farrall, S., Bannister, J., Ditton, J., and Gilchrist, E. (1997). Questioning the measurement of the 'fear of crime' – findings from a major methodological study. *British Journal of Criminology*, 37(4): 658–79.

Farrington, D. P (1995). The development of offending and antisocial behaviour from childhood: key findings from the Cambridge Study in Delinquent Development. *Journal of Child Psychology and Psychiatry*, 36: 929–64.

Fazel, S., and Danesh, J. (2002). Serious mental disorder in 23,000 prisoners: a systematic review of 62 surveys. *The Lancet*, 359(9306): 545–50.

Fazel, S., Bains, P., and Doll, H. (2006). Substance abuse and dependence in prisoners: a systematic review. *Addiction*, 101(2): 181–91.

Feldman, E. A., and Bayer, R. (eds) (2004). *Unfiltered: conflicts over tobacco policy and public health*. Cambridge, MA: Harvard University Press.

Fergusson, D. M., Boden, J. M., and Horwood, L. J. (2006). Cannabis use and other illicit drug use: testing the cannabis gateway hypothesis. *Addiction*, 101(4): 556–69.

Field, M., Mogg, K., and Bradley, B. P. (2004). Cognitive bias and drug craving in recreational cannabis users. *Drug and Alcohol Dependence*, 74(1): 105–11.

Finagarette, H. (1988). *Heavy drinking: the myth of alcoholism as a disease.* Berkeley: University of California Press.

Fleming, C. (1998). *High concept: Don Simpson and the Hollywood culture of success.* London: Bloomsbury.

Foggo, D. (2007). Phone cancer report 'buried'. *Sunday Times,* 15 April. www.timesonline.co.uk/tol/life_and_style/health/article1655012.ece?p; accessed 1 June 2007.

Fong, R. S. (1990). The organizational structure of prison gangs – a Texas case-study. *Federal Probation,* 54(1): 36–43.

Foote, C. L., and Goetz, C. F. (2005). *Testing economic hypotheses with state-level data: a comment on Donohue and Levitt (2001).* www.bos.frb.org/economic/wp/wp 2005/wp 0515.pdf

Ford, J. M., and Beveridge, A. A. (2006). Neighborhood crime victimization, drug use and drug sales: results from the 'Fighting back' evaluation. *Journal of Drug Issues,* 36(2): 393–416.

Forsyth, A. J. M. (2007). From illegal leisure to licensed disorder: rave culture as marketing opportunity for the licensed trade (drinks) industry. Glasgow: Glasgow Caledonian University.

Forsyth, A. J. M., Cloonan, M., and Barr, J. (2005). *Factors associated with alcohol-related problems with licensed premises: report to Greater Glasgow NHS Board.* http://library.nhsgg.org.uk/mediaAssets/library/nhsgg_pilp_main_report_2005–02.pdf; accessed 11 September 2007.

Forsyth, A. J. M., Hammersley, R., Lavelle, T. L., and Murray, K. (1992). Geographical aspects of scoring illegal drugs. *British Journal of Criminology,* 32: 292–309.

Foucault, M. (1980). *Power/knowledge: selected interviews and other writings 1972–77.* New York: Pantheon.

Foy, D. W., Ruzek, J. I., Glynn, S. M., Riney, S. J., and Gusman, F. D. (2002). Trauma focus group therapy for combat-related PTSD: an update. *Journal of Clinical Psychology,* 58(8): 907–18.

Freshwater, D., and Rolfe, G. (2004). *Deconstructing evidence based practice.* Abingdon: Routledge.

Friendship, C., Blud, L., Erikson, M., Travers, R., and Thornton, D. (2003). Cognitive-behavioural treatment for imprisoned offenders: an evaluation of HM Prison Service's cognitive skills programmes. *Legal and Criminological Psychology,* 8(1): 103–14.

Frisher, M., Crome, I., Green, C., Willoughby, R., Smith, A., and Harris, P. (2005). Individual and population risk of drug use among adolescents attending an English Youth Offending Team: an epidemiological approach. *Journal of Forensic Psychiatry and Psychology,* 16(1): 11–23.

Füredi, F. (2006). *Culture of fear: risk-taking and the morality of low expectation.* 2nd rev. edn, London: Continuum.

Galbraith, J. K. (1985). *The anatomy of power.* London: Corgi.

Gallagher, P., Barry, P., and O'Mahony, D. (2007). Inappropriate prescribing in the elderly. *Journal of Clinical Pharmacy and Therapeutics,* 32(2): 113–21.

Galloway, J., Forsyth, A. J. M., and Shewan, D. (2007). *Young people's street drinking behaviour: investigating the influence of marketing and subculture.* Glasgow: Glasgow Centre for the Study of Violence.

Ghodse, H. (2002). *Drugs and addictive behaviour: a guide to treatment.* Cambridge: Cambridge University Press.

Giddens, A. (1991). *The consequences of modernity.* Cambridge: Polity.

Gilhooly, M. L. M. (2005). Reduced drinking with age: is it normal? *Addiction Research and Theory,* 13(3): 267–80.

Gilvarry, E. (ed.) (2001). *The substance of young needs.* London: Health Advisory Service/Home Office.

Glaister, D. (2005). Conservative US braced for drugs and the suburbs. *The Guardian,* 9 August. www.guardian.co.uk/international/story/0,,1545195,00.html; accessed 15 June 2007.

globalissues.org (2007). Poverty facts and stats. www.globalissues.org/TradeRelated/Facts.asp; accessed 17 April 2007.

Godfrey, C., Eaton, G., McDougall, C., and Culyer, A. (2002). *The economic and social costs of class A drug use in England and Wales, 2000.* Home Office Research Study 249. London: Home Office.

Golub, A., and Johnson, B. D. (1994). The shifting importance of alcohol and marijuana as gateway substances among serious drug-abusers. *Journal of Studies on Alcohol,* 55: 607–14.

Golub, A. L., and Johnson, B. D. (1999). Cohort changes in illegal drug use among arrestees in Manhattan: from the heroin injection generation to the blunts generation. *Substance Use and Misuse,* 34: 1733–63.

Golub, A. L., Johnson, B. D., and Dunlap, E. (2005). Subcultural evolution and illicit drug use. *Addiction Research and Theory,* 13: 217–29.

Goodman, J., Lovejoy, P. E., and Sherratt, A. (2007). Consuming habits: global and historical perspectives on how cultures define drugs. London: Routledge.

Gordon, A. M. (1973). Patterns of delinquency in drug addiction. *British Journal of Psychiatry,* 122(567): 205–10.

Gorski, T. T. (2000). *Relapse prevention counselling workbook: managing high-risk situations.* Independence, MO: Herald Publishing House.

Gossop, M., Marsden, J., Stewart, D., and Rolfe, A. (2000). Reductions in acquisitive crime and drug use after treatment of addiction problems: 1-year follow-up outcomes. *Drug and Alcohol Dependence,* 58(1–2): 165–72.

Gottheil, E., McLellan, A. T., and Druley, K. A. (1992). Length of stay, patient severity and treatment outcome: sample data from the field of alcoholism. *Journal of Studies on Alcohol,* 53(1): 69–75.

Graham, H. L. (2004). *Cognitive-behavioural integrated treatment (C-BIT): a treatment manual for substance misuse in people with severe mental health problems.* Chichester: Wiley.

Granfield, R. (2005). Alcohol use in college: limitations on the transformation of social norms. *Addiction Research and Theory,* 13(3): 281–92.

Granfield, R., and Cloud, W. (1999). *Coming clean: overcoming addiction without treatment.* New York: New York University Press.

Grob, C. S. (2000). Deconstructing ecstasy: the politics of MDMA research. *Addiction Research*, 8: 549–88.

Gros-Louis, J., Perry, S., and Manson, J. H. (2003). Violent coalitionary attacks and intraspecific killing in wild white-faced capuchin monkeys (Cebus capucinus). *Primates*, 44: 341–6.

Guyatt, G. (1992). Evidence-based medicine – a new approach to teaching the practice of medicine. *Journal of the American Medical Association*, 268(17): 2420–5.

Hackford, T. (2004). *Ray*. USA: Anvil Films.

Hagan, J., and Foster, H. (2006). Profiles of punishment and privilege: secret and disputed deviance during the racialized transition to American adulthood. *Crime, Law and Social Change*, 46(1–2): 65–85.

Haile, C. N., Kosten, T. R., and Kosten, T. A. (2007). Genetics of dopamine and its contribution to cocaine addiction. *Behavior Genetics*, 37: 119–45.

Hall, W. D., Ross, J. E., Lynskey, M. T., Law, M. G., and Degenhardt, L. J. (2000). How many dependent heroin users are there in Australia? *Medical Journal of Australia*, 173(10): 528–31.

Hammersley, R. (2005). Unthinking drinking. *Scottish Journal of Criminal Justice Studies*, 11: 64–79.

Hammersley, R. H., and Ditton, J. (1994). Cocaine careers amongst Scottish users. *Addiction Research*, 2: 51–69.

Hammersley, R., and Leon, V. (2006). Patterns of cannabis use and positive and negative experiences of use. *Addiction Research and Theory*, 14(4): 189–205.

Hammersley, R., and Pearl, S. (1997). Temazepam misuse, violence and disorder. *Addiction Research*, 5: 213–22.

Hammersley, R., and Reid, M. (2002). Why the pervasive addiction myth is still believed. *Addiction Research and Theory*, 10: 7–30.

Hammersley, R., Jenkins, R., and Reid, M. (2001). Cannabis use and social identity. *Addiction Research and Theory*, 9: 133–50.

Hammersley, R., Kahn, F., and Ditton, J. (2002). *Ecstasy and the rise of the chemical generation*. Reading, MA: Harwood Academic.

Hammersley, R., Lavelle, T. L., and Forsyth, A. J. M. (1990). Buprenorphine and temazepam – abuse. *British Journal of Addiction*, 85: 301–3.

Hammersley, R., Marsland, L., and Reid, M. (2003). *Substance use by young offenders: the impact of the normalization of drug use in the early years of the 21st century*. Home Office Research Study 261. London: Home Office Research and Statistics Directorate.

Hammersley, R., Reid, M., and Minkes, J. (2006). Treating young offenders' substance use problems: systemic, methodological and conceptual issues. *Journal of Educational and Child Psychology*, 23: 41–53.

Hammersley, R. H., Forsyth, A. J. M., Morrison, V. L., and Davies, J. B. (1989). The relationship between crime and opioid use. *British Journal of Addiction*, 84: 1029–43.

Hammersley, R., Minkes, J., Reid, M., Oliver, A., Genova, A., and Raynor, P. (2004). *Drug and alcohol projects for young offenders: the evaluation of development fund projects funded by the Youth Justice Board*. London: Youth Justice Board.

Hansard (2005). *Written answers 4th July: Home Department, cost of imprisonment*. www.theyworkforyou.com/wrans/?id=2005–07–04.4540.h; accessed 16 October 2006.

Hanson, D. J. (2007). *Drug abuse resistance education: the effectiveness of DARE*. www.alcoholfacts.org/DARE.html; accessed 28 March 2007.

Hao, W., Chen, H. H., and Su, S. H. (2005). China: alcohol today. *Addiction*, 100(6): 737–41.

Harré, R. (1970). *The principles of scientific thinking*. Chicago: University of Chicago Press.

Hasin, D., Van Rossem, R., McCloud, S., and Endicott, J. (1997). Alcohol dependence and abuse diagnoses: validity in community sample heavy drinkers. *Alcoholism – Clinical and Experimental Research*, 21(2): 213–19.

Hawkins, J. D., Catalano, R. F., and Miller, J. Y. (1992). Risk and protective factors for alcohol and other drug problems in adolescence and early adulthood: implications for substance abuse prevention. *Psychological Bulletin*, 112: 64–105.

Heather, N., and Richmond, R. (1992). Research into brief interventions for excessive alcohol consumers and cigarette smokers in Australia. *Journal of Drug Issues*, 22(3): 641–60.

Heather, N., and Robertson, I. (1981). *Controlled drinking*. London: Methuen.

Heubner, A. M., and Garrod, A. C. (1993). Moral reasoning among Tibetan monks: a study of Buddhist adolescents and young adults in Nepal. *Journal of Cross-cultural Psychology*, 24(2): 167–85.

Heumann, M., and Cassak, L. (2001). Profiles in justice? Police discretion, symbolic assailants, and stereotyping. *Rutgers Law Review*, 53(4): 911–78.

Hills, J., and Stewart, K. (2005). *A more equal society? New Labour, poverty, inequality and exclusion*. Cambridge: Polity.

Hingson, R. W., Heeren, T., and Winter, M. R. (2006). Age of alcohol-dependence onset: associations with severity of dependence and seeking treatment. *Pediatrics*, 118(3): E755–E763.

Hittner, J. B., and Swickert, R. (2006). Sensation seeking and alcohol use: a meta-analytic review. *Addictive Behaviors*, 1383–401.

Hobbes, T. (1660). *Leviathan*. http://oregonstate.edu/instruct/phl302/texts/hobbes/leviathan-c.html#CHAPTERXIII.

Holdaway, S. (1997). Constructing and sustaining 'race' within the police workforce. *British Journal of Sociology*, 48(1): 19–34.

Holmes, T. H., and Rahe, R. H. (1967). The social readjustment rating scales. *Journal of Psychosomatic Research*, 11: 213–18.

Home Office (1999). www.nationalarchives.gov.uk/ero/browse.aspx?id=3120andlevel=5; accessed 10 April 2007.

Home Office (2003). *Working with offenders*. www.crimereduction.gov.uk/workingoffenders/workingoffenders 3.htm; accessed 28 May 2007.

Home Office (2007). *Our objectives and values.* www.homeoffice.gov.uk/ about-us/purpose-and-aims/; accessed 24 November 2007.

House of Commons Health Committee (2005). *The influence of the pharmaceutical industry: fourth report of session 2004–05.* London: HMSO. www. parliament.the-stationery-office.co.uk/pa/cm200405/cmselect/cmhealth/ 42/42.pdf; accessed 15 May 2007.

Howard, M., McMillen, C., Nower, L., Elze, D., Edmond, T., and Bricout, J. (2002). Denial in addiction: toward an integrated stage and process model – qualitative findings. *Journal of Psychoactive Drugs,* 34(4): 371–82.

Human Rights Watch (1998). *Shielded from justice: police brutality and accountability in the United States.* www.hrw.org/reports98/police/uspo14.htm; accessed 1 June 2007.

Hunt, L. G., and Chambers, C. D. (1976). *The heroin epidemics: a study of heroin use in the United States, 1965–75.* New York: Spectrum.

Husak, D. N., and De Marneffe, P. (2005). *The legalization of drugs (for and against).* Cambridge: Cambridge University Press.

Husserl, E. (1977). *Cartesian meditations: an introduction to phenomenology.* New York: Springer.

Ihlanfeldt, K. R. (2007). Neighborhood drug crime and young males' job accessibility. *Review of Economics and Statistics,* 89(1): 151–64.

Inciardi, J. A. (1979). Heroin use and street crime. *Crime and Delinquency,* 25(3): 335–46.

Inciardi, J. A., Martin, S. S., and Butzin, C. A. (2004). Five-year outcomes of therapeutic community treatment of drug-involved offenders after release from prison. *Crime and Delinquency,* 50(1): 88–107.

Index mundi (2007). *Iraq – death rate.* www.indexmundi.com/g/g. aspx?c=izandv=26; accessed 1 June 2007.

Insight Security (2007). *Knife crime facts – UK.* www.insight-security. com/facts-knife-crime-stats.htm; accessed 1 June 2007.

Institute on Alcohol Studies (2007). *Alcohol and advertising.* www.ias.org. uk/resources/factsheets/advertising.pdf; accessed 15 May 2007.

Jane-Llopis, E., and Matytsina, I. (2006). Mental health and alcohol, drugs and tobacco: a review of the comorbidity between mental disorders and the use of alcohol, tobacco and illicit drugs. *Drug and Alcohol Review,* 25(6): 515–36.

Jarvis, G., and Parker, H. (1989). Young heroin users and crime: how do the new users finance their habits. *British Journal of Criminology,* 29(2): 175–85.

Jarvis, T. J., Tebbutt, J., Mattick, R. P., and Shand, F. (2005). *Treatment approaches for alcohol and drug dependence.* Chichester: Wiley.

Jenkins, R. (1996). *Social identity.* London: Routledge.

Jessor, R., and Jessor, S. L. (1977). The social-psychological framework. In R. Jessor and S. L. Jessor (eds), *Problem behavior and psychosocial development: a longitudinal study of youth.* New York: Academic Press, pp. 17–42.

Jimpix (2007). *Terrorism in context*. www.jimpix.co.uk/words/terror.asp; accessed 10 February 2007.

Johansson, L. (1998) Invisible chains – Sweden tests electronic tagging project for convicts. *UNESCO Courier.* June.

Johnson, B. D. (1973). *Marihuana users and drug subcultures*. New York: Wiley.

Johnson, B. D., Goldstein, P. J., Preble, E., Schmeidler, J., Liption, D. S., Spunt, B., and Miller, T. (1985). *Taking care of business: the economics of crime by heroin abusers*. Lexington, MA: Lexington Books.

Johnson, H., Brock, A., Griffiths, C., and Rooney, C. (2005). Mortality from suicide and drug-related poisoning by day of the week in England and Wales, 1993–2002. *Health Statistics Quarterly*, 27: 13–16. www.statistics.gov.uk/articles/hsq/HSQ27mortality.pdf

Jones, B. T., Corbin, W., and Fromme, K. (2001). A review of expectancy theory and alcohol consumption. *Addiction*, 96: 55–70.

Joseph Rowntree Foundation (2005). Policies towards poverty, inequality and exclusion since 1997. *Findings*, January. www.jrf.org.uk/knowledge/findings/socialpolicy/0015.asp

Kalayasiri, R., Sughondhabirom, A., Gueorguieva, R., Coric, V., Lynch, W. J., Morgan, P. T., Cubells, J. F., and Malison, R. T. (2006). Self-reported paranoia during laboratory 'binge' cocaine self-administration in humans. *Pharmacology Biochemistry and Behavior*, 83(2): 249–56.

Kampman, K. M., Pettinati, H. M., Volpicelli, J. R., Oslin, D. M., Lipkin, C., Sparkman, T., and O'Brien, C. P. (2004). Cocaine dependence severity predicts outcome in outpatient detoxification from cocaine and alcohol. *American Journal on Addictions*, 13(1): 74–82.

Kandel, D., Simchafagan, O., and Davies, M. (1986). Risk-factors for delinquency and illicit drug-use from adolescence to young adulthood. *Journal of Drug Issues*, 16(1): 67–90.

Kandel, D. B., Yamaguchi, K., and Chen, K. (1992). Stages of progression in drug involvement from adolescence to adulthood: further evidence for the gateway theory. *Journal of Studies on Alcohol*, 53(5): 447–57.

Karstedt, S., and Farrall, S. (2006). The moral economy of everyday crime: markets, consumers and citizens. *British Journal of Criminology*, 46: 1011–36.

Kaufman, E., and Kaufman, P. (1991). *Family therapy of drug and alcohol abuse*. 2nd edn, London: Allyn & Bacon.

Keene, J., and Raynor, P. (1993). Addiction as a 'soul sickness': the influence of client and therapist beliefs. *Addiction Research*, 1: 77–87.

Kinlock, P. (1991). Does Phencyclidine (PCP) use increase violent crime? *Journal of Drug Issues*, 21: 795–816.

Klein, N. (2001). *No logo*. London: Flamingo.

Knife Crime Consultation Team (2005). *Tackling knife crime – a consultation: executive summary*. Edinburgh: Scottish Executive. www.scotland.gov.uk/Publications/2005/06/27110255/02566; accessed 1 June 2007.

Knust, S., and Stewart, A. L. (2002). Risk-taking behaviour and criminal offending: an investigation of sensation seeking and the Eysenck personality questionnaire. *International Journal of Offender Therapy and Comparative Criminology*, 46(5): 586–602.

Kohlberg, L. (1969). *Stages in the development of moral thought and action.* New York: Holt, Reinhart & Winston.

Kraus, L., Augustin, R., Kunz-Ebrecht, S., and Orth, B. (2007). Drug use patterns and drug-related disorders of cocaine users in a sample of the general population in Germany. *European Addiction Research*, 13: 116–25.

Kuziemko, Y., and Levitt, S. D. (2004). An empirical analysis of imprisoning drug offenders. *Journal of Public Economics*, 88(9–10): 2043–66.

Labov, W. (2006). *The social stratification of English in New York City.* 2nd rev. edn, Cambridge: Cambridge University Press.

Lamb, H. R., and Weinberger, L. E. (1998). Persons with severe mental illness in jails and prisons: a review. *Psychiatric Services*, 49(4): 483–92.

Lang, E., Engelander, M., and Brooke, T. (2000). Report of an integrated brief intervention with self-defined problem cannabis users. *Journal of Substance Abuse Treatment*, 19(2): 111–16.

Laws, D. R. (1999). Relapse prevention – the state of the art. *Journal of Interpersonal Violence*, 14: 285–302.

Lawton, B. A., Taylor, R. B., and Luongo, A. J. (2005). Police officers on drug corners in Philadelphia, drug crime, and violent crime: intended, diffusion, and displacement impacts. *Justice Quarterly*, 22(4): 427–51.

Lees, J., Manning, N., and Rawlings, B. (2004). A culture of enquiry: research evidence and the therapeutic community. *Psychiatric Quarterly*, 75(3): 279–94.

Lenzenweger, M. F., Johnson, M. D., and Willett, J. B. (2004). Individual growth curve analysis illuminates stability and change in personality disorder features – the longitudinal study of personality disorders. *Archives of General Psychiatry*, 61(10): 1015–24.

Lenzenweger, M. F., Loranger, A. W., Korfine, L., and Neff, C. (1997). Detecting personality disorders in a nonclinical population – application of a 2-stage procedure for case identification. *Archives of General Psychiatry*, 54(4): 345–51.

Levi, P. ([1947] 1991). *If this is man/The truce.* London: Abacus.

Levinson, D. J. (1990). A theory of life structure development in adulthood. In C. N. Alexander and E. J. Langer (eds), *Higher states of human development.* New York: Oxford University Press.

Levitt, S. D., and Dubner, S. J. (2005). *Freakonomics: a rogue economist explores the hidden side of everything.* London: Allen Lane.

Levy, G. (2007). The Duke of Westminister: so rich and so very foolish. *Daily Mail*, 12 February. www.dailymail.co.uk/pages/live/articles/news/news. html?in_article_id=435511andin_page_id=1770; accessed 18 April 2007.

Liddle, H. A., and Dakof, G. A. (1995). Family-based treatment for adolescent drug use: state of the science. In E. Rahdert and D.

Czechowicz (eds), *Adolescent drug abuse: clinical assessment and therapeutic interventions*. Rockville, MD: National Institute on Drug Abuse, pp. 218–54.

Lightfoot, L. O. (2000). *Programming for offenders with substance abuse and dependence problems*. Ottawa: Correctional Service of Canada. www.csc-scc.gc.ca/text/rsrch/compendium/2000/chap_14_e.shtml; accessed 23 May 2007.

Lightfoot, L. O., and Hodgins, D. (1988). A survey of alcohol and drug problems in incarcerated offenders. *International Journal of the Addictions*, 23(7): 687–706.

Lijphart, A. (1999). *Patterns of democracy: government forms and performance in thirty-six countries*. New Haven, CT: Yale University Press.

Linehan, M. M. (1993). *Cognitive-behavioral treatment of borderline personality disorder*. New York: Guilford Press.

Ling, P. M., and Glantz, S. A. (2002). Using tobacco-industry marketing research to design more effective tobacco-control campaigns. *Journal of the American Medical Association*, 287(22): 2983–9.

Linszen, D. H., De Haan, L., Dingemans, P., Van Bruggen, M., Hofstra, N., Van Engelsdorp, H., and ter Smitten, M. (2003). Treatment reluctance in first episode schizophrenia: lack of insight, non-compliance and cannabis abuse predict bad outcome after eighteen months intervention. *Schizophrenia Research*, 60: 325.

Lodico, M. A., Gruber, E., and DiClemente, R. J. (1996). Childhood sexual abuse and coercive sex among school-based adolescents in a midwestern state. *Journal of Adolescent Health*, 18: 211–17.

Logan, T. K., Hoyt, W. H., McCollister, K. E., French, M. T., Leukefeld, C., and Minton, L. (2004). Economic evaluation of drug court: methodology, results and policy implications. *Evaluation and Program Planning*, 27: 381–96.

Lowman, C. (ed.) (2004). Research perspectives on treatment for adolescent alcohol use disorders. *Addiction*, 99: supp. 2.

Luxembourg Income Study (2000). *Relative poverty rates for the total population, children and the elderly*. www.lisproject.org/keyfigures/povertytable.htm; accessed 23 April 2007.

McAdams, D. (1993). *The stories we live by: personal myths and the making of the self*. New York: Morrow.

MacAndrew, C., and Edgerton, R. B. (1969). *Drunken comportment: a social explanation*. Chicago: Aldine.

McCambridge, J., and Strang, J. (2003). Development of a structured generic drug intervention model for public health purposes: a brief application of motivational interviewing with young people. *Drug and Alcohol Review*, 22(4): 391–9.

McCormick, R. A., Dowd, E. T., Quirk, S., and Zegarra, J. H. (1998). The relationship of NEO-PI performance to coping styles, patterns of use, and triggers for use among substance abusers. *Addictive Behaviors*, 23(4): 497–507.

MacDonald, J. M. (2002). The effectiveness of community policing in reducing urban violence. *Crime and Delinquency*, 48(4): 592–618.

MacDonald, R., Shildrick, T., Webster, C., and Simpson, D. (2005). Growing up in poor neighbourhoods: the significance of class and place in the extended transitions of 'socially excluded' young adults. *Journal of the British Sociological Association*, 39(5): 873–91.

MacDonald, Z. (2001). Revisiting the dark figure – a microeconometric analysis of the under-reporting of property crime and its implications. *British Journal of Criminology*, 41(1): 127–49.

McKeganey, N., and Barnard, M. (1992). *AIDS, drugs and sexual risk: lives in the balance*. Buckingham: Open University Press.

McKeganey, N., Bloor, M., Robertson, M., Neale, J., and MacDougall, J. (2006). Abstinence and drug abuse treatment: results from the Drug Outcome Research in Scotland study. *Drugs: Education, Prevention and Policy*, 13(6): 537–50.

McMillan, B., and Conner, M. (2003). Applying an extended version of the theory of planned behavior to illicit drug use among students. *Journal of Applied Social Psychology*, 33: 1662–83.

McPherson, W. (1999). *The Stephen Lawrence inquiry*. London: HMSO. www.archive.official-documents.co.uk/document/cm42/4262/4262.htm

McVay, D. A. (2004). *Drug war facts*. See www.drugwarfacts.org for the latest version.

Malan, D. H. (2001). *Individual psychotherapy and the science of psychodynamics*. London: Arnold.

Mangold, J. (2006). *Walk the line*. Twentieth Century Fox.

Manley, T. (2006). From Columbine, Colorado, to Chicago, Illinois: the criminalization of success and failure by placing white youth at promise and youth of color at risk. Paper given during 'Pathways into and out of crime: taking stock and moving forward', International Symposium at De Montfort University, Leicester, April. www.pcrrd.group.shef.ac.uk/conferences/de_montfort_2006.htm; accessed 3 May 2007.

Marinelog (2003). *Navy nabs Al-Quaida drug dhows*. www.marinelog. com/DOCS/NEWSMMIII/MMIIIDec20a.html; accessed 6 September 2006.

Marks, H. (1997). *Mr Nice*. London: Minerva.

Marsh, D. T., and Dickens, R. (1998). *How to cope with mental illness in your family: a self-care guide for siblings, offspring and parents*. New York: Tarcher Putnam.

Martin, B. (1992). Scientific fraud and the power structure of science. *Prometheus*, 10(1): 83–98.

Martin, S. E., Maxwell, C. D., White, H. R., and Zhang, Y. (2004). Trends in alcohol use, cocaine use, and crime: 1989–1998. *Journal of Drug Issues*, 34(2): 333–59.

Marvell, T. B., and Moody, C. E. (1994). Prison population-growth and crime reduction. *Journal of Quantitative Criminology*, 10(2): 109–40.

Index

9 780745 636184